Social Policy and Risk

FRONTISPIECE

Chance, which was once the superstition of the vulgar, became the centrepiece of natural and social science, or so the genteel and rational people are led to believe. But how can chance ever be tamed? Parallel to the taming of chance . . . there arose a self conscious conception of pure irregularity, or something wilder than the kinds of chance that had been excluded by the Age of Reason. It harked back in part to something ancient or vestigial. It also looked into the future, to new, and often darker visions of the person. (Hacking, 1990: 10)

In all history it would be hard to find such butchery as in World War II, and it is precisely this period, this moment, when the great welfare, public health, and medical assistance programs were instigated . . . One could symbolize such a coincidence by a slogan: Go get slaughtered and we promise you a long and pleasant life. Life insurance is connected with a death command.

The coexistence in political struggles of large destructive mechanisms and institutions oriented toward the care of individual life is something puzzling and needs some investigation. It is one of the central antinomies of our political reason . . . when we ask for support as unemployed, even when we vote for or against a government which cuts social security expenses and increases defense spending, even in these cases, we are thinking beings, and we do these things not only on the ground of universal rules of behavior but also on the specific ground of a historical rationality. (Foucalt, 1988c: 147–8)

When there is a tendency to interpret the incidents or accidents that befall us – opportunely or not – by means of the reintroduction of determinism, necessity or signification, does this signify in turn an abnormal or pathological relation to the real? For example what is the difference between superstition or paranoia on the one hand, and science on the other, if they all mark a compulsive tendency to interpret random signs in order to reconstitute a meaning, a necessity, or a destination? (Derrida, 1984: 20)

Social Policy and Risk

Ian Culpitt

SAGE Publications
London • Thousand Oaks • New Delhi

First published 1999

SAGE Publications Ltd
6 Bonhill Street
London EC2A 4PU

SAGE Publications Inc
2455 Teller Road
Thousand Oaks, California 91320

SAGE Publications India Pvt Ltd
32, M-Block Market
Greater Kailash – I
New Delhi 110 048

British Library Cataloguing in Publication data

A catalogue record for this book is available
from the British Library.

ISBN 0–7619–5885–1
ISBN 0–7619–5886–x (pbk)

Library of Congress catalog card number 98–61883

Typeset by Photoprint, Torquay, Devon
Printed in Great Britain by The Cromwell Press Ltd,
Trowbridge, Wiltshire

To Ginny,
my companion in the risk of it all

CONTENTS

PREFACE AND ACKNOWLEDGEMENTS

All good ideas need room to move: space for their shape and nuances to become more obvious with familiarity. They need, if they are to be any use to us at all, to find ready 'lodging' within our own minds – to raise the cautious yes, the emphatic no, or the maybe. This book is an examination of a set of ideas about risk in relation to social policy. Questions about risks, hazards and dangers seem, increasingly, to be part of the commonality of public discussion. How they have been, and are now being, used to shape our present politics is the focus of this book.

The nature of risk is imaginatively presented by Beck in *Risk Society: Towards a New Modernity* (1992). Relating his thesis of risk society to social policy reveals my other aim, which has been to understand how neo-liberalism used various aspects of risk to attack welfare dependency. Unravelling that has led me to ask whether or not the organizing philosophy of neo-liberalism was based on a valorization of contract and risk. In order to understand the latter I've found myself being drawn more and more into applying Foucault's ideas to that task. This book explores the ways, applying a philosophy of risk, that we might lever the common-sense dominance of neo-liberalism. Undertaking such a critique defines, as Foucault suggested, 'the conditions under which the use of reason is legitimate in order to determine what can be known, what must be done, and what may be hoped' (1984a: 38).

Foucault, of course, is criticized as offering a philosophy that appears to attack the very basis of humanism and thus arguing for a 'subject-less history' (Giddens, 1995: 265). How then could he validly be used to comment on an analysis of neo-liberal social policy, which is so hostile to the welfare 'other'? Decrying Foucault is to miss the radical possibilities that reside in his work. For example, Foucault's question of Paul Veyne, 'how is it that there is so little truth in truth' (1993) appears to be yet one more nihilistic epithet betraying, as his detractors assert, his 'dependence' on Nietzsche (Cousins and Hussain, 1984: 257). However, this epithet, properly understood, is not necessarily nihilistic but 'ethically' challenging. Within it are the seeds of a provocation to 'truthful power' and the hegemony of 'the obvious' that is potentially liberating. It does allow us to look again at subjects and issues we have either become bored by or are so certain of our assumptions that we have stopped thinking. One such issue is welfare and all the ramifications of that 'flawed' political experiment. This book is an opportunity to submit some of those assumptions to yet one more 'gaze' to see whether the apparent 'truths' of neo-liberal politics, clearly at their zenith, actually have so 'little truth in them'!

I want to acknowledge the interest and support I have had for this project from many staff in this department, especially Kevin Dew, Michael Hill, Michael Lloyd and Stephen Uttley. I owe a particular debt to Stephen for his careful and insightful reading of some of the chapters. I have also received some encouraging support from George Pavlich and Patrick Kerans who also read portions of the manuscript. Karen Phillips was enthusiastic about the initial topic and proposal and it has been a privilege to work with her on this book. Her team at Sage have been similarly supportive and helpful.

I would also like to thank the following for permission to reproduce material from their separate publications as epigraphs in this book:

Aldine de Gruyter, Luhmann, N. (1993) *Risk: a Sociological Theory*, page ix; *The Times Higher Education Supplement*, Mottier, V. (1995) 'A tool box of deadly spanners' Volume 1197, October, page 27; The University of Chicago Press, Foucault, M. (1991) 'Questions of Method', in G. Burchell, C. Gordon and P. Miller (eds) *The Foucault Effect: Studies in Governmentality*, page 79; Rose, N. (1996) 'Governing "advanced" liberal democracies', in A. Barry, T. Osborne and N. Rose (eds) *Foucault and Political Reason: Liberalism, Neo-Liberalism and Rationalities of Government*, page 61; Stanford University Press, Hacking, I. (1986) 'Making up people', in T.C. Heller, M. Sosna and D.E. Wellbery (eds) *Reconstructing Individualism: Autonomy, Individuality, and the Self in Western Thought*, page 227; Sage Publications, Baudrillard, J. (1993) *Symbolic Exchange and Death*, page 11; The Johns Hopkins University Press, Derrida, J. (1984) 'My chances/*mes chances*: a rendezvous with some epicurean stereophonies', in J.H. Smith and W. Kerrigan (eds) *Taking Chances: Derrida, Psychoanalysis and Literature*, pages 5 and 20; Suhrkamp Verlag, Beck, U. (1995) *Ecological Politics in an Age of Risk*, page 69; Cambridge University Press, Nietzsche, F. (1997) *Daybreak: Thoughts on the Prejudices of Morality*, page 192; Hacking, I. (1990) *The Taming of Chance*, pages 10, 115 and 169; The University of Massachusetts Press, Foucault, M. (1988) 'The political technology of individuals', in L.H. Martin, H. Gutman and P.H. Hutton (eds) *Technologies of the Self: A Seminar with Michel Foucault*, pages 147–8.

1

WELFARE HAZARD, SOCIAL POLICY AND RISK: AN INTRODUCTION

How do we comprehend our society if we turn the concept of risk . . . into a universal problem neither avoidable or evadable? What is now necessary (necessary for welfare)? And accordingly: What is chance? How does society in the normal performance of its operations cope with a future about which nothing certain can be discerned, but only what is more or less probable or improbable?

(Luhmann, 1993: ix)

This book discusses the 'conduct' and 'practices' of risk within neo-liberal politics. It is polemical, as befits the social policy tradition, about the re-emergence of a moral discourse of welfare that is almost totally pejorative. The political functions of an increasingly strident attack on welfare dependency, and the imputation of 'social' risk this entails, are self-evident. What is not immediately clear is that the rationales used to justify that rejection and invalidation of welfare are reflexive. These numerous denials and exclusions, which seem so self-evidently a representation of neo-liberal common-sense, are not discrete. They reflect the denied obverse of neo-liberal individual self-projection. How this rhetoric is 'manufactured' lies at the heart of neo-liberal political practice. The use of the term *practices* rather than *policies* is significant. It reveals a Foucauldian bias, one *that challenges all our common-sense certainties*. For good or ill, beyond all the complex rhetoric, politics is about power.[1] How risks are perceived and formulated as problems reflects the essentially discursive practices of politics, and 'public debates about risk are debates about politics' (Douglas, 1992: 79). The ability to control and manage public perceptions about the *moral intentions* of a pervasive anti-welfarism may be part of the political 'dark arts'. However, risks are always collective; it is only accidents that are personal (Ewald, 1991).

This obligates social policy 'to investigate the messy realm of practices and relations and the compromised, corrupted, partial ways in which these entities ['neo-liberal rationality', the 'spirit of capitalism'] inhabit the real world' (Garland, 1997: 199). What we create in the structured dismissals of each other may accurately reflect our private perceptions about risk and the need for self-protection. Yet, is that all that we can now say in our marketized, deregulated world? Can we no longer speak of 'mutuality' or 'concern' or 'obligation' beyond that owed to those most intimately involved with us? What world have we fashioned that is so riven with risk and danger? Is it the case, as Hacking has suggested, that 'the central feature of our dangers is that they are rapidly changing' (1982b: 32)? The question, which is always generated within social policy, is how we may act upon the world to enlarge the scope of freedom and respect. To arrogate those qualities of modern life only to the successful seems a very risky project indeed!

Risk and the validity of the 'social': the framework of the argument

The structure of this book is as follows. In this first chapter the issues of risk are set out in relation to the normative debates within social policy about collective concerns about care and justice. The traditional debate has been eclipsed by the profound influence of neo-liberal politics. The second chapter narrows the focus of the debate by centring the discussion on the importance of Michel Foucault's analysis of the uncertainties of late modernity. This chapter is an 'invitation' to consider the value of Foucault's overall *oeuvre* in relation to social policy. As such it seeks to open and not foreclose an interesting inquiry about the policies and practices of government in relation to social welfare. The third chapter extends this analysis of the governmentality literature. The neo-liberal 'language' of risk not only shapes the validity of the discourse about welfare but construes the very domain within which discourse is possible. How that discourse uses the notion of risk to deconstruct the previous justifications for welfare is a central theme.

The fourth chapter sets out an argument that risk was intentionally structured into the core of the new contractual and consensual society. Elements of the Foucauldian 'gaze' and Ian Hacking's thesis about 'making up peoples' extend the governmentality thesis into the area of contract and sanctioned 'expertise'. Chapter 5 examines the validity of citizenship claims-making and relates this to the debate between Habermas and Foucault about the continuing validity of the 'public sphere'. The issues of how we have been governed through society, but society is now seen as obsolete, are considered in relation to neo-liberal 'mentalities of rule'. We consider here some of the questions involved in the presumed 'death of the social'.

Chapter 6 shifts the focus more squarely to an examination of Beck's risk society thesis and its value for social policy, while Chapter 7 critically reviews this analysis. Chapter 8 introduces Axel Honneth's paradigm of the struggle for recognition. It sets out one attempt to refashion a moral and potentially normative debate about the 'social'. Chapter 9 returns more specifically to the overall theme of social policy and risk. The ways in which the various rhetorics of dependency have been aligned with the neo-liberal analysis of risk are revisited and drawn to a conclusion. The Afterword returns to Foucault's imaginative use of Nietzsche's phrase that the state is the 'coldest of all cold monsters'. The shape and nature of the future discourses about welfare and risk are outlined. The hope is expressed that we seek to use our conflictual analyses of risk to reveal ourselves to ourselves and not attempt to eliminate them (cf. Donzelot, 1991: 178). We do need a new genealogy of welfare, risk and social policy.

Hazards and risks: an examination of the rhetorical contexts

Risk and randomness are the twin 'devils' of the chance that is the context of the lived life. Hedging against malign peril, gambling on possible windfall luck, and avoiding unreasonable exposure to risk, govern so much of our personal and social experience. Given the obvious fragility of life, and its randomness, individual perception of risk typically provoked reflex responses to private sets of complex fears about health, safety and survival. These latent personal fears, sentinels against the possibility of haphazard chance, were perceived to be an inevitable aspect of life's dangerousness. So universal are these common threads that the concept of risk is integral to the idiosyncratic knowledge of who we are. Indeed, surviving and dealing with inescapable risks had commonly been defined as part of the unique and archetypal process of solitary reflection fundamental to an awareness of self. Traditionally, discussions about risk were associated with the idiosyncrasies of separate personal fate and identity. Framed within this general purview, each individual could, in most instances, be presumed to have had some responsibility for what befell them. However, risk is no longer just associated with personal fate. It is now used to summon up a complex political debate about power, governance and the nature of personal freedom. Risk is no longer part of the normal possibility of random fate associated with individual life. It is now part of our fears about possible technological pollution and biochemical destruction. Risk has become public, pervasive, compelling and inescapable.[2]

That which was private, but part of the common order, now stands over the whole, raising the spectre that our self-preoccupations about risk actually magnify and engender risk. These assumptions are colloquially expressed in the canard that fear begets fear. Questions are increasingly raised about whether various emphases on 'dangerousness' and 'threat' have actually intensified a generalized sociological awareness of risk (cf. Harris, 1997). This current investigation offers an opportunity to reflect on how the narrower individual perception of risk has ineluctably widened to encompass the arguments now made about a risk society. In his radical treatise Beck (1992) set out the dilemma that risk, generalized and global, must now take into account not just the fear of what might be but also the terrifying knowledge of what we have created. He contends that:

> sources of danger are no longer ignorance but *knowledge*; not a deficient but a perfected mastery over nature; not that which eludes the human grasp but the system of norms and objective constraints established with the industrial epoch. (1992: 181)

Risk, conceptualized in this sense, is no longer about private fears of the random unknown. It now involves public perception of universal dangerousness and threat (cf. Bauman, 1997: 204). This shift from ignorance to knowledge is crucial to an understanding of Beck's thesis about the ubiquity of terrifying risk. Establishing risk as a central defining motif of late modernity offers a new perspective for social policy theory. Currently the debate is much more about minimizing risk than ensuring justice. As Gordon argued, the 'task of justice, as social defence . . . consists . . . not so much in deterrence as in neutralization and prophylaxis' (1991: 39). This new dynamic of risk (the boundary between private and social fears) creates an opportunity to rework the apparently foreclosed debate about the viability of welfare systems.[3]

Setting out his arguments for a social theory of risk (encapsulated in his phrase 'risk society') Beck suggests that 'risks become the motor of the *self-politicization* of modernity in the industrial society' (1992: 181). How that conjunction between risk and individual awareness has become politicized provides a new perspective on the future viability of the welfare state/society. One aspect of the 'motor' of self-politicization is how successful neo-liberalism has been in fashioning a tight 'armour' of *practicality*, *obviousness* and *common-sense* around its political rhetoric (cf. Mouffe, 1995). The practical expediency that arises from a rhetoric of common-sense defines any opposition as 'unreasonable'.[4] The substance of such opposition is not intrinsic to modernity. As Procacci argues, soon after the French Revolution in 1789 'traditional forms of assistance started to appear *as themselves a cause of poverty* because they opposed the absorption of poverty into labor. This recognition in turn made possible a moral rehabilitation of the poor, one that was expected to open the way to their economic and social integration' (1994: 207, my italics). The seeds of the tenet that 'moral hazard' could be generated into a critique of those institutions (read 'welfare state') that sought to ease poverty is clearly nothing new! As Castel confirms, 'today's lack of security is also an echo of earlier structural components of the condition of the disadvantaged classes: fragile ties to employment, the vulnerability that arises from constant uncertainty about the future' (1994: 250).

The concerted attack on the validity of the welfare state is not just confined to an epistemological debate. It has a historical narrative coherence. It cannot be solved solely in discourses about ideas. Habermas has indicated that, if it is to be successful, 'neo-conservatism' (as he terms it) will need to 'find a political base in the social Darwinism of the split society' (1986: 12). In Procacci's analysis it has already found it! It represents an increasingly divided society of 'haves' and 'have nots'. Sundry social constructions of welfare 'crisis', pivoting around demands for prudent fiscal management of the modern state, have, seemingly, become powerful and watertight.[5] The vigour of market-oriented economic policies has eviscerated the social democratic reform policies which sustained prior welfare state mandates. A new pattern of political and administrative reform has been struck which has 'socially contained' and weakened the interventionist welfare state. The medium for such radical political change was the widespread adoption of contractualism that presaged a dramatic revision of the practices of governance.[6]

Habermas: arrival of the 'new obscurity'

What we are witnessing, as Habermas indicated, is a 'completely altered relationship between autonomous and self-organized public spheres on the one hand, and sub-systems steered by money and administrative power on the other' (1986: 13–14). That this indicates a new crisis in welfare politics is clear.[7] Any effective challenge to neo-liberal policies will have 'the difficult task of making possible a democratic generalisation of interest positions and a universalistic justification of norms *below* the threshold of party apparatuses' (1986: 14). Neo-liberalism has successfully forestalled the social democratic left from constructing an interlocking set of political beliefs that operate 'below the threshold' of political parties. Habermas makes the interesting observation that 'a pluralism of [these new] defensive sub-cultures' would ignore the 'norms of civil equality'.[8] We are now witnessing a drastic revision of our 'life-worlds' where widespread contractualism has assumed the dynamism of common-sense. Some would even argue that these neo-liberal fiscal reforms, yoked to the international 'demands' of capital in a globalized world, might 'threaten the foundation of . . . formal democracy' (Huber et al., 1997: 339). Despite the difficulty in seeing how to reinvigorate the 'exhausted utopian energies' of social democracy, the debate is not over. Habermas (1986) may well be right in describing the hackneyed debates between left and right as evidence of a 'new obscurity', but that must not blind us in seeking new tools with which to work upon our world.

This investigation into the usefulness of risk, as a means with which to rejoin the classic debate, does have an exploratory, epistemological and normative aim.[9] As Habermas contends, the drying up of the 'utopian oases' leads to 'a desert of banality and helplessness' (1986: 16). If we cannot easily revitalize the social we still need to argue for the legitimacy of the marginalized and excluded (cf. Cooke, 1997). If Habermas is correct in arguing that 'self assurance in the modern world continues to be spurred on by a consciousness of the present in which historical and utopian thought are blended' (1986: 16) then normative debates about welfare needs and rights may yet be possible.[10] Any valid social inquiry must challenge the watertight obviousness of the neo-liberal stance on welfare. This is not to pose the superior validity of the discredited social democratic policies, but rather to argue that all policy positions are only approximate. They are by definition political and thus open to question. Trying to foreclose the debate is understandable – part of the totalizing aim of any hegemony. Any rational challenge to this apparent obvious-ness must prove that these assertions of common-sense reveal an ideo-logical bias (cf. Hewitt, 1992: 41ff). However, such challenges, as Foucault (1984b) argued, ought not to be specifically aimed at trying to change what is in people's heads or to deny their legitimate consciousness. The critical task of 'revealing an ideology' is not to challenge the *belief* of common-sense but to reveal its *practices*. Counter-posing the various assumptions about risk alongside the neo-liberal hegemony of an obvious common-sense, thus revealing its 'practices', provides new tools of social critique. My purpose is to outline the possible elements for a philosophy of risk, one that encompasses the paradoxes implicit in the separate personal and social notions of risk. Such an analysis will re-examine the ideological split between private and public 'realities' and shed some light on the 'new obscurity'.

It is the intersection and overlapping of overwhelming public risk with the individualized search for a 'perfected mastery' that have led to this relentless process of self-politicization. There is a remorselessness in this process that undermines the political rhetoric that legitimated previous welfare state mandates based on some basis of mutual social obligation.[11] It will be useful to ask how the distributions of risks, hazards and dangers, now the fundamental elements of a risk society, have contributed to the 'crisis' of welfare. My intent in doing this is to locate the rhetoric about welfare state change in a wider philosophical frame.

Arguments against the welfare state do not just depend on the accumulated weight of the incontrovertibly negative social indicators. The dominant rhetoric about the perils of welfare dependency, arising out of the imperative of self-politicization, has exacerbated the 'fear of the other'.[12] The notion of risk has been used to support an anti-welfare rhetoric and to contextualize a form of neo-liberal individualism that is hostile to the legitimacy of the 'other'. So much so that it could defensively frame any welfare dissensus as having the appearance of an 'anti-society'.[13] This investigation will offer a reconsideration of the power of that neo-liberal rhetoric, which Shklar (1989) perceptively called the 'liberalism of fear', and of how that general politicized fear construes the debates about social policy and welfare provision.

Can social policy mount an effective dissensus?

Social policy no longer has command of a rhetoric that can galvanize political and public opinion. The moral gravity of Titmuss, in writings such as *The Gift Relationship*, which established an intellectual position for an independent social policy theory, remains but seems rather an echo of an ethical social world that has been superseded. In this, arguably the most famous of his books, he set out to dispute the 'philistine resurrection of economic man in social policy' (1970: 14). He suggested that social policy must be concerned with the 'unquantifiable and unmethodical aspects of man as well as with those aspects that can be identified and counted' (1970: 224). Titmuss' intent was to invite consideration of the assumption that anonymous voluntary gift giving elevated us all and would serve to overcome individual alienation. It was an eloquent manifesto for social obligation. His conclusions, about the risks associated with a comparative analysis of American and British blood donors, are that altruistic concerns 'derive from our own characters and are not contractual in nature . . . [and that] it is these concerns and their expression which distinguish social policy from economic policy' (1970: 212).

The rhetorical power of those arguments that collapse the distinctions between economic and social policy, so central to the initial rhetoric of welfare states, needs to be respected. Social policy theory which cleaves, as an essential part of its argument, to the maintenance of a juxtaposition between the venality of the market and the morality of social justice concerns will not suffice. This is not to deny the place and the power of such distinctions in the history of social policy thought. For the moment, however, attempting to resurrect them as the mainstay of contemporary debate condemns social policy to marginality. The dominance of the neo-liberal, deregulated contract state, with its emphasis on market-based solutions to the distribution of social goods, has collapsed the force of this previous distinction: the paramount reality is competition and risk. Railing against the 'blitzkrieg' speed of these public sector reforms, or decrying their 'philistine' intent, is no substitute for trying to understand the force of the intellectual imperatives that uphold them.

There is an important paradox at work here. When contentions for social justice claims-making remain stubbornly normative, clinging to a 'false nostalgia' for those institutions that have been so powerfully socially deconstructed, the innately defensive rhetoric of individualism is reinforced. In the current policy climate such normative claims, even when acknowledged, are quickly dismissed, are not engaged with or debated. If we are to find ways to re-establish the traditional concerns of social policy we must enter the debate and not stand outside it.[14] If social policy remains yoked, in its theorizing, to a normative epistemology – to what ought to be rather than to an analysis of what is – then we will remain isolated and marginal (cf. Hewitt, 1992).

We need to understand the power of the neo-liberal political rhetoric that so swiftly captured the public policy debate during the 1980s[15] and established rationales for the deregulation of the public sector welfare and health bureaucracies. Overturning these bureaucracies that had institutionalized social security, swept away the former justifications for welfare states.[16] Neo-liberalism stands apart from any evaluation of the normative debate and insists only on the relevance of practical and manageable solutions. As Hewitt has argued, part of the appeal of neo-liberalism was that 'its political plausibility lies in the claim that the market, if given free rein, limits the persuasive power of ideology' (1992: 40).[17] The apparent excesses of social justice claims-making are either relegated to the past or projected out into the future. They are seen either as the remnants of a former socialist perspective that is defeated, or as possible future goals, only feasible as a by-product of a strong economy.[18] In either case, the rhetoric depends upon the manner in which the practical and common-sense are subsumed within the 'frame' of managed risk.

The structure of that dominance depends upon the use of definitions of social life that are appealed to as basic and incontrovertible. Typical of such rhetoric is the expression of an instinctive pragmatism. The gist of these basic assumptions, from public choice theory, is that people are primarily selfish; they are presumed to be 'rational utility maximizers',[19] and are better equipped themselves to rank order the priority of their needs. In the light of this analysis of risk we can also add 'subjective probability utilizer' (Reddy, 1996: 234). Similarly, it is argued that only through clear specification of contracts – the mechanism of purchaser/ provider split – and by applying the reward system of agency theory can the true nature of market exchange be realized. The rhetoric of liberal deregulation depends upon an assumption of obviousness. What is being created in our economic and social exchanges can derive meaning only from *what is*, not from what *ought to be*.[20]

Obviously, the vigour of the neo-liberal orientation to risk has been its ability to restrict contemporary discussion, not only to issues of common-sense but also to concerns about the future. Focusing the concept of risk on the possibility of overwhelming or 'undesirable outcomes' has captured the rhetorical high ground (Kemshall et al., 1997: 223). Redirecting the connotation of risk, away from the common ground of the usual, toward the future, escalates the possibility of threat so that it comes to represent a 'wildness lying in wait' (Bernstein, 1996). The equation of risk only with predictive possibility, or menace, is further sharpened by Kemshall et al., as they rely on Douglas' valuable insight that the contemporary usage of risk is best defined as 'forensic' (1992: 27). All cultures, Douglas argues, require 'a common forensic vocabulary with which to hold persons accountable' (1990: 1). This is particularly so when generalizing risk in terms of the global consequences of Beck's risk society. The 'forensic' aspect of a cultural approach to risk implies that (in respect of universal risk) someone must be held to account – that blame be laid and protection from further risk obtained. All cultures, Douglas argues, need some symbol system to recognize risk, and establish accountability. The terrifying aspects of risk can be lessened and generalized into a cultural norm. As Rayner has stated, 'there is a consensus that the essence of risk consists of the probability of an adverse event and the magnitude of its consequences' (1992: 93).[21] Common usage of risk still reflects a desire to ascribe and allocate accountability. This point is well expressed by Pratt who contends that it is this application of blame, and the demands for protection, that reinforce the new views of governance. He argues that the

> shift in political rationalities – from welfarism to neo-liberalism . . . has both mediated and reformulated the nature and extent of this 'right to protection', involving, inter alia, the creation of new risk groups and new strategies for risk management. (1996: 245)

The state, not the individual, must now be held accountable for resolving these situations of overwhelming threat. Emphasizing a globally protective conception of risk, involving this forensic aspect, reinforces a particular approach to governance that empowers the neo-liberal view of the individual. Consequently, the proper role of the state is redefined as security not welfare – protection of individual autonomy. Risk management is institutionalized as an essential aspect of the residual duties of government. Accountability, not responsibility, is the theme that undergirds the neo-liberal patterning of governance. There is a hidden normativeness in the neo-liberal position that is able to restrict discussion of risk to a predictive and forensic category of understanding.

The language of risk and chance: general or particular?

The nature of risk involves the possibility of random fate, whether individual or social, shrouded in the intellectual and political dilemmas of endless rationalization about cause and responsibility. The language of risk, however, is also full of interesting paradoxes. Risk is about individual fears and social rights. Risk is something chosen and something imposed. Risk is manageable and can be insured against or, alternatively, is overwhelming and uncontrollable. Risk is about ensuring survival and avoiding contamination. Risk assessment involves the protection of assets and the maximization of profit in complex market exchanges. Risk analysis has always been part of the strategic considerations of organizations, corporations, groups and nation-states. Given the obviousness of risk and personal insecurity, an exploration of 'risk in social policy' might be seen to require a detailed examination of the range of services and policies that represent complex patterns of response to individual and social need. Such an exploration might equally start from a respect for the belief that the welfare state had already achieved its high expectations, that it symbolized a consensual, caring society of mutual obligation, and that all it needed was a watchful defence.

While detailed quantitative depictions of risk analysis are an important aspect of an overall approach to social policy, their power to compel in the current climate of deregulation, contracting and privatization has been blunted. I agree with Hewitt that 'the very criteria for appraising the welfare state have been lost under a welter of statistics, where each series is subject to constantly changing definitions of reality' (1992: 3). Defending the welfare state, in the present neo-liberal climate, through careful statistical research about needs and rights, or by mounting a 'romantic' defence of welfare as a superordinate moral ideology, is vapid. The obvious facts of social inequality and the daily evidence of personal trauma have often confined discussion of risk to the practical aspects of policy analysis, to the procedural and the particular and not the general. Concepts of risk, particularly of Beck's thesis of risk society and the various meanings associated with it, have not been explored fully in relation to social policy. Risk discourse does not represent a fixed point of analysis and cannot be narrowly construed as assessment, prediction and consequence. Risk is not just about the analysis of a potential threat, or a by-product of failure to implement specific policy. Risk is antecedent and not only consequential. It is part of the organizing ground of how we define the personal and the social. What is required is a more thorough analysis of the crises of modernity that is represented, in part, by Beck's analysis of risk society. Such analyses of risk in relation to social policy must encompass wider political discourses about the construction and maintenance of ideologies of need and welfare – to examine the practices of the modern neo-liberal project.

Luhmann's question about how we are to understand our society if we do generalize risk as a universal problem is significant. It points to the increasing use of the possibility and fact of risk as a common generalization of social life. However, as Giddens argues, in contrast to Beck, it

> is not that day-to-day life is inherently more risky than was the case in prior eras. It is rather that, in conditions of modernity, for lay actors as well as experts in specific fields, thinking in terms of risk and risk assessment is a more or less ever-present exercise. (1991: 123–4)

If these generalizations about risk as a universal problem are correct and can be presumed to be part of the obvious, part of what must be assumed and taken for granted, what do we make of chance and risk as archetypically individual realities? How are we to understand the idea of risk if it is increasingly generalized into a category of sociological explanation, a risk society? The reflexivity of that debate provides an opportunity to re-examine risk as it relates to the individual, to the idiosyncratic and particular as well as the universal.

Welfare resistance: insurance, risks and providence?

The particular examples of welfare states, which have sustained major neo-liberal pressure, are either those that espouse a social democratic model, or those loosely termed 'residual'. The rampant power of neo-liberal critique of welfare 'slows' considerably when faced with the inertia of the social insurance model. They have not been so hospitable to the neo-liberal rhetoric. As Esping-Andersen argues, the 'neo-liberal right is, on the Continent, a truly marginal player' (1996: 66). Why neo-liberalism has been ineffectual in challenging this social insurance system needs some comment. How that presumed solidarity fares when confronted with Beck's arguments about the imminent social collapse of the previous social arrangements that sustained welfare states is equally important.

Esping-Andersen said that 'Bismarck's aim was not a welfare state but a welfare monarchy' (1996: 66)! The success of that has not generated much impetus for change. As Esping-Andersen stated, the

> perceived adequacy of social insurance across most strata implies also very little demand for private sector coverage, especially in pensions. And since contributory social insurance instils a sense of individually earned contractual rights, these social security systems have enjoyed unusually broad public legitimacy. (1996: 67–8)

However, it was an 'authoritarian, étatist, and corporativist' state which represents, of course, exactly the combination of unreflective and traditional expertise that Beck argued was no longer possible within the radical transformation of risk society. Offe argued that 'the institutional structures of the German social security system are suited to channeling participants' motives towards conformity and acceptance' (1996: 185). It was not a fundamentally redistributive system and therefore risk mirrors the existing order. Risk could not be used to agitate for change. Social insurance is an entitlement system: it makes no 'cognitive or moral claims'. Characteristically, a social insurance system reduces 'the demands of *risk acceptance* (or of trust in the future) and moral demands for solidarity (or for trust in "others") to such an extent that rationally grounded reservations towards the social security system as a whole cannot easily be made' (1996: 187). As Esping-Andersen said, 'the realm of solidarity and risk-sharing is narrower and more particularistic'. These combined reasons made it hard for neo-liberalism to make any inroads. Such political change requires a more diffused sense of either incapacity or incompetence; neither was true of social insurance systems. It is an interesting reflection on the resistant power of social insurance systems. It reveals how rationales for the acceptance of neo-liberal reforms in the other systems could not simply be presumed to rest on the superior logic of neo-liberalism.

All of Beck's assertions about the contradictory nature of risks, contained in his thesis of risk society, raise these important questions about the relationship of risk, insurance and welfare security. Does Beck's thesis void the social insurance model of welfare, intrinsic to his native Germany? This question is significant not the least because it is often asserted, as Offe said, that the Bismarckian model has shown a 'remarkable robustness' and has retained most of its institutional features for more than 100 years! So this overall discussion, relating risk to social policy, must consider how effectively Beck's thesis has undercut this enduring system of welfare. The essence of Beck's argument is that risk society 'negates the principles of its rationality. It has long ago left this behind, because it operates and balances beyond the insurance limit'. He continues his theme of the 'rupture' of the steady state: 'perhaps risk society only begins where the sound barrier of insurability has been broken *and* this has been understood, noted and made into the theme of conflict which is superimposed on everything' (1996b: 41). It is clear that he wishes to introduce into the 'comforts' of a predictable insurance state all of the insecurities typical of other welfare states.

Freedom, risk and security?

This book is an invitation to engage in an analysis of the sociology of risk and to see how a certain concept of risk is woven into the heart of the libertarian imagining of individualism. Marketplace liberalism is so dominant that clever articulations of need are forced to 'stumble over' the more urgent logic of costs and the apportioning of limited economic resources. We have come to a new impasse in our social arrangements whereby demonstrated and expressed need no longer merits a reflex assumption of social responsibility (cf. Giddens, 1994b). This inquiry into the universality of risk also provides an opportunity to reconsider the relative decline of the former welfare state patterns of social obligation – to examine the rhetorical context in which the political demand to abandon justifications for the welfare state has been successful. A reconsideration of risk can illuminate how the logic of that imperative, to recast the welfare state, has resulted in the creation of a new set of justifications for a welfare society – the provision only of a minimal 'safety net'.

The universality of risk, as both social and individual threat, establishes the premises within which the current conflict about personal freedom, self-sufficiency and social obligation is debated. Hacking suggests that:

Our public fears are endlessly debated in terms of probabilities: chances of meltdowns, cancers, muggings, earthquakes, nuclear winters, AIDS, global greenhouses, what next? There is nothing to fear (it may seem) but the probabilities themselves. This obsession with the chances of danger, and with treatments for changing the odds, descends directly from the forgotten annals of nineteenth century information and control. (1990: 4–5)

Both the libertarian right and the social democratic left use the concept of risk to reinforce the logic of their separate positions. Unravelling the origin of this struggle allows us to reconsider the perennial conflict between the one and the many.

However, as Hacking has argued, the real nature of the debate may be structural. It may have to do with how information is used and produced, about the nature of the world that both left and right must negotiate. This debate reflects something of the purpose of Beck's risk society, which we cannot but inhabit, where risk is inescapably universal and not especially personal. Within this perspective, any discussion of risk must first consider Beck's operating assumption that the inevitability of change, consequent upon risk society, is beyond political control. However, while a possible sociology of risk involves the contemplation of overwhelming future threat it must also consider that risk involves aspects of control. Risk and control are conjoined.[22] The future is threatening, even apocalyptically so (at least in Beck's formulations), but it also offers the opportunity to plan for and hedge against risk. Reactions to risk involve coping with the fear about the 'wildness' of the 'unknown' by anticipation, planning and even insuring against the possibility of the 'overwhelming'. It is, however, the ideologues of neo-liberalism who have used such analyses to their advantage. Beck's notion that 'reflexive modernization' means 'the possibility of a creative (self)-destruction for an entire epoch: that of industrial society' (1992: 2) strikes hard at those who would defend the welfare state using the previous rhetoric of mutual support and social obligation.[23]

Such is the force of this anti-welfare rhetoric, premised on a valorization of risk, that it has not only changed the locus of the debate but also refashioned what is an acceptable 'language of welfare'. We can no longer easily talk of welfare as 'opportunity', 'responsibility' or 'obligation'. Welfare has been pejoratively recast as welfare dependency, and risk is one of the underlying themes of the new rhetoric. The emergence of the more brutal aspects of risk, when allied intrinsically to individualism and random fate, are used as generative reasons for the obvious imperative of that very individualism. Recent analyses of social risk from writers like Beck, that envisage a rampant and uncontrollable sociology of risk, are allied with the brutality of individual suffering. A perverse cycle exists where the more risky life seems, the more individuals are expected to manage and insure against that risk. The hurts and losses of others (the citizen-strangers) awaken compassion or revulsion and even fear. They are no longer used to generate a collective response to the risky nature of life but rather prove the new mandate that it is the solitary individual, and not the state, who must guard against risk.

The evidence of personal distress no longer has the same power to compel collective state responses, or generate any real social obligation beyond that offered to a 'tribalized' minority (the citizen-friend). Whether we can still talk of an epistemology of risk and how it intersects with the current philosophy of individualism is an important question. Another is whether there is a deeper structural issue surrounding the dominant assumption that freedom is associated with self-sufficiency. Placing risk at the centre of this analysis provides a new opportunity to examine some of the structures of these assumptions. This involves discerning the patterns by which a supposed obviousness dominates and construes the nature of social discourse. What is discussable and germane in the context of any current social analysis is never internally intrinsic. There is always an obverse, a reversal, something hidden, a non-admissible and non-discussable element that must be weighed as well as the obvious, the certain, the new.

While the rhetoric and fact of individualism are dominant, even rampant, there remains something unsatisfying and unpersuasive about the social and personal reductionism inherent in such a position. An analysis of risk requires an investigation of how freedom and self-sufficiency were originally woven together and form our present understanding of individualism. We cannot assume that such contemporary assumptions reveal an irreducible truth about risk and individual life. Our social theories are never fixed and cannot express immutable assumptions. They represent our attempts to understand the world, perhaps also to manoeuvre and dominate it, but cannot be seen as ineluctably true. Debates about the so-called 'crisis of welfare' have led some social policy theorists to return to an analysis of social rights and citizenship.[24] This often involved an attempt to understand the epistemology of welfare in order to challenge the dominant beliefs of neo-liberalism. Exposing or elucidating these sets of beliefs, while important, has not altered the ideological power of the welfare reform agenda. It will be important to find other 'tools' to comment upon and challenge this agenda.

The search for normative 'closure'

Epistemological analysis has some usefulness, since various theoretical attempts to remove normative assertions from discussion about power can be questioned. We still require 'normative criteria for distinguishing acceptable from unacceptable forms of power' (Fraser, 1989b: 33). It will be important, nevertheless, not just to focus the debate on an analysis of beliefs but also to establish whether the 'everyday politics' of welfare and benefit administration provide a more valuable starting point to consider these ideas about risk and social policy. If it can be argued that the ideology of welfare change lies not so much in beliefs, but in practices and action, then perhaps it is to the act of giving itself that we must turn our attention. Various arguments for a return to the values inherent in charitable giving highlight the issues that surround how a society gives to those who fall into its 'safety net':

- What are the 'practices' of welfare, and how do these 'practices' reinforce the risky nature of life for those who must survive on them?
- How do welfare beneficiaries give up their autonomy and become recipients rather than contributors in the social arena?
- How is the status of victim reinforced by the administrative act of giving?
- In what ways do the new arguments for contracted social services sever the former link between the perception of needs and rights for service?

Private narcissism and public management

One of the reasons for the current ascendancy of neo-liberal ideas in social and welfare policy debates may well be that the supporting philosophies (such as public choice and agency theory) have a better and more coherent understanding of risk. Those sets of communitarian and social obligation imperatives espoused by the left are now eclipsed. One significant reason for this may have been an inadequate conceptualization of risk or a failure to understand the inevitability of change. The apparent practical rigour and common-sense truism of public choice (or rational choice) theory is that every individual must manage and take responsibility for the risks inherent in social life. Much of the rhetoric supporting a change in the pattern and structure of welfare states typically argues that in respect of risk, individuals should bear more and the state should carry less. Consequently, not only the 'risks of welfare' but also the costs are now the common threads of public discussion.

Part of the conundrum is that neo-liberalism seeks to diminish the state's role in respect of welfare while maintaining that the state ought more properly to be involved in dealing with the consequences of a risk society. Typical phrases that form this rhetoric are that we need to move from a 'welfare state to a welfare society' and that social wellbeing and not welfare ought to be emphasized.[25] As Hewitt has argued:

> the Right has sought to overturn the old common sense of Social Democracy, with its standards of collective regulation, public ownership and state benevolence, and to replace it with a new morality based on private enterprise, wealth and self-reliance. (1992: 42)

Public choice theory has countered the communal ideas of welfare states with a powerful restatement that fundamentally social life is made up of solitary, self-interested individuals who must perforce make rational choices after weighing all the possible alternatives. Perhaps it was because the left had abandoned the notion of an arbitrary and random world, and subsumed risk into the state, that it was easy for neo-liberalism to take over the language of social policy's traditional concerns? This is not to argue that the welfare state cannot be defended but to suggest that essentially new arguments, and a new rhetoric, must be found in order to do this. One of the 'less conventional arguments' (Goodin, 1988: x) that can elucidate the shape or outline of a new rhetoric draws on an understanding of the concept of risk. Relating an analysis of risk to social policy allows for the development of new forms of discourse (cf. Hillyard and Watson, 1996). It provides an interesting opportunity for the development of a view of welfare and social responsibility that does not ignore the fragility of the modern world. Welfare rhetoric must address the needs of individuals as they make sense of their experience and also demonstrate how social institutions are constantly involved in the process of change.

Risk and social policy: asking the right questions?

As well as examining a particular set of questions about risk, this discussion considers the patterns of rhetoric that are used either to defend or to challenge previous welfare mandates. What is often an accepted part of the public critique of welfare does not reveal the real nature of the ideological forces that demand change. Little effort has yet been made to evaluate Beck's thesis of risk society in relation to changes in welfare ideology. While there have been valuable attempts to develop a sociological theory of risk (cf. Beck, 1992; Beck et al., 1994; Giddens, 1990; 1991; Luhmann, 1993) there have, as yet, been no separate attempts to develop a comprehensive analysis of risk that is germane to social policy.

One of the curious aspects of the purchase of service contracting and welfare privatization debate is that the drive to cost, accurately, the provision and delivery of services leads us into societal changes the consequences of which are not clear. Hacking has pointed out that 'enumeration requires categorization, and . . . defining new classes of people for the purposes of statistics has consequences for the ways in which we conceive of others and think of our own possibilities and potentialities' (1990: 6). Such 'counting', as Foucault also argued, is essential to modern government: 'The art of governing, characteristic of reason of state, is intimately bound up with the development of what was . . . called either political *statistics*, or *arithmetic*' (1981b: 245–6). The demand to provide accurate financial accounting for the operation of government seems incontrovertible. Nevertheless, the theorists of risk society would argue that the consequences of such rational decision-making are not yet understood. As Luhmann suggested, the 'fear that things could go wrong is therefore growing rapidly and with it the risk apportioned to decision-making' (1993: xii).

The result may well fulfil Derrida's postulate that the 'continuous process of making explicit, moving toward an opening, risks sinking into the autism of closure' (1982: 135). Consequently, a more specific set of questions can be generated:

- What are the grounds for an assessment of risk in social policy?
- How relevant is it to associate sociological theorizing about risk with the particular sets of problems that social policy faces in redefining the values of welfare?
- Can the current ideological power of neo-liberalism be challenged?
- And if so, what will such a discourse and analysis look like?

The social freedoms and protections that were allied with the growth of welfare states are no longer possible. Those traditional welfare institutions constructed a particular response to social and individual threat, based upon an analysis of class inequality and consciousness. They now find themselves unable to deal with the increasing burden of a society where all are 'expected to live with a broad variety of different, mutually contradictory, global and personal risks' (Beck et al., 1994: 7). It seems timely to take current discussions about risk and to extend them into an analysis of how such ideas impact on social policy. Beck's recentring of risk sociologically provides a different but no less important focus for this discussion. Honneth's (1995a; 1995b) paradigm of recognition offers a variant on Beck's structural analysis of risk, enabling a reconsideration of social obligation and whether it might yet have some rhetorical mileage. Foucault's influence in the debates about modern society has fashioned new ways in which to discuss the discourses of power and knowledge that shape that debate, as well as those of freedom and risk. He 'invents a philosophy not of foundation but of risk; a philosophy that is the endless question of freedom' (Rajchman, 1985: 124). In the next chapter we focus on some aspects of Foucault's overall *oeuvre* in order to see what impact his ideas might have in shaping our understanding of risk and social policy.

Notes

1 Perhaps the most important subtext in this analysis of risk and social policy is the observation made by Procacci that while poor people exist that 'is not a sufficient warrant for treating poverty as a "social question" ' (1994: 208). That our current social debates treat welfare dependency as a 'social question' should

give us pause. How neo-liberalism has valorized risk and reified the legitimacy of individual 'dependency' into a 'social question' is central to my analysis.

2 According to Giddens, common usage of 'risk' did not appear in English philosophy or social theory until the seventeenth century. While Machiavelli's theory of power emphasized *fortuna* and divine intervention, his depiction of *fortuna* still left space for human calculation. In the exigencies of such calculation Machiavelli postulated a world which foreshadowed risk. Risk did not lose its French spelling until the nineteenth century. Its usage, as Giddens argues, was first applied to the nascent insurance industry and was used alongside the French word *risqué*. As he says, the 'term *risqué*, meaning a joke that risks giving offence, still retains the old form' (1991: 111). Ewald suggests that 'risk' developed as a neologism of insurance and was derived 'from the Italian word *risco* which meant "that which cuts", hence "reef" and consequently "risk to cargo on the high seas" ' (1991: 198–9). Luhmann also confirms this (1993: 9–10).

3 The neo-liberal critique is structural as well as personal. This investigation into risk could have focused more explicitly on risk expressed as a structural problem of the maintenance of viable social security and employment policy. While aspects of this will be considered, my focus is more on the 'personal' critical rhetoric of neo-liberalism. Applying aspects of the Foucauldian analysis reveals how integral this personal anti-welfare rhetoric has been in undergirding the 'practices' and the justifications of neo-liberal politics.

4 One of the points that Foucault makes with respect to 'the will to knowledge', the kinds of inflexible certainties that lie hidden in this rhetoric of common-sense, is the presence in that 'hiddenness' of an unacknowledged violence. He said, imaginatively, that we are

> not given an exact and serene mastery of nature. On the contrary, it ceaselessly multiplies the risks, creates dangers in every area; it breaks down illusory defences; it dissolves the unity of the subject; it releases those elements of itself that are devoted to its subversion and destruction. Knowledge does not slowly detach itself from its empirical roots . . . it creates a progressive enslavement to its instinctive violence. (1984c: 96–7)

5 While it has often been argued that welfare reform is motivated ideologically there are sets of economic, political and social factors that cannot be narrowly construed as ideological. Summarizing and paraphrasing George and Taylor-Gooby (1996: 22–7) the following key points reflect the tangible challenges facing the welfare state:

- Demands and needs for services are outstripping resources. There is an almost universal contraction in service provision.
- Different social environments now create a demand for a more participatory and user-friendly welfare society.
- Unforeseen changes in patterns of family life have combined with the power of the political demand to reduce sexist social divisions.
- Major changes in labour and workforce patterns have occurred.
- National economies are increasingly subservient to the decisions of transnational corporations.
- Diminished working class solidarity is associated with a more mobile and fragmented society.

- There are complex issues relating to individual consumer choice – the effects of a 'designer-label' culture.
- There is an increase in indices of crime statistics and an increase in the objective levels of poverty and social dislocation which the welfare state was expected to have solved.

6 This term indicates the complex critique of power that is associated with Michel Foucault.

7 It is important however to 'unpack' the use of the word 'crisis'. It is a much overused word and this volume cannot escape from the consequences of that. Nonetheless, the intent of my analysis of risk and social policy is to set out a critique of neo-liberal political reason which depends so heavily on presenting the crisis of welfare dependency as given 'fact'. Crisis and contradiction are, as Hewitt suggested, 'sieve-like concepts' (1983: 82) subject to various epistemologies of rule.

8 The issues of governance, the possibility of the 'public sphere' and Habermas' further discussion of how to defend this aspect of 'civil society' are taken up in Chapters 3 and 5.

9 Habermas in jocular but serious manner describes such aims as entering a 'no-man's land' (1986: 15).

10 See Turner for a synthesis of the debate about human rights. Especially useful is his discussion about how rights extend beyond the boundaries of the nation-state and how that intersects with citizenship theory. Turner concludes that 'there is a dynamic relationship between human vulnerability and the precarious character of social institutions' (1993: 508). He argues that analysis of risk is vital to maintaining a lively examination of rights.

11 It is clear that there is no 'single' welfare state model and welfare states involve many functions other than the achievement of equality. I am not intending this analysis of risk and social policy to be an occasion to relate these themes of risk to a comparative analysis of its varied functions across all of the many 'forms' and 'models' of welfare states. My intention is narrower and considers, first, how risk has become the leitmotiv of a neo-liberal socio-political attack on the welfare state and, secondly, how that social reconstruction is often 'framed' as a 'moral crisis' (cf. Offe, 1996: 150). This particular focus allows me to consider how varying perceptions about risk have contributed to the 'crisis that the advanced welfare states now face [which] is almost certainly linked to their projection of a set of egalitarian principles that no longer command broad consensus' (Esping-Andersen, 1996: 263).

12 Foucault suggests that unmasking the 'face of the other' requires attention to 'petty malice' in all its hiddenness (1984c: 80).

13 See Procacci (1994). Gordon describes how in pre-modern times the poor were seen as the

> purest form of *social danger*, not only as the obvious political threat of riot and sedition, but also, and more profoundly, as the danger of an anti-society, a zone of unchecked instinct incompatible with truly social being, blocking the free circulation of labour and capital which is the *sine qua non* of liberal welfare. (1991: 38)

How that 'other' is viewed will vary according to the general nature of particular welfare states, ranging from the comprehensive and universal social democratic model, through various models of a social insurance welfare state, to residual models. In the first, the welfare 'other' is an equal citizen with 'rights'. The second regards welfare as a necessary disciplinary activity of nation building and treats the welfare 'other', accordingly, as an 'object' of moral suasion and social pacification. The third regards the welfare 'other' as having failed to take up 'obvious' opportunities for personal success and therefore as being personally responsible for their impoverished situation.

14 Not that these concerns were always about normative issues. The traditional concerns of social administration in the Titmuss *oeuvre*, for example, had been strongly empirical and positivist. I am indebted to my colleague Stephen Uttley for the following comments: 'It is only since the late 1960s that the push to strengthening theory has led to a turning away from the detailed accounts of policies and services as they exist. One could, of course, counter that neoliberalism has almost totally ignored what is – as evidenced by the lack of data for decision-making and evaluation of policy prescriptions' (personal communication). Garland supports this point of view when he suggests that governmentality study 'takes it as axiomatic that government is a "problem-solving activity"' and 'tends to conceptualize these problems and fields *through* the perceptual grid of the programmes and rationalities that the authorities generate to deal with them. There is no concern to establish an independent analysis of its own' (1997: 200–1).

15 This is certainly true of New Zealand where I live and work.

16 This analysis of risk and social policy is more applicable to those welfare states that fall more specifically within a social democratic model or those that may be defined as residual. See below for a fuller discussion of the different justifications that social insurance models espouse and how that works against the imperative of a neo-liberal revision of the welfare mandate.

17 See note 19 of Chapter 4 for a description of Foucault's objections to the lax use of ideology.

18 For an excellent discussion of claims-making in welfare see Drover and Kerans (1993).

19 Honneth traces the origin of this view of politics back to Machiavelli who introduced into Florentine politics the idea that humans are 'egocentric beings with regard only for their own benefit'. Honneth also suggests that 'Machiavelli set in place a socio-ontological foundation that amounts to the assumption of a permanent state of hostile competition between subjects' (1995b: 8).

20 Squires, however, validly argues that social policy needs not to avoid the 'common-sense'. He attacks social policy rhetoric which expresses a 'virulent form of idealism' (1990: 41).

21 The role of the shaman in migratory cultures was to encapsulate tribal fears within complex rituals. The shaman could be held to account. Once nomadic cultures became settled the risk bearer (or the sin eater) became the priest whose different rituals transposed the consequences and accountabilities of risk within the signs and symbols of the Eucharist. God's will became a different 'schedule' of accountability! The essence of the priestly craft was to absorb communal fears and point away from the particular to the numinous for any possible resolution.

22 Though Beck argues that some risks are so potentially overwhelming and out of control that no feasible insurance is possible (cf. 1996b: 31).

23 I do not intend to traverse the debate about the correct 'origin' of welfare states. Most interpreters, in social policy, have preferred to locate its development in the pressure of class interests, political visions of social order or the maintenance of a productive workforce. Social obligation is only one possible factor, and not necessarily the most important. I use it here to emphasize the salience of security and risk. The endurability of the welfare state *after* unions have been effectively controlled by the politics of deregulation, and the enactment of employment contracts has vitiated national awards, indicates that its survival, at least, does not solely depend on the political clout of unions. As indicated in note 11, my intent is to see whether we might consider the complex issues of security to be an important factor in the development of welfare states. If my argument holds, that refashioning the public rhetoric of risk is part of the fundamental nature of neo-liberal politics, then any political argument about mutual support and social obligation must challenge the neo-liberal denial of otherness to those groups whom it defines as politically unacceptable. We can then examine the issues of how security and risk became central to the view that the welfare state is also a disciplinary state serving wider political ends.

24 See Burchell (1993; 1996), Culpitt (1992: 25–47), Fraser and Gordon (1992), Jayasuriya (1996), Meredyth (1997), Mouffe (1995), Saunders (1993), Taylor-Gooby (1993), Turner (1993).

25 While neo-liberalism has appropriated the term 'welfare society', the use of that term has not been the sole preserve of the right. See for example William Robson's earlier book (1976) *Welfare State and Welfare Society: Illusion and Reality.*

2

FOLLOWING FOUCAULT: GOVERNANCE, SECURITY AND RISK

> All my books . . . are, if you like, little toolboxes. If people want to open them, to use a particular sentence, a particular idea, a particular analysis like a screwdriver or a spanner to short circuit, to discredit, to break systems of power, including perhaps even those that my books issue from . . . well, so much the better.
>
> (Mottier, 1995: 27)

The 'language' of Foucault, which I use to think more deeply about risk, is often recondite and operates at several levels. In general terms the question is whether we consider Foucault to be a historiographer of knowledge (as Rorty [1982] suggests) or a philosopher (as Deleuze [1988] argues). In an interesting review article discussing this question, Descombes (1987) suggests that there are indeed several 'Foucaults'. One is a 'French philosopher whose unfinished system is reconstructed by Gilles Deleuze . . . the second is a sort of perennial visiting philosopher in the US'! Descombes goes on to argue that the 'French Foucault and the American Foucault are not two sides of one and the same thinker: they are philosophers who hold entirely incompatible doctrines' (1987: 20). The elusive prose of the 'Masked Philosopher' is well captured by Merquior who suggested that Foucault's writings are 'strewn with gnomic utterances, tantalizing hints, and a taste for verbal drama rather than logical argument' (1985: 56). His ideas need to be approached in a novel way. Like all social theorists we can use them indiscriminately, as bits and pieces out of his 'toolbox'.[1]

What I think a 'reading' of Foucault requires is a willingness to embrace not only the logic but also the 'playfulness' of his ideas. For example, he wrote that 'genealogy is history in the form of a concerted carnival'. Or consider this: 'knowledge is not made for understanding: it is made for cutting' (1984c). They are 'word-pictures' which engage the mind deeply *below* the logical. They evoke a 'yes' that is not rational but comes from the 'otherness' to which he often refers.[2] Together with the allusive conception of 'otherness' is Foucault's significant insight about 'rarity' or 'scarcity' which implies that our 'speaking' can never be finished. This is 'the postulate that everything that it is possible to say, in terms of the rules and lexical resources of language, is not in fact said; that the field of utterances . . . is spotty and full of gaps' (Goldstein, 1984: 171–2). The value of his *oeuvre*, ultimately, is that such insights enliven our imaginations. He seeks to *dance* at the carnival of knowledge as well as deal with the *sharp and possibly dangerous* consequence of so doing. There is a *cost* to ideas. As Descombes concludes, the 'American Foucault may take our concerns and practices very seriously. Yet it may be the "anarchist" Foucault who keeps fascinating his readers' (1987: 21).

The 'Foucault effect' in social policy: preliminary forays?

Garland (1997) suggests that Foucault has had 'a huge impression' on criminological studies and allowed the discipline to develop a new theoretical language. Foucault is yet to have the same effect on social policy. However, a new literature is emerging in social policy which sees in his theorizing an opportunity to think freshly about welfare epistemologies (cf. Hewitt, 1983; 1992; Hillyard and Watson, 1996; Squires, 1990; not excluding Donzelot's earlier classic *The Policing of Families*, 1979). A consideration of the meaning of risk in relation to social policy theory provides an opportunity to re-examine the obvious and common-sense assumptions that the real issues of market exchange are about the necessity to manage the possibility of risk. The following investigation into the 'archaeology' and 'genealogy'[3] of risk sets out an alternative position that the primacy of the solitary, self-regarding, individual is not such an incontrovertible 'fact' of social life.[4] Social policy needs to find new theoretical justifications to articulate the currently unfashionable but vital safeguarding 'of basic needs, as well as opening up opportunities for different individuals and groups to encounter the otherness of need in each other' (Hewitt, 1994: 54). The possibility exists, within social policy, to use Foucault to develop a new theoretical language.[5] Procacci sets out a convincing argument that while Foucault did establish a valid genealogy of madness the same is yet to be done for poverty (1994: 207).

   Applying some of Foucault's critical thinking about power/knowledge to establishing a history of the philosophy of risk reveals that risk also conditions that individual consciousness: it is antecedent and formative. Risk cannot be construed just as a potential threat to the self. Risk perception also involves the ways in which the self is able to perceive the self. Because risk constitutes that consciousness, as well as threatening it, it becomes reflexive. Power, and knowledge about the 'practices' that reveal it, is not the possession of any one specific dominant political 'group'. As Foucault wrote:

power . . . is not that which makes the difference between those who exclusively possess and retain it, and those who do not have it and submit to it. Power must be analysed as something which circulates, or rather as something which only functions in the form of a chain. It is never localised here or there, never in anybody's hands, never appropriated as a commodity or piece of wealth . . . individuals are the vehicle of power, not its points of application. (1980: 98)

If we can argue that the idea of risk is fundamental to the formulation of that belief about the singularity of individual consciousness, and is not just an aspect of it, then the whole basis and rationale for neo-liberal individualism can be re-examined. If 'power' can be seen as that which affects us all then its potential to dominate is lessened, not because it is weakened, but because it is something that inevitably 'circulates'. Another way to 'understand' what Foucault meant by the ubiquity of power, and its elusive nature, is to reflect on his significant question to Paul Veyne, 'how is it that there is so little truth in truth?' (Veyne, 1993: 8).

Foucault's techniques of the self: the 'psychology' of social policy

If individualism is now the nodal point of how risk is to be defined, allied to the imperative of the market, then it is even more important to ask questions about the origin of such immutable and irreducible imperatives. The essence of all ideological dominance is the contention that 'truth' is not only so for the speaker but must also be so for all others. That there may be 'so little truth in truth' is still a rallying point for critical theory. It calls common-sense assumptions into question and suggests a method to challenge current political hegemonies. Analysing various reifications of the 'process' of power was central to Foucault's task. The concept of risk has now been used to reinforce and generate the power of an all-pervasive colonizing of our self-consciousness, such that the 'solitary', 'self-regarding' individual is the dominating symbol of our times. We need to ask not only why this image has such normative power in economic theory but also why it has assumed such prominence in social policy theory.[6] Placing this discussion of risk alongside aspects of Foucault's thought is one way to establish an answer to this question.

For Foucault, the state developed 'institutions of discipline and confinement which are constitutive of knowledge' (Said, 1991: 4). This analysis of the institutions that constitute knowledge is not, for Foucault, an opportunity to engage in a debate about meaning – to search for reliable and trustworthy norms. It was rather a search for how we construct *patterns of meaning*. He sought a vantage point from which to examine the 'taken-for-grantedness' of modern governance. His reluctance to determine lines of causal inquiry is expressed in his phrase that he was pursuing 'conditions of possibility'. His thought provides some necessary tools to challenge the implicit obviousness of neo-liberal arguments about risk, protection of the self and the proper role of political intervention. His work is especially useful in elucidating not just how the archetypal 'solitary individual' is a cultural symbol but how it has become such a cornerstone of contemporary theories of governance. It is interesting to note that Foucault believed that:

> since Kant, the role of philosophy is to prevent reason from going beyond the limits of what is given in experience; but from the same moment – that is, since the development of the modern state and the political management of society – the role of philosophy is also to keep watch over the excessive powers of political rationality. (1983: 210)

Foucault's mechanism for 'keeping watch' was to elucidate an 'archae-ology' of how certain 'knowledges' establish specific patterns of govern-ance – the 'practices' of specific genealogy. Attempting to 'constrain' reason to what can be observed experientially, to the *how of practice* and not the *why of reason*, formed the core of his research method (cf. Hacking, 1986a). Keeping watch over the 'excessive powers of political rationality' is a valuable touchstone in trying to set out the elements for a philosophy of risk within social policy. It allows us to challenge some aspects of the taken-for-granted assumption in neo-liberalism that risk is fundamental only to the depiction and defence of a rigorous individualism.

The valorized 'self' and some ontological temptations!

Foucault created a methodology of inquiry that would not get 'bogged down' in the intricacies of ontological claims-making. He stood outside the 'ethical polarization of the subject–object relationship' in order to challenge those assumptions that privileged individual subjectivity as the source and ideal form of moral autonomy. Descombes commented that Foucault sought to address 'the issue of the morality which characterises our time – the morality of autonomy ... Autonomy means that our conduct cannot be governed by motives of the common good of the group or of a sacred law' (1987: 20). Foucault's task also involved rejecting 'the assump-tion that domination falsifies the essence of human subjectivity'. This is so important in challenging those rationales for the rejection of the welfare 'other'. Equally, he wanted to stand apart from the universalizing claims of humanism – to avoid the potential tyranny of 'ascribing to them the teleology of progress' (Gordon, 1980: 239). What Foucault sought was a 'morality with no claim to universality' (Veyne, 1993: 4). We need to hold in mind this dual task (which he set himself) as we consider how the emergence of risk became a defining aspect of modern neo-liberal self-

reflection. Our 'subjectivity' is not often essential to anyone else but ourselves (and our immediate intimates) and cannot really be used to 'name'
the world. Similarly, our drive to find a universal ethical touchstone for our
coveted social 'utopias' cannot easily be generalized into dependable
political forms. There is a reflexive challenge in his theorizing to the
excesses of both radical individualism and uncritical claims for the pre-
eminence of 'the social'.

Foucault's 'genealogy', or hermeneutics, of the self describes how the
opening up or 'knowledge' of the self was premised originally on the
notion of sacrifice. This valorization of sacrifice created an aspect of individual reflection that reinforced a process of 'indefinite interpretation'.
Such meditations about individual meaning accelerated personal hopes
for how it might be possible to transcend individual contingency and thus
make possible the extension of the self towards another. I quote Foucault at
length because this luminous paragraph contains so much of the reasoning
behind his explanation for how political belief systems (neo-liberalism in
this discussion), perhaps vainly, seek to emphasize the positive aspects of
self-autonomy. 'Vainly' in the sense that they ignore the contexts out
of which the 'selves' emerged, and deny the formative power of the
'historical technologies' that shaped the experience of the 'self'. The search
for a positive philosophy of the self has recursively set out to deny the
'other' who inevitably becomes a *competitor* and not a *companion* in the
avoidance or minimizing of risk.

> I think that one of the great problems of Western culture has been to find the
> possibility of founding the hermeneutics of the self not, as it was the case in early
> Christianity, on the sacrifice of the self but, on the contrary, on a positive, on the
> theoretical and practical emergence of the self. That was the aim of judicial
> institutions, that was the aim also of medical and psychiatric practices, that was
> the aim of political and philosophical theory – to constitute the ground of the
> subjectivity as the root of a positive self, what we could call the permanent
> anthropologism of Western thought. And I think that this anthropologism is
> linked to the deep desire to substitute the positive figure of man for the sacrifice
> which for Christianity was the condition for the opening of the self as a field of
> indefinite interpretation. During the last two centuries, the problem has been:
> what could be the positive foundation for the technologies of the self that we
> have been developing during centuries and centuries? But the moment, maybe,
> is coming for us to ask, do we need, really, this hermeneutics of the self? Maybe
> the problem of the self is not to discover what it is in its positivity, maybe the
> problem is now to discover that the self is nothing else than the historical
> correlation of the technology built into our history. Maybe the problem is to
> change those technologies. And in this case, one of the main political problems
> would be nowadays, in the strict sense of the word, the politics of ourselves.
> (1993: 222–3)

It is the 'politics of ourselves' which is significant in showing how various
attempts to establish the ground of a positive, subjective, non-sacrificing
self have resulted in the neo-liberal arguments for self-autonomy. The

'politics of ourselves' has been derailed by a preoccupation with risk. The passion for change, to articulate a positive view of the world, now intersects with a passion for protection from the ill consequences of invasive risk. When the individual could be subsumed within the greater perspective that it was sacrifice which created individual meaning, what Foucault called the 'ontological temptation' of Christianity, then risk was simply part of the sacrificing 'truth technology' of confession.

The paradox is that self-sacrificing individuals did not in fact lose themselves but the intense personal reflection involved implicitly reinforced the politics of individual autonomy. The notion of risk emerges out of the search for 'subjectivity as the root of a positive self'. It is this search for autonomy, within neo-liberalism, that establishes risk as a separate category of possibility. The search for it cannot be captured by the previously all-consuming possibility of sacrifice. As Foucault suggests, watching 'the most imperceptible movements of our self' is now the dominating feature of the epistemology of the self. Its rhetorical strength, as Hacking has suggested, depends on the 'cunning of conscience and self-knowledge . . . to make it *feel* private' (1986b: 236). Speculation that the 'self is nothing else than the historical correlation of the technology built into our history' raises the spectre of a contingency that is, seemingly, too hard for us to bear.[7] This counter-defensive self-regard has found risk at every turn since it is the perception of risk that is intrinsic to the minute observation of the self. With the emergence of Protestantism, salvation became 'privatized' through all the intricacies of personal devotion and reflection so that 'religious care was no longer care for others . . . it was care for one's own sole salvation' (Luhmann, 1986: 315). This was the 'engine' for the massive historical shifts in how 'being poor' was reified into 'poverty' (cf. Procacci, 1994).

The politics of governance: Foucault's legacy?

A more considered understanding of how social institutions are constantly involved in the process of change requires an examination of Foucault's idea that power is not repressive (as radical liberationists would argue) but 'productive' (Gordon, 1986; Weberman, 1995). While controversial, Foucault's ideas offer a useful challenge to the notion that it is beliefs that drive social change. For him the important questions are not really epistemological (i.e. about beliefs and meanings) but rather about the patterning of how knowledge and ideas are used to create systems of governance. For example Fraser argues that Foucault, in establishing his 'genealogy of knowledge/power', is not interested in whether knowledge 'is in any sense true or warranted or adequate or undistorted. Instead of assessing epistemic contents, he describes knowledge production procedures, practices, apparatuses and institutions' (1989b: 21).

A genealogical analysis of the 'procedures, practices, apparatuses and institutions' of public choice theory and agency theory, which does not engage in epistemology, provides an opportunity to locate this inquiry into risk and social policy within aspects of Foucault's theory of how knowledge is produced.[8] He called this an 'ontology of the present' rather than an 'analytic of truth'. Applying this analysis to the current sets of welfare rhetoric generated by the dominant neo-liberal political assertions raises an interesting set of questions:

- How does the concept of risk relate to these knowledge production procedures?
- What practices have been adopted with respect to the provision of welfare benefits?
- How have these procedures contributed to a distinct, pejorative and hostile reaction to welfare?
- What changes in the established welfare bureaucracies have contributed to this 'new knowledge'?

These discourses about risk are powerfully centred on the logic of a presumed rationality that is, as Foucault argues, better understood as the 'subjectivity' of the self. Placing the concept of risk in relation to Foucault's theory of 'knowledge/power' reveals another important focus. If epistemological examination of welfare ideologies is no longer possible, we can perhaps advance the debate by relating how 'knowledges' about welfare are structured and patterned to Beck's discussion of reflexive modernization. Previously, seeking the irreducible and defendable core of social policy's concerns has led us away from the paradoxical. The empirical and positivist tradition had no time for such speculation. The brutalities of disadvantage needed no philosophical 'hair splitting'! So much of the effort was to establish the actual legitimacy of need and to argue that legitimacy rationally. However, as I have argued already, social policy must ground its rhetoric not only in reshaping epistemology and the urgent practicalities of social disadvantage but also in considering the way that social knowledge is constructed. Focusing only on 'meanings' has been unsuccessful in confronting neo-liberalism. It will be important to understand how, while 'breaching the normal form has to be registered as chance because it is not anticipated', all explanations of these events seek to return to a basis of rationality. Events may be seen as arbitrary but explanations 'must be shown to have an order of . . . [their] own, a secondary normality as it were' (Luhmann, 1993: vii).

Deconstructing and revealing the false imperatives of such reasoning must remain the core task for critical theory. Foucault's analysis of the 'practices' of how power/knowledge constructs patterns of political discourse provides fresh analytical tools for social policy to confront the hegemony of neo-liberal welfare policy. As de Oliveira stated:

For Foucault it is thus understandable that capitalism had to fabricate the mechanisms that would secure the protection of wealth, through the moralization of the working subjects, just like the institution of the police, based on the fear of the criminal, or the welfare state in socializing techniques of normalization. (1997: 143)

Linguistic paradoxes: silence, 'side effects' and knowledge

This analysis of risk provides a new way to comment on the ideologies that have been used to support current beliefs about the perils of 'welfare dependency' and the value of promoting self-reliance. The exciting aspect of Beck's analysis of risk is that his thesis reaches deeply into the paradoxical nature of our social world. He considers

> that it is not knowledge but rather non-knowledge which is the medium of 'reflexive' modernization. To put it another way: we are living in the *age of side effects*, and precisely this is what is to be decoded – and shaped – methodologically and theoretically, in everyday life or in politics. (Beck et al., 1994: 175)

An examination of the paradoxical leads us into a discussion of Beck's 'side effects' and how to decode them, while an examination of the implicit aspects of public welfare rhetoric leads us into the significance of what is not said as well as that which is asserted. The search for 'non-knowledge', and the gleaning of 'side effects', is a productive way to re-examine how social policy theory has formulated risk in the past and how the concept of risk reveals the paradoxical nature of welfare dependency rhetoric. Associating Beck's notion of 'side effects' with another set of ideas about the importance of 'silences' in social policy gives us a vantage point to examine the implicit rhetoric as well as the politics of governance espoused by neo-liberalism. Consideration of the elusive silences of social policy will allow us to comprehend why so many social programmes (so full of good intent) have become implementation failures. Rational explanations for such failures are unsatisfying, precisely because they ignore the irrational and the paradoxical.

What is refreshing in Beck's thesis of risk society is his willingness to embrace the significance of the irrational as a valid concern of sociological theory. The power and hostility with which the successful can pillory the dependent is derived from the presumed rationality of market attainment. There is little room in those particular calculations for either the irrational or the paradoxical. Promoting his notion of 'reflexive modernization', Beck thought, would assist to break an important taboo about

> the tacit equation of latency and immanence in social change. The idea that the transition from one social epoch to another could take place unintended and unpolitically, bypassing all the forums for political decisions, the lines of conflict and the partisan controversies, contradicts the democratic self-understanding of this society. (Beck et al., 1994: 3)

He poses the significance of social change that operates at the interstices of customary politics – one that is not bounded by an explicit historicist viewpoint. Katznelson is equally interested in the notion of change resulting from the interplay of ideas *below* or *outside* what is commonly discussed. Some of the most significant aspects of social change, he suggests, lie apart from the generally accepted levels of political and social discourse. They are found in the 'silences of social policy'. All political systems, he suggests, have boundaries 'between that which is discussed and disputed and that which is not discussed and disputed' (1986: 310–11).

Reconsidering the power of the unspoken (the silences), the occluded, is not typical of social policy theorizing. Nevertheless, it is these silences, part of the non-knowledge to which Beck refers, that dictate current realities and future possibilities that social policy needs to consider. Foucault too would often argue that we were looking in the wrong places! As he said, it 'seems to me that the possibility exists for fiction to function in truth, for a fictional discourse to induce effects of truth' (1980: 193). We are constrained by the perceptions of what is appropriate social analysis. For example, he said of his overall 'project' that 'where no word is heard any more one can still hear the deep buried murmur of meaning, that what men do not say is a continuation of their speaking' (1991a: 61).

The 'speaking' to us in 'fictions' that Foucault does in order to 'induce effects of truth' challenges our perceptions of the normal. His prose, maddening to some, is suggestive of those elements of how we might 'revision the social' which lie outside our intellectual grasp. The idea that there might be a 'deep buried murmur of meaning' which is not reducible 'to language and speech' suggests that knowledge of the 'social' is most likely to 'be discovered lurking in signs and discourses' (Said, 1991: 5). This seems to find an echo in Katznelson's 'silences' in the sense that no matter how sophisticated our social knowledges, no matter how certain the findings in a rhetoric of our social research, there is a 'more' we might yet understand.

Foucault had an 'uncanny ability to invent whole fields of investigation'. These new areas of social inquiry 'come from Foucault's everlasting effort to formulate otherness and heterodoxy without domesticating them or turning them into doctrine' (Said, 1991: 5–6). For Pavlich this means 'pursuit of the unthought' (1995: 555) and Goldstein's reflections on 'rarity' or 'scarcity' mentioned previously. Katznelson, reflecting a different aspect of the 'shape' or 'feel' of such knowledge, considers that we must

> explore the construction and changeability of the always present division between the domains of political speech and political silence. By making this problem the centrepiece of analysis, we can widen the domain of empirical studies, make a place for counterfactual analysis, and develop a taste for

thinking about possible worlds that are not very far away, but seen to be just beyond our grasp. (1986: 325)

Post-modern theory might well create the legitimization of difference and destroy the basis for normative epistemology but it doesn't destroy the search for the 'other', the elusive 'non-knowledge' that is not antagonistic as Foucault argued. He can be allied with Katznelson in suggesting that some of the most important levers of change in a society, dominated by 'reflexive modernization', lie outside the notion of 'democratic self-understanding'. Foucault argued that 'power is tolerable only on condition that it masks a substantial part of itself'. This is the basis for the hegemony of neo-liberalism: the political substance is 'masked' in the rhetoric of common-sense. As Foucault continues, the force of such hegemony 'is proportional to its ability to hide its own mechanisms. Would power be accepted if it were entirely cynical? For it, secrecy is not in the nature of an abuse; it is indispensable to its operation' (1981a: 86). So perhaps it is not to the 'noise' of social change (the strident anti-welfare rhetoric) that we must look for understanding but to the 'silences'. This refocuses our investigation into risk. What is it that contemporary political and social debate defines as the vital issues, and how do these obvious concerns relate to those imperatives that are not framed as part of public discourse?[9]

Unmasking these assumptions that dominant political power 'hides itself' exemplifies Beck's argument that 'the institutions of industrial society become the producers and legitimators of threats they cannot control' (Beck et al., 1994: 5). Risk society, he suggests, has two important aspects: the means by which cumulative decision-making produces a sense of residual risk; and, perhaps more importantly, how the perceived dangers of modern society become the dominant aspect of public social and welfare discussions. By postulating the notion of 'reflexive modernization' Beck wishes to highlight what he calls the concept of 'self-confrontation'. He describes this as the social mechanism by which the 'transition from the industrial to the risk period of modernity occurs undesired, unseen and compulsively in the wake of the autonomised dynamism of modernization' (1992: 5). How that idea of self-confrontation has developed and how it supports public choice theory is an important question to be debated. Associated with this concept that societal institutions are responsible for the creation of risk is Luhmann's complementary analysis that:

the dependence of society's future on decision-making has increased, and nowadays so dominates ideas about the future that all concepts of 'forms of being', which – as Nature – intrinsically limit what can happen, has been abandoned. Technology and the concomitant awareness of capability has occupied nature's territory, and both surmise and experience indicate that this can more easily prove destructive than constructive. The fear that things could go wrong is therefore growing rapidly and with it the risk apportioned to decision-making. (1993: xii)

The rhetorical ground for massive social reconstruction, typical of those states that have defined themselves as moving from a welfare state to a welfare society, is generated by a new/old concept of social risk. Public choice theory, used to articulate the rationale for massive social reconstruction, has valorized the concept of individual risk to reinforce the 'whittling away of the state'. Katznelson, commenting on this, suggests that the

> most analytically powerful of recent policy studies are grounded in choice theory drawn from the parsimonious postulates of neoclassical economics about isolated, self-interested persons who choose rationally between alternatives after computing their costs and benefits. (1986: 312)

The intent of this rhetoric is to develop a more self-responsible, self-risk-managing citizenry who will not look to the state to be rescued from the inevitable vagaries of life. Neo-liberalism considers that a welfare society must reflect only the interplay of social and political structures forged out of the harsh logic of self-interest. Benevolence and social concern can only occur tangentially in private altruism. Such politics reflects Foucault's 'game of citizen and laws, rather than the pastoral game'. These were later concepts that Foucault developed to explain aspects of governance. Foucault argued that the pastoral

> form of power is salvation oriented (as opposed to political power). It is oblative (as opposed to the principle of sovereignty); it is individualizing (as opposed to legal power); it is coextensive and continuous with life; it is linked with a production of truth – the truth of the individual himself. (1983: 214)

Gordon describes how Foucault's argument that the 'daemonic coupling' of 'city-game' and 'shepherd-game' reinforced a 'form of secular pastorate which couples "individualization" and "totalization" ' (1991: 8). The supremacy of neo-liberalism has been its theoretical ability to combine these two 'practices' of government: to articulate the clearest support for the political expression of individualism on the one hand, and on the other to surround this with an all-encompassing rhetoric that admits of no legitimate difference.

In the next chapter we consider how the previous justifications for social obligation and welfare have been defined as an unwarranted burden. It will be important to consider how the idea of risk not only fashions the discourses about welfare but also controls the language of the debate. We can seek some explanation for the power of this linguistic hegemony in relation to Foucault's theory of governance. We might do well to keep sight of Foucault's allusive maxim that 'liberty is what must be exercised . . . [the] guarantee of freedom is freedom' (Gordon, 1991:

47). The idea that we are governed through our freedom is, as Garland argues, 'at once critical and revelatory'. It is 'analytically audacious and devastating in its political implications'. However, he then mounts a very considerable objection to the cavalier use of this Foucauldian paradox, not the least being his observation that to use 'freedom' too simply 'tends to repeat the propaganda of the advocates of neo-liberal reform' (1997: 196–7). In the next chapter we shall consider how accurately we can apply this notion of being governed by our freedom and whether it does reflect a compelling aspect of Foucault's *oeuvre*.

Notes

1 Applying Foucault's ideas to this analysis of risk and social policy inevitably faces the jeopardy that it is only 'bits and pieces' of his ideas that I have used. Nonetheless, I take some comfort in his acknowledgement that using these 'bits and pieces' widely was acceptable.

2 See Deleuze ('What is a dispositif?') where he discusses Foucault's sense of the 'other': 'it is necessary [as he says] to distinguish what we are (what we are already no longer), and what we are in the process of becoming' (1992: 164).

3 I agree with Hewitt that the translation of these terms 'jars in the mind': they are not naturally terms of our English social philosophy. He sees *archaeology* as a 'method of analysis that sites knowledge and its subjects by excavating the rules that form a particular discourse . . . [such] rules establish both the boundaries dividing discourses and the continuities traversing [them]'. Alternatively, Hewitt sees *genealogy* as a way to trace discursive information 'to bring us a fuller understanding of presently constituted knowledge, a history of the present, and of its deployment as an instrument of power to promote authoritative pro-nouncements and mask criticism' (1983: 68). See the following note for a similar view of genealogy as providing a means to criticize the hegemonic 'masking' of the present.

For Foucault, genealogy records 'the singularity of events . . . in sentiments, love, conscience, instincts; it must be sensitive to their recurrence' (1984c: 76). The allusion to respect and recognition that is represented here finds an echo in Honneth's paradigm (see Chapter 8). Goldstein, reviewing the meaning of these terms, suggests that 'genealogy arises from the background of archaeology . . . genealogy accentuates the "horizontal" dimension: its hallmarks are "eventuality" and narrative process'. She emphasizes that genealogical narrative is *not* teleo-logical: 'events are eruptions; outcomes are local and radically contingent, never adhering to a global necessity' (1984: 14). This presupposes the possibility of a welfare genealogy, which is not necessarily collective and constitutive of the welfare 'other' as a collective grouping.

4 My application of Foucault's notion of 'genealogy' accords with O'Malley et al. (1997). They seek, in this significant article, to emphasize

genealogy as criticism/critique: a renewal of interest in the role of historians of the present as public intellectuals; and a conceptualization of politics as relations of contest or struggle which are constitutive of government rather than simply a source of programmatic failure and (later) redesign. (1997: 505)

Burchell, who suggests that these analyses can have a 'diagnostic value', also endorses the critical possibilities of genealogical research. It draws attention to the contingent nature of these specific 'mentalities of rule' (Miller and Rose, 1990), that typify neo-liberal governance strategies, which might allow for an estimate of the 'costs' associated with these specific rules of governance (Burchell, 1993: 279). The possibility of using Foucault in this critical way is the major subtext of my inquiry into social policy and risk.

5 Although that task is not easy given Foucault's stricture that the 'emergence of social science cannot . . . be isolated from the rise of this new political rationality' which, as he expressed it, 'results from a constant correlation between an increasing individualization and the reinforcement of this totality' (1988b: 162). His point, which he made often, was that social science must confront its role in the 'mentalities of rule'; it cannot stand outside for it is part of the governing process.

6 Le Grand's recent depiction of the range of human motivation surrounding those who receive and those who deliver welfare services is fascinating. 'Knaves' are self-interested actors in the welfare drama; 'knights' retain the stance and practice of altruism and public spirit; while 'pawns' are passively recipient of others' actions or largesse (1997: 154).

7 Foucault's thinking about the 'self' is not entirely consistent. In his early work it seemed that he was concerned to 'free the self' from the consequences of disciplinary governance. But in his later work (when he does turn explicitly to describing an 'ethics of the self') he saw the possibility of an ethics 'that is no longer supported by either tradition or reason; as an artist of itself, the self would enjoy that autonomy that modernity can no longer do without' (Veyne, 1993: 7).

8 However, for Foucault, the 'will to knowledge' was not simple. He found many 'forms' in knowledge; namely, 'instinct, passion, the inquisitor's devotion, cruel subtlety, and malice'. Knowledge, he says,

> discovers the violence of a position that sides with those against those who are unhappy in their ignorance, against the effective illusions by which humanity protects itself, a position that encourages the dangers of research and delights in disturbing discoveries. (1984c: 95)

9 Habermas was impatient with how the 'foreground contingencies *in the world*' were denied any legitimacy and replaced with 'mysteriously encoded contingencies found in the *disclosure of the world*'. Certainly for him such 'other' reasoning had 'the effect of extinguishing the last sparks of utopian thinking and western culture's confidence in itself' (1986: 3). See White (1988a; 1988b) for a different perspective on Habermas' pessimism and the possibility of creating a 'legitimate commonality'.

3

WELFARE OBLIGATIONS AND SAFETY NETS: THE LESSENING OF RISK

> My problem is to see how men govern (themselves and others) by the production of truth (I repeat once again that by the production of truth I mean not the production of true utterances, but the establishment of domains in which the practice of true and false can be made at once ordered and pertinent).
>
> (Foucault, 1991b: 79)

Neo-liberal social policy has successfully eclipsed the former moral imperatives of mutual obligation that sustained political support for welfare states. A new rhetoric of governance argues for the lessening of risk, not the meeting of need. Welfare states are being refashioned into residual welfare societies with appropriate 'safety nets' (cf. Barry, 1997; Culpitt, 1992;[1] Garland, 1997; Hewitt, 1992; Hoy, 1991; Rose, 1996a; 1996b). The advocates of this new welfare society disdain the old ethos of 'welfarism' which reflected patterns of need analysis and social provision defined as collective state responsibility. Clearly, the new 'more marketized, entrepreneurial, consumerist forms of social organization is a major fact of our time' (Garland, 1997: 183). Rhetorical arguments about the 'evils of welfare dependency', and the political necessity to find new responses to the 'crises of welfare', are presented as if they are self-evidently true. Any attempt to raise the contestability of these issues confronts the fact that neo-liberal 'explications of rule' are encapsulated within an idealization of specific programmes as 'perfect knowledges'. These new 'mentalities of rule' (Miller and Rose, 1990) 'provide an image of rule so consistent, coherent and integrated, so univocal, that it becomes difficult to prise apart a space for any political intervention' (O'Malley et al., 1997: 513).

The 'domain' of neo-liberal welfare practices

Both the character of the domain and the language deemed appropriate to a discussion of welfare are circumscribed. For neo-liberalism the nature and contours of that domain are self-evident, as is the common acceptance that an appropriate language to describe welfare must now be couched in terms of risk and threat. Contemporary concepts of risk, 'parsed now as danger' (Castel, 1991; Douglas, 1990), are invoked to protect a culture of individual autonomy and justify an expanding industrial system. This 'dialogue about risk plays the role equivalent to taboo or sin, but the slope is tilted in the reverse direction, away from protecting the community and in favor of protecting the individual' (Douglas, 1990: 7).

The rhetoric of possible catastrophe also reveals how deeply embedded consideration of risk has become. Using such language as minimal 'safety nets' to describe acceptable patterns of welfare claims suggests the impact that thinking about risk has had in furthering that rhetoric.[2] It is risk that is the dominant theme of a political language which depicts welfare dependency as a 'semiology of catastrophe' (Barry et al., 1996: 7). The rhetoric for and against welfare is linguistically similar in that both discourses base their argumentation on some striving for normative superiority. The rhetorical difference is that neo-liberalism embraces a hidden normativeness (presented as rational practicality) while simultaneously attacking the obvious normativeness associated with arguments about needs and social rights. Donzelot suggests that:

> Society is no longer the *subject of its evolution* so much as the *object of a promotion* devised over its head and aiming to bring freedom to each and security to all. Essentially, at the basis of the reversal of relations between State and society we find an operation which *elides the notion of responsibility* in the field of social relations. (1988: 424)

The debate is not only about the saliency of the relevant issues but about who, apparently, has the *truth*. The neo-liberal dominance in welfare policy has been successful, in part, because it has identified the real problems that welfare systems have had in responding to massive structural change in the labour market. It has also altered public perception of the proper role of government. Ways have been found to 'market' an ideology of power and develop viable sets of expectations about how welfare needs and claim rights are to be interpreted. The regulation of personal conduct, part of Foucault's 'technology of the self', described in the previous chapter, is no longer the responsibility of the state. Donzelot is right: notions of social responsibility have been elided and 'the social' is no longer the *subject* but an *'object of promotion'*. The notion of responsibility has been 'deconstructed' from any social nexus. Welfare needs are reified into the personal. As Rose argues:

> the disadvantaged individual has come to be seen as potentially and ideally an active agent in the fabrication of their own existence. Those 'excluded' from the benefits of a life of choice and self-fulfilment are no longer merely the passive support of a set of social determinations: they are people whose self-

responsibility and self-fulfilling aspirations have been deformed by the dependency culture, whose efforts at self-advancement have been frustrated for so long that they suffer from 'learned helplessness', whose self-esteem has been destroyed. And, it thus follows, that they are to be assisted not through the ministrations of solicitous experts proffering support and benefit cheques, but through their engagement in a whole array of programmes for their ethical reconstruction as active citizens – training to equip them with the skills of self-promotion, counselling to restore their sense of self-worth and self-esteem, programmes of empowerment to enable them to assume their rightful place as the self-actualizing and demanding subjects of an 'advanced' liberal democracy. (1996b: 59–60)

The full extent of this new approach to welfare and dependency is explored in Chapter 9. Here it is important only to note how such rhetoric has been used to define the domain of welfare, to interpret valid needs and limit rights. We need to understand how our political institutions, with their particular patterns of governance, have construed the overall debate in order to discern the shape of the 'domain' within which these issues can be discussed. It is all couched in the language of obviousness, certainty and risk.

Foucault: a pessimistic 'activist' or a buffoon of God?

Foucault's thinking about power and governance offers new intellectual tools to examine such certainties and elucidate how risk has been used to frame them.[3] His stance was not to contend for the truth or falsity of such propositions. His aim was to explicate the particular 'domains in which the practice of true or false can be made at once ordered and pertinent'. Garland argues that:

the point of Foucault's genealogical approach was to make it possible to view such facts in a critical, historical perspective. It also so happens that concepts such as 'action-at-a-distance', 'governing through freedom' and 'the active subject of power' are particularly apposite for the analysis of neo-liberal policies which are explicitly designed to maximise entrepreneurial activity, to empower the consumer and to replace state or professional governance with market mechanisms. (1997: 183–4)

In *The Archaeology of Knowledge and The Discourse on Language* Foucault describes four 'themes', or 'methodological demands', that will determine further work on the archaeology of knowledge. These are a principle of reversal; a principle of discontinuity; a principle of specificity; and, most usefully for this discussion about domains of welfare, a principle of exteriority. This fourth principle

holds that we are not to burrow to the hidden core of discourse, to the heart of the thought or meaning manifested in it; instead, taking the discourse itself, its appearance and regularity, that we should look for its external conditions of existence, for that which gives rise to the chance series of these events and fixes its limits. (1976: 229)

In this chapter the discussion is more clearly oriented to how the idea of risk has been used to fashion such domains. Our perceptions about risk have not only dictated the domain within which speech is possible but also controlled the language that might be used within that domain. The linguistic hegemony is almost complete and it is this that requires some explication. However, as Foucault cautions, analysis of that hegemony ought not 'to burrow to the hidden core of discourse'. To do that is to argue at the level of normative truths: both left and right are naturally protective of the core, the heart of their rhetoric.[4] The critical task is to detach 'the power of truth from the forms of hegemony, social, economic, and cultural, within which it operates at the present time'. That is not achieved, Foucault suggests, by trying to change 'people's consciousness – or what's in their heads'. What is amenable to change is the 'political, economic, institutional regime of the production of truth' (1984b: 75).

Patterns of welfare governance and discipline: clinical relationship or risk profile?

Another important reason for the dominance of neo-liberalism is that not only did it circumscribe the domain within which discourse about 'welfare' is possible but it also refashioned the domain itself. For example, part of the ethos of the drive to construct a welfare and health system based upon the perceived 'transparency' of contract reflects an antagonism to the professional privacy of the social-worker/client relationship. That which was premised on a relationship of *meaning* has now become part of the relationship of *power*. A paradox is established in that while neo-liberalism is essentially possessive, private and individual it denies the individual otherness of the welfare client. Individual success is reified into a 'quality' of the individual and is therefore able to be used pejoratively to exclude the welfare other. Huge rafts of empirical 'facts' are adduced about welfare 'recidivism'. Assumptions are made that welfare has become a 'life-style of choice'.

Reviewing Young's *Justice and the Politics of Difference* (1990), Mills observes that 'the premise of possessive individualism in theories of distributive justice *precludes* a conceptual analysis of social groups, thus foreclosing any understanding of the way oppression actually functions in society' (1994: 212). It is not that neo-liberalism denies the legitimacy of social groups so much as that it does not accord those who are 'different' the same rights. Hence oppression arises out of policies and practices that are aimed at the welfare constituency as a whole – an example of Foucault's 'action-at-a-distance'. Similarly to Foucault, Young argues that such control over the 'domain of welfare' is structural, demonstrating how such constraints are intrinsic to the 'norms, habits, and symbols in the assumptions underlying institutional rules and collective consequences of following those rules' (1990: 41).

This change in patterns of governance reveals the dominance of neo-liberal political rationalities – what Foucault referred to as *techne* – and how these rationalities were actually organized into new welfare practices. As Garland has argued:

> The discretionary powers of clinical experts are being displaced by central management decisions based upon actuarial expertise. New diagnostic practices apply risk factor analysis to the 'profile' of a case rather than engage in face-to-face examination of individual patients. Strategies of care or control fix increasingly upon 'population flows' rather than individual cases, ushering low-risk groups into low-cost care in the community, reserving institutional care for groups defined as high risk. (1997: 182)

This movement away from the validation of the 'helping relationship' is an aspect of governance – the mechanism by which welfare clients, collectively, are 'disciplined', away from dependency towards risk. The current preoccupation is with case management and not casework (cf. Dean, 1995: 568–9, 575; Parton, 1996: 112–13; Rose, 1996b: 54–5). Case management demands clarification about input and outcomes, which constitutes the dominance of contract. Such contract protocols highlight a significant aspect of modern neo-liberal governance that (particularly in respect of welfare services) prefers action 'at a distance' and not face to face. Merquior describes Foucault's analysis of how the 'transcription' of human life moved from the 'chronicle, with its accent on the heroic and memorable . . . [to] the file, measuring up observance as deviation from the norm' (1985: 95). The face-to-face involvement with the case manager is effectively narrowed to brokering services contractually supplied by the state. The client strikes an implicit contract with the case manager. However, another vital but implicit contract with the state is also being ensured (Davis et al., 1997: 230). This pattern institutionalizes a new welfare practice that abandons the notion of the private healing and empowering relationship of casework (the registering and recognizing of a personal 'chronicle') and, instead, institutionalizes (and files) the welfare client as a *risk group and not a risk individual*. The distinction is crucial. In summary, the core tasks of the case manager are 'risk profiling' – an assessment of individual need against a pre-established analysis of risk factors (cf. Parton, 1996: 111). As Rose (1996b) argues, these changes in the 'regulatory technologies' of welfare emphasize measurement and calculation over the previous norms of service. The current norms are no longer about the therapeutic nature of the caseworker/client relationship but rather 'those of competition, quality and customer demand' (1996b: 56).

Consequently, the emergence of risk society focuses politics on the protection and securing of individual autonomy and not on social obligation or cohesion. Various disjunctions between how individual success will be protected, and escalating social need denied, has significantly altered our contemporary politics. Actively responsible individuals are obliged to fulfil their wider political obligations 'not through their relations of dependency and obligation to one another, but through seeking to *fulfil themselves* within a variety of micro-moral domains' (1996b: 57). As Gordon also comments, the 'contemporary question of government is . . . the problem of presenting rules of the game for a society of individuals in a world where the civic and commercial strata of individuality fail to harmonize' (1996: 267).

The typical discourses of social policy have been confined to this 'civic strata of individuality' which has led to their relative marginalization. So much of the normative cast of this discourse hangs on the idea of a 'good citizen'. When confronted with the power of rational choice theory to depict not the *good* but the *rational* citizen, social policy has had no effective means to challenge the 'commercial strata of individuality'. Ultimately the power of neo-liberalism resides in its ability to persuade governments that it is their responsibility

> to *actively* create the conditions within which entrepreneurial and competitive conduct is possible. Paradoxically, neo-liberalism, alongside its critique of the deadening consequences of the 'intrusion of the State' into the life of the individual, has none the less provoked the invention and/or deployment of a whole array of organizational forms and technical methods in order to extend the field within which a certain kind of economic freedom might be practised in the form of personal autonomy, enterprise and choice. (Barry et al., 1996: 10)

Much of the normative focus of social policy discourse implicitly disdains the rhetoric of the commercial world and so is caught in an impossible position of seeking to influence from outside. Attempting to reconstruct social obligation as a norm and therefore an imperative for welfare betrays, as Gordon (1996) argues, no real awareness of the 'art of government', no fundamental understanding of the *techne* of neo-liberal purpose. The concerns of social policy, however, while inevitably normative and universalizing, can be recast within a reworking of the notion of risk. Analysis of the nature and fact of risk provides an intellectual tool to harmonize the divergent strata of civic and commercial individuality. The task is to prove that they are not so inalienable as they appear. We need to argue that the inevitability of risk, dramatized in Beck's risk society, is at the core of how the 'arts of government' are fashioned. Having done that, it becomes possible to argue further that an analysis of the perception of risk challenges both the civic and the commercial notions of individuality.

The presumption of common-sense sets the ground of the rhetoric which, of itself, can provide no harmony in the debate. We need to examine separately how neo-liberalism and the left have fashioned a former discourse about risk that contributed to the great divide. The left abandoned an adequate understanding of risk and this has contributed to its relative isolation as a viable government.[5] Beck concluded that:

> One can take up the case of one social institution after another: economic restitution; attributability; medical, cultural or religious provision. Everywhere the result is the same: protection from catastrophe is to the threat of catastrophe as a sticking plaster is to a mushroom cloud. That however, exposes a yawning gap in prior provision in the welfare state, annulling its rubber-stamped safety claim quite independently of catastrophic occurrences. (1995a: 177)

The singular visions of neo-liberalism

It is generally assumed that neo-liberalism, as a political ideology, drew the substance of its position from the development of nineteenth century liberalism.[6] As Burchell argues:

> It is, perhaps, not surprising that there should be a 'return' to liberal themes in the contemporary politics of both the left and the right, since we seem to be witnessing a significant mutation of liberal governmental rationality which aims to modify the relation of individuals to political power by seeking, in part, to get them to economize on their expectations of or demands of government. A change in the political objectification of ourselves as individual subjects accompanies current modifications in the relation between the state's centralized power and the techniques by which we are governed as concrete individuals. A new figure of rational-'economic' subjectivity seems to have emerged as the proposed correlate-partner of this modern version of liberal governmental reason. (1991: 145–6)

It has become a commonplace truism that, in seeking to modify a welfare state mandate, neo-liberalism was reimposing aspects of a former political philosophy. In effect, it sought to define the welfare state as an anachronism, an aberration in the ineluctable drive of free enterprise and the logic of the free market. Regarding neo-liberalism as only an expression of some form of revamped liberalism is a mistake. To see such an unbroken strand of liberal logic as the intelligent bedrock of a fundamental political reality is to miss the point. As Garland significantly argues:

> The crucial feature of the social policies implemented by the liberal reforms of the 1900s was the establishment of mechanisms of security and integration, which could overlay and reorganise the effects of the labour market while maintaining its basic capitalist terms. The provision of pensions, state-subsidised insurances, labour exchanges . . . ensured that the harshest consequences of the market system were tempered, and the inequalities of distributional effects

modified. The degree of risk and insecurity encountered by the worker and his family was significantly reduced. (1985: 231)

The old conservative liberalism is nothing like its modern counterpart![7] The nineteenth century was still resolving the principles of governance that were essentially feudal in origin. Notions of 'individual' power were still understood as an expression of some pattern of alignment with, or accommodation to, a powerful other. It was the 'lord' or the 'prince' whose patronage conferred political power. Thus the individualism that the nineteenth century espoused was, in part, to be understood in relation to patronage. It reflected a conferred power, or power held on behalf of another whose status instituted power as a sovereign right. Neo-liberalism, however, is now 'understood not so much as a substantive doctrine or practice of government in itself, but as a restless and dissatisfied ethos of recurrent critique of State reason and politics' (Barry et al., 1996: 8). It may well be restless and dissatisfied but there is a basic antinomy in the notion of modern neo-liberal contractual power which, as Doxiadis points out, arises from the fact that modernity relegates 'the source of all power to (pre-modern) sovereignty' (1997: 534).[8]

Construing the welfare state as a historic aberration reveals an epistemological sleight of hand that conceals how the power of the argument is framed. To do this is to be swayed, in fact, by that mantra-like assumption of neo-liberalism that there is no alternative. Neo-liberalism conceals its reliance on pre-modern notions of sovereign power. It is the reliance on the hidden sovereignty of power in modernity that Foucault illuminates. The phrase 'there is no alternative' really reflects the construction of a Foucauldian 'domain'; it is not a 'true utterance'. That it is powerful is not in question. The impetus of such assumptions depends on the ability to define and control the 'domain' of speech. It does not naturally occur as a 'true utterance' of an intrinsic truth. Such arguments interpose an interpretation on our current understanding that reinforces the power and hegemony of neo-liberalism. Whatever legitimate criticisms we might make about welfare states, to imply that they were an aberration, and that somehow we have returned to previously held truths, is a fallacy.[9]

A new understanding of power is required: power defined as the ability not just to 'speak the truth' but to influence the 'domain' of truth utterances. The shaping of this 'domain', as we saw earlier, depended upon the rhetoric of risk. It is not satisfactory to assume that discussions about risk can be tied solely to a revalorization of the pre-eminent power of individuals. In all of this it is the 'knowledge' *of*, and *about*, power that Foucault is attacking. Effective critique depends not so much on who has or does not have knowledge (defined as an intrinsic 'sovereign' possession). It does not depend on a sovereign/servant matrix. It is not about the power of *inside* knowledge *vis-à-vis outside knowledge*. It is rather about the *structures and patterns of knowledge itself*. What we must do is to take the risk, as Foucault suggested, 'to transform the critique conducted in the form of necessary limitation into a practical critique that takes the form of a possible transgression' (1984a: 45).[10] The phrase 'there is no alternative' stands revealed as a 'necessary limitation' that merits all possible 'transgression'!

Risk is not just the gamble with loss or the joust with fate that typifies an individual's preservation of autonomy and protection of the self. It is that, but living in a risk society also emphasizes the collective nature of risk. The fallacy of a purely contractual approach to the formation of a minimalist state is to assume that individual autonomy is somehow a precursive covenant of autonomous individuals to agree to a system of mutual protection. For example Hindess suggests that:

> the principal obsession of modern political theory is with the idea of a community of autonomous persons whose consent provides their sovereign (or the government) with both the right and the capacity to rule. The idea of such a community is widely . . . regarded as something of a fiction. We should not be surprised then, to find the western ideal of a political community consisting of autonomous persons is such a fertile source of confusion and dispute. (1996b: 21–2)

As Hindess asserts, a tightly argued contractual assumption 'clearly implies that those individuals are formed independently of the sovereign power they agree to constitute' (1996b: 43). Power does not reside antecedently in individuals alone, whose political actions constitute the minimal society required for social protection; it inheres in the nature of that mutual decision. Individual autonomy is not enacted in a social vacuum but arises out of the pattern of political assumptions current in any given society. Ultimately, the point is whether we infer that individual freedom is *granted* or *taken*. The more we assume that individual freedom is taken, define it as an act of defiance or equally as part of an individual act of autonomy, we embrace a concept of risk that requires only an individual solution. If we can argue that the essence of individual freedom is not taken, but granted, then we can validly argue for a concept of risk that requires a collective and not only an individual response.

Another way to consider this is to reflect on whether we characterize power as a 'right' or as a 'capacity'. Hindess defines the context of modern politics as the arena where there are 'slippages between the idea of power as capacity and the idea of power as a right' (1996b: 55). If the power that resides in individuals is defined as a capacity, an *opportunity* to act rather than a *right* to act, then we can locate the essence of that individual consciousness and action within a political system. It would not be necessary that it be defined as antecedent or external to it. If, however, the right to individual autonomy presumes a primal onto-logical consciousness then that argument depends upon a definition of power as a right. But how are we to understand rights apart from the context in which they are to be exercised and the 'practices' that reinforce them? If we define power as a capacity then that assumption establishes a context for the expression of individual rights, as well as validates the need for social obligation. Both are still possible. As Taylor argues, 'the patriotism of a free society has to celebrate its institutions as realizing a meaningful freedom, one that safeguards the dignity of citizens'. Freedom does not, by definition, exclude some aspect of citizenship. While, as he continues, 'the modern notion of the dignity of the person is essentially that of an agent, who can affect his or her own condition', it is also clear that the 'dignity' of citizenship 'involves a notion of citizen capacity' (1995: 200). Nevertheless, in the contemporary discussion of risk it is the valorization of individual rights, rather than individual capacity (which might lead on to legitimizing a collective approach), that is dominant.

As Hindess suggests, power defined as political right plays a major role in contemporary debates about the proper nature of the state and the exercise of political action. It leads inexorably to a definition 'that the most important activities of government – at least with regard to the internal affairs of the community – are the making and enforcing of rules' (1996b: 57). They are important because they reinforce the structural significance of individual or personal qualities of our experience and establish the normative basis for intervention by the state in the lives of autonomous individuals. This is crucial to a discussion about risk because it strengthens the idea that the only legitimate intervention by the state must be to protect or guarantee the right to individual autonomy.

However, we cannot leave the debate there. Government cannot just be defined instrumentally as 'the making and enforcing of rules'. To do that is to ignore the normative implications of government action. Such a definition of governance reflects the hidden norms that are implicit in assumptions about the precursive reality of individuals. The function of these norms is to assume that the only valid aspect of governance is to protect individual rights and secure legitimacy for state intervention, based only on the securing or protection of those individual rights. We can move forward in this debate if we can agree that the *business* of government is not only to make and enforce rules but also to establish the more subtle issues of how government *is to be done*. That is to say that we consider not just the function of government as a protector of rights – which is to look only at the contractual end-point of government action and policy. We can also look at the process by which policy options are defined and alternatives found. We can, in effect, ask questions about how we are governed and what the *practices* and *arts* of government might entail. This is to critique both their epistemology and their self-referent immanence.

Foucault and governmentality

To further expand on this idea of government as process I want to turn to some of the insights that Foucault has charted in commenting on modern governance.[11] There are many excellent discussions of Foucault's theory of governmentality (Burchell, 1993; 1996; Garland, 1997; Gordon, 1991; Hindess, 1997a; Rose, 1996a; 1996b; Turner, 1997).[12] I do not intend to rework the full debate about these issues; I intend only to use it to highlight the focus on how risk is used in this analysis.[13] The important conceptual question is whether defining the welfare state as a 'disciplinary state', in Foucault's terms, has condemned any reconsideration of it. Reasons for this question can be found in Foucault's theory of governmentality, in which it is possible to see

> the substitution for a society of sovereignty of a disciplinary society by a governmental one; in reality we have a triangle: sovereignty–discipline–government, which has as its primary target the population and as its essential mechanism apparatuses of security. In any case, I wanted to demonstrate the deep historical link between the movement that overturns the constants of sovereignty in consequence of the problem of the choice of government; the movement that brings about the emergence of a population as a datum, as a field of intervention, and as an objective of governmental techniques; and that which focuses on the economy as a specific sector of reality, and on the political economy as the science and technique of intervention of the government on that field of reality. (1979: 19)

While he clearly postulates the notion of a triangle, involving some aspects of an interlocking system, there is an inertial residuum in our political thinking about the historicity of the movement from sovereignty to disciplinary society to governmental. The last in the sequence carries more perceptual 'weight' and appears to be superior. Challenging the hegemony of neo-liberal common-sense, the internal logic of its criticism of welfare and its multitude of 'dependencies' and 'risks', requires an analysis of the dynamism of this 'historical inertia'. Posing the 'system' of the interlocked triangle is useful but perhaps not totally satisfying. Neo-liberalism is arguably the most potent and effective system of governance. We need not be naïve in understanding what challenging that 'hegemony' entails. As Ewald has argued, what 'makes society, as it were, disciplinary is precisely the fact that disciplines do not create partitions. On the contrary, their diffusion, far from dividing or compartmentalising, *homogenises social space*' (1992: 170, my italics).

Interpreting Foucault is not an easy task, but the very allusiveness of his thought offers different patterns about how we might reconsider the hegemonic isolation and intransigence of political certainties. Foucault's notion that we are governed by means of the processes by which we assert our freedom *from* government is quintessentially part of his deliberate aim to alter 'taken-for-granted' perceptions. Garland argues (as I also quoted him in the previous chapter) that the 'central critical claim' of the governmentality literature – 'audacious and devastating in its political implications' – is that we are ruled 'through our freedom'. He goes on to say that 'what we cherish as our autonomy, our individuality, our independence of power relations, is precisely the basis for our being governed by others' (1997: 196). Garland nevertheless has some cautions about the usefulness of this approach.

He argues that applying this governmentality 'literature' to an analysis of criminology (and equally for me within social policy) it is possible to conflate *freedom* ('the capacity to choose one's actions without external constraint') with *agency* (the 'possession of the power to act'). Not all neo-liberal reforms of the public sector health and welfare services can be seen as examples of 'governing through freedom'.[14] There are procedural constraints that are imposed and, as he says, we 'are obliged to be choosers but . . . are not therefore made to be free'. Granted, but is this not to apply a narrow 'sociological' frame to the issue? Does Foucault mean to apply his paradox that we are 'governed through freedom' to refer to an *overall* construct of autonomy, independence, individuality? Is this not a debate about 'where' and 'what' rather than proving a conceptual flaw by arguing that it involves the conflation of agency and freedom? Whatever Foucault meant by this he doesn't mean it to apply in some conceptual vacuum. Practices and arts are just that and no more! They operate in the 'real world' and not in the mind. I do agree with Garland that an exuberant, uncritical overuse of these ideas does allow neo-liberal advocates to 'repeat their propaganda'. Mantras of common-sense, which surround neo-liberal rhetoric, are very clever marketing ploys against the 'florid' and 'fanciful' excesses of social democratic theorizing.

Garland's strictures about misusing 'agency' are a very different and valuable critical reflection. Requiring agents to take managerial respons-ibility for the outcome of decisions that were formerly a 'shared risk' of the total welfare or health bureaucracy can produce adverse effects. At the very least it is an interesting comment on how managerial risk (within organizations) is altering the 'mentalities of rule' about respons-ibility for the dispersal of risk in major welfare institutions.[15] The practical managerial issues involve the typical neo-liberal restructuring processes of devolving 'budgetary allocation powers while cutting budgets . . . [which] often means that subordinates in organizations have to take on the unwelcome task of imposing cuts' (1997: 197–8). This small instance of Foucauldian 'genealogy'[16] involving current managerial practice, within an environment of constant risk, is writ large all over the deregulating public policy sectors of the Western world. It is an inter-esting example of the globalization of a governing 'practice' that has assumed wide significance.[17] These aspects of practical management demonstrate how 'risk' is used as a dogma for, and a rationalization of, institutional change. If freedom and agency *are* conflated, then deconstructing the rhetoric around agency and its effects is crucial to this analysis of risk.

Elucidating *how* government is done and not just *what* it does provides a new way to look at risk. Certainly, as Garland suggests, we need to understand 'the pragmatics of programme-implementation and the processes through which rationalities come to be realized (or not) as actual practices' (1997: 200). It is facile to argue that individual risk is not part of the common-sense reality that we all must deal with. The point rather is to establish that the genesis of risk arises from the social structure, part of the actual pattern of governance, and not as integrally part of some individual consciousness superordinate to social process. For Foucault, analysing the conduct of government provides a way to move beyond the recursive debates about individual rights and autonomy. One of his concerns is to

> challenge the idea of a sovereign subject which arrives from elsewhere to enliven the inertia of linguistic codes, and sets down in discourse the indelible trace of its freedom; to challenge the idea of a subjectivity which constitutes meanings and then transcribes them into discourse. Against these ideas I would advocate a procedure which maps the roles and operations exhausted by 'different' discoursing subjects. (1991a: 61–2)

The assumption, which dominates the contemporary debate, that risk is an integral part of individual consciousness, arises from this fetish to articulate 'the indelible trace of its freedom'. We do not 'arrive from elsewhere', nor are our meanings constituted out of some pre-existing ontological subjectivity. Mapping the process of how individual subjectivity seeks to maintain an illusory freedom provides some new 'tools' with which to comment on the nature of risk.

Foucault describes the capillary nature of power as an exemplar of conduct and not an articulation of rights. The nature of contemporary politics is about power as process and not simply contractual rights. Foucault was always concerned to argue that power as consent, as representative only of a mutual contract, could not be seen to justify the normative 'rules' of state intervention (Hindess, 1996b: 138). Foucault would rather argue that 'the founding contract, the mutual pledge of ruler and subjects, [is] to function as a sort of theoretical matrix for deriving the general principles of an art of government' (1991c: 98). The 'art of government' implies patterns not rules, processes not policies – the raw material for Foucault's 'archaeology of knowledge'. How those patterns and processes have refashioned our thinking about risk in order to alter welfare state rhetoric warrants more investigation. One aspect of this, the emergence of 'contract' as part of the autonomous rationality of government, will be covered in the next chapter.

Social security, risks and limits: Foucault's exegesis on welfare

It is interesting to note how Foucault accepted that one of the 'perverse effects' of systems of social security was that they inevitably led to a 'growth in dependence'. While he argued that the typical view of social security was that it ought to give 'each individual autonomy in relation to the dangers and situations likely to lower his status or subject him', nevertheless, he thought that the crucial change in welfare rhetoric arose from the linking of security with independence (1988a: 160–1). As we have seen earlier, the valorization of risk has been an important element in how the previous rhetorical undergirding of 'security' was attacked.

Hindess, describing Foucault's analysis of Bentham's Panopticon, concluded that Bentham's argument, that liberty is conceptually a 'branch of security', must be balanced with the converse – that 'liberty is a condition of security' (1997a: 262). The importance of this distinction is that it sets out the ground for Foucault's governmentality thesis that liberalism established a rationality of government distinct from an 'ideology or normative political standpoint'. Distinguishing between liberty as a *branch* of security and liberty as a *condition* of security is not mere wordplay. The former allows for all the issues of risk to be depicted as issues of ideology or norms. For example, within this purview, welfare is contestable on the binary distinction between the 'deserving' and the 'undeserving'.[18] Within an ideological or normative function all the excesses of moralism and judgement can appear. In Foucault's depiction of liberty, as a condition of security, we can see the elements of the argument about how intrinsic the obverse welfare 'other' is to the self-description of neo-liberalism. In this respect, the 'failure' of the welfare dependent is the obverse of the successful. As Hindess concludes, 'the freedom of members of the governed population is seen as an artefact of effective government' (1997a: 262). The 'welfare wars' are a justification of rule – the necessary obverse of the autonomous claims of individualism. Expressed in this way the debate is not about morality but politics – the ways in which concepts of risk are used to alter how we are governed.[19]

The notions of protection and care, which were allied with a general or social security against risk, have been destroyed. It is the shift in language that is significant: social security became welfare.[20] That is the mechanism for the change in welfare governance. Using aspects of risk to associate security with independence, and not protection, is significant. Welfare became a pejorative term allied with dependency. Security needed to be dissociated from its social associations in order that it could be used to focus on risk and independence. As Foucault outlines, social security was initially allied with the notion of finding remedies to accidents, responding to the perversity of happenstance. The association of security with independence alters the way that risk is perceived in the 'practice of security'. The cycle of linguistic change is complete; risk is no longer about happenstance but now encapsulates threat. This is an aspect of the 'semiology of catastrophe' mentioned earlier. Issues of security are also linked to the demands for marketization where 'economic efficiency now appears as a more important element of security, and it does so at a time where the earlier techniques of macroeconomic management are regarded as ineffective, if not indeed as counterproductive' (Hindess, 1997b: 25).

The problem is that autonomy can be discussed only within the frame of threat. It is not easy to see how autonomy and independence can ever again be associated with a general system of social coverage. Foucault states that 'we completely lack the intellectual tools necessary to envisage in new terms the form in which we might attain what we are looking for' (1988a: 166). Nevertheless, deeper unpacking of the rhetoric about welfare change can offer us ways to challenge the stance of neo-liberal 'truth' that there can be no other alternative to the particular association of welfare with dependency.

Despite himself, Foucault suggested a way to analyse dependency that is significant. He thought that such an analysis ought to 'distinguish between two tendencies: an effect of dependency *by integration* and an effect of dependency by *marginalization or exclusion*' (1988a: 162). Prior to the neo-liberal attack on welfare states, Foucault argues, dependency was perceived to operate not between the individual and the state but rather at a personal level between people. One consequence of the promulgation of 'welfare crisis' was that beneficiaries of various social security systems might now recognize that dependency was not intrinsically personal. It could now be associated with 'an institution whose decision-making powers . . . had hitherto only [been] dimly perceived'. Consequently, a new/old variation of the 'deserving and undeserving poor' is established. It maintains the paradox of an individual critique of welfare beneficiaries while treating them as a 'welfare population'. The association of dependency with marginalization shows how the new focus on risk, as threat, created a 'separation between an "assured" population and an "exposed" population' (1988a: 163).

Part of the success of the former welfare state was to 'hide' its functioning, particularly aspects of access and availability, in what Foucault called a 'cloud of decisions' (1988a: 174). The system worked through an explicit set of 'silences' – things done but not talked about (cf. Katznelson, 1986). Reliance on the 'authority' of the state was part of that 'cloud of decisions'. Now that such 'authority' has been challenged and a principle of competence and transparency adopted, making the 'hidden rules' explicit has seemingly led to a paralysis of the former sustaining metaphor of welfare. Certainly the function of this destroyed any sense of the implicit (or silent) paternalism of social security.

The withdrawal of the state from the provision of full public access to
health and social services raises the spectre of the limits of state provision. This re-emphasizes the fact of risk and curiously increases the
sense of dependency. What was part of the organic taken-for-grantedness
must now be negotiated. A new contractual relationship of the individual to the state is forged out of the increased perception of limits.
Foucault's response to the broad issues of social security is helpful in
seeking new directions for social policy in an age of globalized and
universal risk.

Welfare discourses: some comments

The idea that neo-liberalism has re-established the 'truth about politics'
in reaction against the aberration of the welfare state reflects a particular
aspect of that discourse which needs examination. We need rather, as
Foucault suggests, to see 'how effects of truth are produced within
discourses which in themselves are neither true or false' (1984b: 60). The
search for a former truth and its reinstitution sets up patterns of action
regarding certain key ideas. It establishes 'that the functioning of discursive regimes essentially involves forms of social constraint' (Fraser,
1989b: 20). That those current political epistemologies are essentially
about constraint rather than freedom is important. The theme of constraint, as essential to governance, is vital to my overall analysis of the
philosophy of risk. Whatever the rhetoric, the patterns of constraint that
are instituted to express these dominant ideologies may reveal how
power is really exercised. What Fraser is suggesting, which is relevant to
my argument, is the existence of the following:

> the valorization of some statement forms and the concomitant devaluation
> of others; the institutional licensing of some persons as authorized to offer
> authoritative knowledge claims and the concomitant exclusion of others;
> procedures for the extraction of information from and about persons involving
> various forms of coercion; and the proliferation of discourses oriented to
> objects of inquiry that are, at the same time, targets for the application of social
> policy. (1989b: 20)

The arguments for eliminating the 'passive' welfare state and establishing an 'active' welfare society can be evaluated against this process of
valorization (cf. Dean, 1995). Hence the pejorative assertions about the
problems of welfare dependency. This examination will not just untangle
these patterns of belief but also consider how current assumptions about
'power/knowledge' (to apply Foucault's term) establish certain forms of
'institutional licensing'. How the idea of risk permeates the creation of
these new patterns of power sets a new standard for how to respond to
and evaluate both need and dependency. Fraser argues that the 'formation and functioning of incommensurable networks of social practices . . .

[involves] the mutual interrelationship of constraint and discourse' (1989b). That the arguments of neo-liberalism about risk can be seen as a discourse about constraint is significant. Questions about the patterning of this constraint are more useful than continuing 'slanging matches' about the 'new right' and public choice theory being an outmoded philosophy of individualism. An effective analysis needs to move past the frozen rhetoric of either individual or community bantering.

Foucault's theorizing about power/knowledge, and his argument that contemporary power discourses are in fact reflections of a discontinuity, casts doubt on this historical lineage of neo-liberalism. Claiming the significance of an unbroken or evolving tradition of political power is not possible within his perspective. Foucault states that his work is 'an attempt to introduce the diversity of *systems* and the play of *discontinuities* into the history of *discourses*' (1991a: 61). Neo-liberal political discourse creates the 'practices' of welfare. They determine the bureaucratic mechanisms by which needs are assessed and benefits delivered. These discourses are not about the uncovering of inalienable truths so much as about revealing processes and procedures – what Foucault calls 'their rules of formation' and 'their conditions of existence'. Foucault calls into question the notion of an 'infinitely receding origin, and the idea that, in the realm of thought, the role of history is to reawaken that which has been forgotten, to uncover the occluded, to rejoin what has been blocked from us' (1991a: 62). All forms of political discourse which reify practical expressions of some pre-existing rationality (or ontological given) need to be deconstructed.

We deliver welfare services in precise ways because it suits us to do so – in order to create the discourse of access and to keep salient the more fundamental discourse about risk. As I have argued earlier, it is this discourse about risk that removed 'security' from the social and aligned it with independence. Attacking welfare dependency is revealed as an essential prop to the more fundamental use of risk as threat, rather than happenstance – which is the bedrock of the neo-liberal position.

The other aspect of this discourse, which needs unpacking, is the notion that 'communities' of autonomous individuals can and should be governed through consent of their members. To enjoin the same acceptance of risk responsibility of welfare recipients is to invite them into the singular vision of neo-liberalism. Processes by which welfare clients are 'disciplined' on account of their dependency are hidden in this notion of governance through consent (Dean, 1995: 567; Hindess, 1997b: 24–5). Countering implicit aspects of such analyses requires careful articulations of difference. It will also require us to see the implication of Foucault's manifest paradox that the history of such discourses (about apparent mutual consent) represents 'a set of specified and descriptive forms of non-identity' (1991a: 62). Generalized welfare discourses create a disdained 'population' that has no specific individual identity. Challenging the power of such social 'discrediting' depends upon making the implicit aspects of such generalized and apparently obvious welfare discourses explicit. We need, as Beck argues, 'an eye for the rule-governed character of what is apparently, natural . . . so that the train of argument and action will travel in the opposite direction' (1995a: 171). Relying on the political metaphors of the past will not assist us to understand the real reasons for the dominance of neo-liberalism.

If it is the case that the demand that politics and policy respect an irreducible individualism cannot be tightly linked to the past, then we may turn to an analysis of risk in order to highlight the essential aspects of this new but not old right. As we have seen, it is the argument that individuals must accept responsibility for dealing with risk that has helped shape the anti-welfare lobby. While this needs to be described as a set of beliefs, epistemological analysis will only take us so far. Revealing hidden meanings has not proved an effective strategy so far in challenging the dominance of neo-liberalism. This is to argue not that such analysis has no value but that we must respect the limitations of this form of 'exegesis'. The anti-welfare discourses of neo-liberalism are not easily amenable to argument. Those sets of ideas about the 'perils of welfare dependency', the failure of the state as a 'guardian of our best interests', are more like mantras. Unpacking this epistemology will be useful but so too will an attempt to situate these assumptions in a wider analysis of 'power/knowledge'.

What has brought about this sea change in an acknowledgement of legitimate social need? The crisis of affordability is an important strand in seeking answers to this question. What I want to do is to discuss these arguments, not just as if they had a coherent internal logic, but in the context of the changes that we see in how the individual interacts with and relates to the state. As Foucault suggests, the political power of these discourses depends not so much on the espoused systems of belief but on the actions and processes engendered by these beliefs. Epistemological challenge does not reveal action and debate process. The questions stimulated by such a requirement are as follows:

- What are the imperatives of 'tribal' knowledge that are revealed in the new social movements?
- Can we have a legitimate separate or 'tribal' knowledge in a world increasingly globalized?
- What unique 'knowledges' are possible for us in the new risk society?
- Does neo-liberalism represent an expansion of a political logic or a constraint and contraction into the solitary perception of individual risk?
- What are the institutional and managerial forms of how power is exercised and legitimated that alter not only our beliefs, but also how states must practise welfare?

- What does it mean for states to define the proper role of the individual in terms of managing their own risk?
- Why has 'being dependent', previously part of the natural cycle of life, become so pejorative?
- How has the very notion of 'welfare' become so derisory?

Answering these questions requires a dual focus: on the sets of normative ideas but also on the practice of these ideas. It will be important to join Foucault in refusing to place the notion of a power, which is based on consent, at the centre of an analysis of government. Neo-liberal reliance on 'governance through consent', which sustains an attack on social risk management formerly assumed through systems of social security, needs disproving. Foucault argued that 'the idea of a sovereign power based on the consent of its subjects should be regarded simply as one rationality of government amongst others that are at play in contemporary societies – and as one that need be accorded no special analytical or explanatory privilege' (Hindess, 1996b: 145). The next chapter continues with the theme that risk was intentionally structured into the core of the new contractual and consensual society. The intent is to show that an attack on welfare dependency is no by-product of a marketized and contractual rhetoric but is essential to the maintenance of that political philosophy. Exposing the crucial nature of that linkage is one way to challenge such dominant systems of belief.

Notes

1 In Culpitt (1992) the proposition was made that the old sustaining assumption of a moral and political obligation on those who had to give to those who had not, which was typical of an 'old welfare paradigm', had given way to a new rights-based paradigm of welfare. The new imperative of welfare rights was that those who had not, had rights to receive.

2 While the phrase 'welfare safety net' is now commonly associated with neo-liberal restructuring of state welfare systems, it has been argued that it was an essential element of the early welfare state policy framers that welfare assistance be short term and therefore a 'safety net' (cf. Barry, 1997).

3 Foucault said that his task was to 'know what to make of . . . [the] masquerade' of history; thus discovering 'a realm where originality is again possible as parodists of history and buffoons of God' (1984c: 94).

4 They both, respectively, have 'sacred' internal 'languages' and 'profane' descriptors for the language of the other. See the Afterword.

5 For a good description of the costs of modernization and how this led Habermas to discuss his theory of 'cultural impoverishment' see White (1988a: 116).

6 See Hindess (1996a; 1996b).

7 For an excellent discussion of this see Barry (1997).

8 These issues are taken up again in the next chapter.

9 I'm aware that the current governmentality literature does establish neo-liberalism as a very new political methodology. The use of *neo-liberal*, however, is important in that it does presume some sense of a historical lineage with classic liberalism. It has been suggested that neo-liberalism is the 'perfect' political expression of the Enlightenment project of reason.

10 It is in the application of such 'transgressions' that we can see aspects of the socially active Foucault.

11 Of the many available definitions of govermentality, Garland's is the most succinctly clear. He states that governmentality 'focused particularly upon the relations between two poles of governance: the forms of rule by which various authorities govern populations, and the technologies of the self through which individuals work on themselves to shape their own subjectivity' (1997: 174). See also Foucault's own paper 'On governmentality' (1979: 20).

12 The governmentality 'literature' is, perhaps, still fashionably new. However, there are some significant critiques emerging that seek to set these important ideas in a more considered context. The best of these is O'Malley et al. (1997).

13 This preliminary analysis of risk and social policy provides an avenue for critical theory to rework aspects of its normative critique. The possibilities of this are canvassed in Chapter 8 in relation to Honneth's paradigm of recognition.

14 See the Afterword for some examples of how 'governing through freedom' might evolve.

15 These governance 'practices' are revealed in the application of perpetual cycles of administrative review.

16 Which Foucault teasingly describes as 'gray, meticulous, and patiently documentary' (1984c: 76)!

17 The international exchange of managerial ideas about how to make the new deregulated managerial system work has all the hallmarks of a 'crusade'! The gurus of the new order are regularly featured on TV and in the popular press. How these ideas are 'marketed' is extraordinary. It can hardly be seen though as a conspiracy, which some left-wing writers are prone to assume; it is too open and relentless for that! Tangential but related to this marketing of ideas is Hermer and Hunt's preliminary explorations of official graffiti as 'an exemplary form of governance in post-modern modernity' (1996: 477).

18 Hillyard and Watson refer to the 'tyranny of the binary structuring of thought in modern society. In each binary opposition there is a hierarchical privileging of one side against the other. The discipline of social policy is replete with oppositions with one side carrying overtones of moral superiority' (1996: 324).

19 This topic will be explored further in the next chapter, especially in relation to the emergence of contract and how *the family* has been so central a part of the changes in governance.

20 One of the practical expressions of 'individualized' welfare is the explosion in home security firms and the demands for prudentialism – now the hallmark of the 'responsible individual' (cf. O'Malley, 1996: 201–2).

4

CONTRACT, FREEDOM AND CHOICE: THE REDISCOVERY OF RISK

It may be a fact about human beings that we notice who is fat and who is dead, but the fact itself that some of our fellows are fat and others are dead has nothing to do with our schemes of classification.

(Hacking, 1986c: 227)

National balance sheets now merely retrace a numerical and statistical growth devoid of meaning, an inflation of the signs of accountancy over which we can no longer even project the phantasy of the collective will.

(Baudrillard, 1993: 11)

My discussion about the relationship between risk and neo-liberalism examines two separate strands of inquiry. The first considers whether Beck's thesis about reflexive 'risk society' might have implicitly re-inforced neo-liberal rhetoric attacking 'welfarism'. The apocalyptic view of risk perception, generated by Beck's ideas, has significantly contributed to an increased fear of the future. Neo-liberals, fashioning an anti-welfare stance, have found this general culture of fear well suited to their task.[1] The second examines the vitality of contemporary fears about reducing welfare dependency and emphasizes an inherent structural connec-tion between risk and neo-liberalism. The validity of this perspective depends upon an analysis of governance and the presumption that risk was structured into the very core of the neo-liberal contractual society. Both strands indicate how various perceptions of risk have been used to produce the current anti-welfare politics.

This chapter emphasizes the second strand: examining how the con-temporary politics of contract, involving agency theory (and rational or public choice theory), emerged and became an essential aspect of modern governance. There are two additional sets of ideas that are applicable to this discussion about the salience of contract and risk. The first follows from Foucault's philosophical exegesis about the elaboration of a medical/professional 'space', the 'birth of the clinic' and its associated 'powers'. The second demonstrates how the advent of an 'avalanche of numbers' (Hacking's evocative phrase) dovetails with Foucault's theory of governmentality. Donzelot depicted the growth of statistical analysis – the ability to 'count deviance' – as a new aspect of governance, revealing a 'numerical capacity for enterprise and intimidation' (1979: 175). Statistics, it is now argued, serve and sustain the disciplinary surveillance of professionals. The internal logic of this new social science sought to create a 'population' rather than understand 'persons'. Such surveillance methodologies 'rendered [subjects] governable through simplification, codification, deconstruction and the imputation of order' (Harris, 1997: 162). Prototypically, the *family* became the focal point of these new 'social investigations'.

Foucault described the emergence of the 'clinic' in the late eighteenth and nineteenth centuries as a response, in part, to the escalating 'fear of popular movements' (cf. Donzelot, 1979; Procacci, 1994). Foucault argued that a new political context was forged 'for the preservation of both hospitals, and the privileges of medicine, that was compatible with the principles of liberalism and the need for social protection' (1973: 82). For the first time, a link was formed between the creation of a powerful and intrusive professionalism and how this new power might be politically defended (cf. Goldstein, 1984). The method for achieving this, Foucault suggested, had to link the 'right that invests sovereignty, and . . . the mechanics of the coercive forces whose exercise takes a disciplinary form' (1980: 107). The social justifications for this new professionalism were 'found' in the privileging of its nascent expertise. Further protection was guaranteed by licensing procedures.

A powerful new social 'practice' was instituted, which led to what Foucault called a 'society of normalization'.[2] He wished us to see that the power associated with this general 'medicalization' of life was the greater because it operated at the interstices between sovereign power and the emerging disciplinary mechanisms of the state.[3] In its clinical 'gaze' it was neither sovereign 'prince', or tactic, but a clever blend of both. The trust given to the doctor represented a new form of power – one balanced on risk. The power that resided in healing and knowledge, rather than the sanction to remove (or control) through jurisprudence, was more subtle. The 'doctor' came to represent an articulation of power that was almost incontrovertible, since the linking of sovereignty and discipline are two absolutely integral constituents of the general mechanism of political power. An identifiable 'population' was necessary (*vide* Hacking) for modern political power to operate. The clinical activity of investigation, 'watchfulness' and institutionalized care was the means by which such 'populations' were secured. These new 'practices' were not discrete. They are part of the *techne* of governance. It is interesting to observe that the managerialist revolution in the public service bureaucracies, the 'handmaiden' of neo-liberalism, sought to broach the power of the 'doctor/specialist nexus' – with varying success, as we shall see later.[4]

Governance procedures hallowed professional expertise: by implication, denying legitimacy to a whole coterie of 'lay knowledges' (cf. Wynne, 1996). Professional expertise developed a coded language and 'its norms and values [were] . . . compelling because of their claim to a disinterested truth' (Miller and Rose, 1990: 10). The lures of expertise and the conjecture about efficiency, first associated with the burgeoning medical profession, heralded the possibility of rule that was not dependent upon previous assumptions about power. It is the presumption of discreteness that is significant. It marked a shift from the sovereignty of status power to the sovereignty of expertise. The professions were the mechanisms of governance, not its product: they were not discrete. The professional hallowing of expertise was an integral part of the new governance – the mechanism by which certain knowledges were translated into bureaucratic power. Medical knowledge was, in its clinical respect, the application of knowledge not to the *genus*, to the disease, but to the *individual*. It is this personal, clinical, aspect of medicine that created and reinforced the notion of contract. How this was achieved (as Hacking demonstrates) was to link the normative power of the individual medical 'gaze' to the development of 'populations' of countable disease. The new politics of contract can be seen as a herald of the means to achieve social order, so implicitly part of modernity's triumph of rationality.

Mastering time and disciplining the future: contracts, insurance and risk

The classical notion of contract within market economies, extended to all aspects of social life, allows for the 'management' of governance (the arts of government) to be devolved to the market and away from the 'limiting' control of sovereign power. In the precise agreement of the contract 'economic and juridical sovereignty can alike be situated as relative moments' (Gordon, 1991: 22). Once established, these 'relative moments' become 'partial moments' of a political dynamism that has its own momentum. Hence Foucault's respect for neo-liberalism as the practical political expression of this conjunction. It creates, for him, the outlines of a 'methodology of security'. The subtle power of neo-liberalism rests in its ability to assign political significance to the 'partial moments' of contract agreements. Contract specification effectively establishes the politics of differentiation: the ability to define those who are within and those who are without the political compact. The welfare claimant/beneficiary is perceived to have broken the great contractual law of independent survival! Establishing individual responsibility for security means that we cannot easily talk of the *needs of society* under threat of risk. This occurs, as Gordon (1991) argues, because the actions of a multitude of players subject the 'totality' of social need to their own interpretation or qualification. Within this perspective the specific nature of 'social need' can never be articulated. It may be conceptualized in variations of 'the social' or 'civil society' but it is always altered by varied personal interpretations of the social. Foucault would argue that we have only the 'variable and floating quality of . . . accidental needs' (Gordon, 1991: 23).

We can now see how powerful such neo-liberal rhetoric is, which sets its 'face against the social'. It rejects the notion of 'civil society', and the 'public sphere', and rests its case on the always elusive multiplicity of individual needs. It is a wider perspective on the 'politics of needs interpretation' than Fraser (1987) would allow. Security for neo-liberalism is, therefore, only an individual, an autonomous, private 'security', gained by self-responsibility through the market: which, by definition, is part of the hazard of the ever changing dynamism of the world. Security for neo-liberalism is *from* the world not *within* the world. It is this that informs the rhetoric. How can we be secure or elude the risks that are seen to be unavoidable and which generate the need to protect the self? Within neo-liberal thought the moral duty to care is understood as a *'duty of man in society*, rather than as a *duty of society'* (Gordon, 1991: 23). Nevertheless, the 'intricate workings' of the market allow the 'largely privatized micro-power structures' to participate 'in a coherent general policy of order' (1991: 27). Interestingly, the notion of contract became aligned with protection *in* the market. It was not to be an abrogation *of* the market by promulgating the pre-eminence of 'civil society'. It creates a 'circuit of interdependence between *political security* and *social security'*.

The tangible mechanism for creating this order was the development of the insurance industry – where the indemnity contract is the archetype of a social contract. The irony is that insurance makes risk a collective reality since logically an individual can only be insured against a collective backdrop – a generalized risk pool. Insurance socializes risks and makes everyone part of the whole (1991: 203). As Ewald (1991) argues, risk is collective; it is only accidents that are personal. Gordon concludes his examination of the origin of neo-liberal contractualism by stating that:

> The fulfilment of the liberal idea in government consists – over and above the economic market in commodities and services, whose existence founds the classic liberal attribution of an autonomous rationality to the process of civil society – in a recasting of the interface between state and society in the form of something like a second-order market of governmental goods and services. It becomes the ambition of neo-liberalism to implicate the individual citizen, as player and partner, into this market game. (1991: 36)

Perhaps the quintessential second-order market is insurance. Insurance guarantees the prospect of autonomy against the possibility of hazard. Ewald argues that risk is not only collective, it is calculable and it is 'a capital'. What is insured against is not that which happens, but the guarantee of capital reparation. As he says, this is a contract to acknowledge 'the uniqueness of the irreparable' with an indemnifiable amount of money (1991: 204). What this means is that every personal hazardous possibility can be insured against – until now, Beck would argue. A price can be set upon personal risk but the price will not be the same for all, given the 'uniqueness of the irreparable'. Insurance is individual, unique, and yet infinitely generalized.[5] The generation and licensing of contract arrangements become almost infinite.

These are the processes, as Bauman (1992; 1997) later described in his theory of post-modernism,[6] in which the modernist creation of order meant neither the extirpation nor the cultivation of differences so much as the *licensing* of them. Bureaucratic power established order through enumeration and specification – all the tangible requirements for satisfying the terms of a contractual agreement. Risks were lessened through the mechanism of consequential agreement. Contract thus implied a mutual repercussion in the event of failure to comply. Power expressed in this way meant both the sanctions to impose a contract, and the authority to compel, on the basis of expertise. It was an interpretative and defining power.[7] Bauman, interestingly, suggests that political usage of contracts also posed the creation of an obverse. This implies the 'de-legalising [of] unlicensed differences', since order 'can be only an all inclusive category' surrounded by the 'belligerent camp' of those excluded from such contractual order (1992: xvi). Strategies of social order could now ostracize those who did not adhere to the given contractual patterns. Social stigmatization had found a new and implicitly more menacing 'tool': the disciplining and circumscribing of contract relationships. This required the creation of welfare 'populations'.

The sequestering of the insane and the custodial surveillance of the criminal (Bentham's Panopticon)[8] required watchful physical exclusion.[9] The advent of professional and bureaucratic contracts altered the administration of social power. A new form of social 'surveillance' was generated. Institutional mechanisms for enacting and monitoring contracts instituted new normalizing procedures. Patterns of social surveillance, implicit in adhering to a contract, were more insidious because they were less obvious. Adherence to expertise was ultimately more compelling than responding more crudely to status power. The other important aspect about the introduction of contracts was that they were personal – isolating individuals within patterns of contracted obligation. That this sense of obligation was first developed in the *family* is significant (see below). Reliance on the salience of contract helped shape the subsequent politics of neo-liberalism. It set the seal on the condemnation of the political or welfare 'other' as intrinsic to the disciplinary power of neo-liberalism. These insights have been vital in demonstrating how the entrance of social sciences 'into administration was not guided by humanitarianism, but by the advent of disciplinary technologies which sought to apply normalising judgements' (Hewitt, 1983: 76; see also Squires, 1990).

The 'clinic': the shape of contracts to come?

Foucault's assumption that the guardianship of private medical professionalism was related to general aspects of 'social protection' is significant. It was a crucial mechanism for how the ideas of risk and protection were generalized from the private to the public arena: private fears were overlaid onto the public. With this shift, Procacci argued, the notion of pathology was used to define poverty 'as a social question'. Poverty was now pathologized and 'placed among the collective phenomena accompanying the life of a *population* – birth, death, sickness, hygiene and accidents'. The experience of being poor was reified into the category of poverty. As Procacci argued, this 'shift opened what Foucault called "the era of epidemics", the medical configuration of a society centered on *security* techniques' (1994: 213). This transposed the notion of risk from that which might imminently happen to individuals to being an intrinsic part of the burgeoning and fearful 'social question'. Risk and security were co-joined. Consequently, risk now became essential to the 'colonising of the future' (Giddens, 1991: 111).

A complete account of this social history is not relevant here. I'm wanting only to counter-pose Foucault's instructive insights about the development of professionalism and the 'gaze' with the general context of late eighteenth and nineteenth century fears about poverty and the possibility of revolutionary 'Bolshevism'. Foucault's ideas about power and governance, and how these are played out in the sets of 'disciplining technologies', allow us to see below the 'surface' of the grand political designs being shaped at the time. Fashioning the context for professional medical surveillance – 'the era of epidemics' – created a different set of obligations and compensations about poverty, success and risk. Developing assumptions about the precedence and protection of medical privacy forged a new intellectual alliance in favour of a limited contractual sense of social responsibility. As Foucault argued:

> The system of obligation and compensation between rich and poor no longer passed through the law of the state, but by means of a sort of contract, subject to variation in space and suspension in time, it belonged more to the order of free consent. (1973: 83)

If he is correct, that the relationship between the successful and the socially dependent is no longer to be resolved solely 'through the law of the state', then the issues of poverty and need could not be depicted as solely a state or civic responsibility. The origin of the 'contract versus charity' debate[10] can now be associated with the history of the development of a theory of governance and professionalism. Any new attempt to 'demystify this ideological dichotomy' between contract and charity must now recognize that these issues are not just about the benefactor/beneficiary moral nexus. They are more antecedent.[11] They not only relate to the use of contract as an exemplar of the 'private handshake' of market transactions but go to the heart of the adumbration and protection of private professional privilege.[12]

The reification of 'contracts': risks and rationality

Rational choice theory sets out the intellectual supports for irreducible individualism. Part of the surrounding epistemology of rational choice theory is dependent upon positing the relationships of contract as the only reasonable way to organize political activity. Within this perspective politics is defined as the amalgam of choices people make in 'moving out from their private needs and sufferings to create a public world where each can appear before the others in his or her specificity' (Young, 1996: 479). The grand vision of public choice theory to create and maintain a collectivity of autonomous agents has commanded enormous respect. There are vast and important literatures about these separate topics; my purpose here is limited to how risk can be seen to be part of this politic of the autonomous self.

The arrogation and empowering of a professional 'space' marked the shift to a new politics of contract. The liberal vision, that it was possible to emerge from suffering and satisfy private needs through individual or familial effort, undergirded the politics of contract. Foucault showed that the creation and ordering of professional knowledges and powers was not discrete. They were rather the bedrock of a new politics that would reify success and pillory need. This impacted very powerfully on how chance and risk were defined as inhering in the self of the patient or the personal character of the 'poor'. A new way had been found to deal with fears about poverty and the potential 'swamp of social need' (Young, 1996: 480). The great liberal question about how to govern freely and morally had found a significant political 'tool' in contractualism. As Miller and Rose argue, this arose from the

> part accorded to the self-regulating activities of 'private' social actors under the guidance of expertise, [such] that the possibility has emerged for governing the economic life of the nation in ways consonant with liberal democratic ideals. (1990: 11)

The emergence of the idea of 'contract', the structure of the relationship between the observer and the observed in the 'gaze' of professionalism, altered the politics of the social.[13] Here it is important to note that the 'language of expertise', which reinforced the locus of the clinic as a focus of medical surveillance, was also used to strengthen the notion of contract as a fundamental aspect of the new politics of governance.[14]

This discussion about the relationship of contract to medical 'surveillance' is only one aspect of the normative 'gaze' of professionalism. We must not lose sight of the obvious legal significance of contract formulation. Contract is not only the guarantor of the norms of a 'professional space'. It was also the political mechanism used to stake out bourgeois privileges, property, and the laws surrounding inheritance. The whole complex of labour and employment contracts is part of this association of contracts with the nature of governance procedures. This has been a contested arena in which organized labour has strenuously fought against collapsing the distinctions between 'oppressors and oppressed' into procedures requiring 'medico-social legislation'. The contest was, in part, about the proper locale for how to deal with risk. The further growth of neo-liberalism is reflected in the recognition that 'part of the unexpected political acceptability of mass unemployment can be plausibly attributed to the wide diffusion of the individual as enterprise' (Gordon, 1991: 44). The 'social wars' involving the legalization of unions marked the resistance to a bourgeois politics, and those aspects of modern governance, which sought to govern through the individual.

Family governance and risk: from patriarchy to rationalities of rule

As Donzelot argues, 'the issues carrying the greatest passion' coalesced 'around the juridical status of the family' (1979: 177). The significance of the 'family' in the discourses about social policy and risk is obvious.[15] One aspect of the remoralization of welfare within neo-liberalism is the common project to 'resurrect' the *family* as the fundamental unit for social policy initiative. It is the key site for the clash of social theory (Squires, 1990). The *family* is also used rhetorically as exemplar – as a means to further stigmatize those who have no family or whose *family* falls outside the norm of respect. Attempting to control the deviant family is part of the implicit aims of normative welfare. This will be discussed in the next chapter in consideration of Habermas' theme of juridification.

The development of an 'autonomous rationality of government' required a significant change in perception about the *family*. The *family* was appealed to in the early modern period to provide an exemplar for government. The epistemologies of the *family* and the *firm* were mutually coherent.[16] The microcosm of the *family* was extrapolated out into how governments might be expected to act. As Donzelot outlines, social control through the *family* was achieved by 'its craving for betterment'. The bourgeois ideal *family* represented the key for social integration which was the 'private pursuit of well-being' (1979: 94). This private pursuit was not to be narrowly associated with market consumption. Being able to measure and assess the 'success' of these private pursuits created the welfare antinomy. It allowed for a new view of marginality: those who were not successful because of their own efforts (rather than fate) were to have their private rights stripped away under the 'gaze' of the disciplining welfare professionals. If this antinomy was simply about access to goods and markets the power to create these negative conceptual differences would not have been so great. The lack of goods had still to be larded with morality: the moral dissuasion was essential to the politic.

What is at work in the construction of autonomous rationality of government is how to achieve this without obvious resort to the notion of sovereignty formerly expressed in the notion of Machiavelli's 'prince'.[17] One of the 'arts' of modern government was initially to do this through the *family*, but then shift the ground. This shift in governance was given philosophical substance by Locke who denied 'any similarity between political and parental authority' (Miliband, 1994: 41). The modern 'genealogies' of power that facilitated this shift involved developing new conjunctions of expertise and risk. The decay in the sovereign power of the 'prince' was accomplished by endowing a whole new matrix of social experts with the ability to determine 'types of crime, sexual aberrations and states of grace, health and mind' (Hewitt, 1983: 68–9; see also Garland: 1997).[18] These myriad social experts, Foucault argued, established the *raison d'état* as an end in itself. Political rationality no longer devolved from the 'prince'. The new political rationality sought 'to increase the scope of power for its own sake by bringing the bodies of the state's subjects under tighter discipline' (Dreyfus and Rabinow, 1982: 137). Hewitt demonstrates a vital aspect of this form of genealogical criticism in outlining how the locus of this new control by experts was always directed at corporeality. Threats to the 'body' are, of course, powerful persuaders of the mind! The genius of these corporeal shifts in governmentality was that their implicit and explicit use of risk to compel allegiance could 'not be inscribed with the exactness of law' (Hewitt, 1983: 69). This very inexactness located the politics of risk within 'the body' from which, given our innate sense of self-protection and narcissism, they are almost impossible to dislodge.

It is 'the conjunction which Foucault establishes between the question of government and the fabrication of the individual within a range of practices which allows him to overcome the difficulties . . . with the concepts of domination and ideology' (Miller, 1987: 157).[19] Foucault required a definition of power that depended neither on sovereignty nor on governance systems defined as structures of ideology. His task was to get *below* the obviousness of ruler and subject. Sovereign power did not fully explain the allegiance to authority, nor did the suasion of ideology. The 'something else that was going on' was the essence of his genealogical researches into capillary power.[20] That these forms of coercion and control, premised on risk, involved our corporeality more than our minds is significant.

What Foucault sought to establish was his assumption that power 'exists only in action', in the manner of its 'doing'. It cannot be 'given', 'exchanged' or 'recovered', it can only be exercised (1980: 89). Foucault was interested in the 'how of action' – the mass of shaping and defining 'practices'. He had, as Gordon argues, a 'predilection for "how" questions, for the immanent conditions and constraints of practices' (1991: 7). Power, expressed as some aspect of reified exchange between sovereign ruler and subject, facilitates an attitude to risk that frames the resolution of risk as mutual obligation. How that is altered in the neo-liberal articulation of governance is significant. Power expressed as that which is *done or exercised* reinforces the singularity of the resolution of risk. While we are not necessarily architects of the risks that befall us, modern governance seeks to make us personally responsible and so to cut the legitimacy of any wider claims. Hence the concerted attack on general systems of risk pooling such as accident compensation schemes.

Autonomous rationality had to stand apart from the court of the prince and 'all the other appurtenances of the ruler' and establish its own principle of rationality. One way this was achieved was to suborn the uniqueness of the *family* as a model of patriarchal rule. The development of the autonomous rationality of government (which is not the same as government's separate principle of rationality) 'requires that families and households be seen . . . as components of the population which is now to be governed' (Hindess, 1997a: 258–9). The key word in this phrase is *components*. The issue for modern governance was how to intervene in the *family* ('a sphere of natural association'). For Donzelot, the

> concept of organic solidarity justified this intervention by allowing the prin-
> ciple of the interdependence of the individuals composing society to override
> the state of dependence in which they were placed inside the framework of so-
> called natural associations. (1991: 172)

It was an assumption of organic solidarity (the opportunity to organize for greater security) that made this intervention possible. Dealing with the potential for risk by 'reaching outside' the *family* for solidarity led to various justifications for complex juridical and welfare bureaucracies whose task was to contain risk.[21] The concept of solidarity thus repres-ents the 'organization' of what was a generally diffused individualism, often loosely caught up with aspects of romantic patriotism. Now the 'subjectification' of the family, as a component within a governance framework, increases risk perception and reinforces the need for solidarity. No longer was the *family* intrinsic and protected in and of itself. That could only arise now through alignment with the disciplinary power of the governance structures of the state. The collapse of this social compact, which allowed state intervention, occurred because of the obvious fact that risks were not contained.

Let us summarize the sequence of this. The *family* was constructed as a model for the newly developing nation-state (Donzelot, 1979). The use of exemplar *family* models allowed for distinctions to be made between archetypes of the good and successful bourgeois *family*, and welfare *failure families* whose manifold problems stood them in opposition to the norm. The emergence of contracts and enumeration were seized upon by a fledgling statistical 'science' to winnow out those whose life-styles were an affront to the bourgeoisie. These processes were intrinsic to the subtlety of the use of binary oppositions to create a modern version of governance. It depended not so much on the matrix of sovereignty but rather on the driving force of autonomous rationality that could be developed out of the binary process. The mechanism for this process was based on all the complex ways that risk was used to force and justify this change. It was the ability to *divide* and *measure* that formed the substance of this power. Consequently, the *family* as a microcosm of the whole became now *only one of the components*. The divisive neo-liberal compact was set!

The unit of risk was not just an individual (that was an essentially premodern assumption) but now it included the *family*. Trying to institutionalize risk in the early modern era, through changes in the governance of individuals alone, would not have achieved this, as the contra-appeal could always be back to the 'prince' or the 'king'. The issue for modern governance was not to use the obvious powers of sovereignty, and risk counter-reaction (or be embroiled in aggressive judicial legitimization), but to instil the new political arts as contract management.[22] It was this new contractualism which allowed for the growth of a 'multitude of regulative agencies . . . and, the advent of the empirical human sciences [*vide* Hacking] making possible these new technologies of control' (Hewitt, 1983: 68). Governance thus stands apart from the previous political legitimizations. Once families had been separated out as exemplar, all individuals could be drawn into these new powers of governing (Foucault's capillaries 'pumping furiously'!). The new 'mentalities of rule' had indeed suborned the family for its own ends. The antinomies of welfare were essential to the growth and defence of neo-liberalism. New mechanisms for translating this politically were found in the administration of the current 'welfare' bureaucracies. Probability and the 'science' of risk analysis became integral parts of government.

The arrival of numbers: managing destiny or guaranteeing progress

Translating contract discourse into all sections of the public arena established the intellectual ground for the emergence of rational choice theory – the calculation of individual risks. Creating the 'social' as an opportunity for the rational pursuit of private choice is consequent upon being able to enumerate and evaluate contractually (Hacking, 1982a). The debates about *the family*, which Donzelot describes, show how integral it was to the emergence of a contracted world that the family could be measured and divided. A new moral calculus was made possible by the 'science of numbers' and the emergence of the *family* as a core social unit. The deserving and undeserving could now be measured, and once measured, be 'removed'. As Hacking argues:

> Ethics is in part the study of what to do. Probability cannot dictate values, but it now lies at the basis of all reasonable choice made by officials. No public decision, no risk analysis, no environmental impact, no military strategy can be conducted without decision theory couched in terms of probabilities. (1990: 4)

Castel's important thesis about risk is that current usage of it marks a drastic 'rupture' with the previous ascription of risk as dangerousness. Put briefly, his argument is that the new governance 'strategies dissolved the notion of a *subject* or a concrete individual, and put into place a combinatory of *factors*, the factors of risk' (1991: 281). It represents an explicit denial of recognition (see Honneth's discussion of this in Chapter 8) and a valorization of statistical correlation as the means for analysing risks.

The ability to enumerate such previously private and personal aspects of living (Hacking's thesis) establishes a new view of morality, one driven by epistemologies of management and not specific care or service. The normative neo-liberal rhetoric summed up in the canard that the 'poor ought not to be a charge against the state but an opportunity for the altruism [sic] of private charity' is dependent on such major shifts in how power and responsibility are constantly being reshaped.[23] For Hacking, these shifts were directly associated with the new science of numbers. This science was 'obsessed with *analyse morale*, namely the statistics of deviance . . . the numerical analysis of suicide, prostitution, drunkenness, vagrancy, madness, crime, *les misérables*' (1986c: 222–3).[24] Processes of enumeration and categorization institutionalized a division between the successful and a nascent welfare 'population'. A different relationship between benefactor and beneficiary could now be made – suggesting that the real issues of welfare ought, more properly, to be opportunities for the successful to exercise charity and not the social validation of need. Welfare beneficiaries needed to 'prove their moral worthiness'![25] The significant point is how these nascent 'disciplining technologies' developed. For Hacking, the answer was that the application of enumeration to the idea of contract hid 'opinion with a veneer of objectivity' and thus replaced 'judgement by computation' (1990: 4).

The sense that some form of 'social' agreement (contract?[26]) could be struck with the poor served to reindividualize the resolution of poverty by emphasizing the moral relationship between benefactor and beneficiary. Such agreements contextualized these exchanges outside the moral act of charity and surrounded them with a 'law-like regularity'. At the heart of this particular example of governance there is a contradiction – yet to be fully exploited. Neo-liberalism does require that these welfare exchanges approximate the nature of a 'moral' contract, as a way to reify the poor as a 'social problem'. However, as Procacci (1994) describes, if it can be argued that the fundamental welfare exchange is moral *and not contractual*, then satisfying those 'needs' becomes a moral and not a contractual question! The contemporary remoralization of welfare, which takes aim at welfare dependency, requires a conjunction of morality *within* the welfare exchange. However, if we can decouple this linkage, using a Foucauldian genealogy of welfare, then the political intent of welfare moralization stands revealed as a disciplinary activity of neo-liberalism for its own political ends.

Irrespective of whether this moral equation was the most significant aspect of the nascent welfare exchange, the more fundamental point is that it posited the absolute significance of a mutual contract in law and economics. Lauding the supremacy of contract in public policy and the private sector shaped the 'order of free consent'. Valorizing personal freedom and autonomy was fundamental to neo-liberalism and, in association with risk, explains how rhetorical supremacy in current political debates was achieved. It is also crucial to an analysis of how neo-liberalism established a pejorative view of welfare dependency and argued for the creation of an active welfare society rather than be forced to maintain a passive welfare state (cf. Dean, 1995). Resolving the risks of society could now be associated with the procedures of contract such that the solutions that might be sought 'belonged more to the order of free consent' (Foucault, 1973: 83). Hacking goes on to explain that most of these contractual exchanges

> were first perceived in connection with deviancy: suicide, crime, vagrancy, madness, prostitution, disease. This fact is instructive. It is now common to speak of information and control as a neutral term embracing decision theory, operations research, risk analysis and the broader but less well specified domains of statistical inference. We shall find that the roots of the idea lie in the notion that one can improve – control – a deviant subpopulation by enumeration and classification. (1990: 3)

Hacking's thesis is given an earlier 'shape' in Merquior's explication of a classical *episteme* of Foucault's where he discusses the shift in an archaeology of knowledge from analogy to representation. Merquior outlines Heidegger's notion that *'correspondence . . .* [was] the law of pre-modern thought and *representation . . .* the norm of modern knowledge' (1985: 44). As Merquior argued, this 'substitution of analysis for analogy' created the 'objectifying, reductionist glance of . . . modern representation' (1985: 44). This 'demand' for accurate, representative knowledge involved two complementary processes: *'mathesis,* a "universal science of measurement and order",* and *taxinomia,* the principle of classification, of ordered tabulation . . . knowledge sought to replace infinite resemblance by finite differences' (1985: 46). Consequently, the power of this new intellectual coalition against poverty and social disadvantage required that it be aligned, measured, understood and mediated by a 'sort of contract'. The state was now to be seen as a 'manager of destiny' not a 'guarantor of progress' (Donzelot, 1991: 176). Everything was now subject to the logic of 'free consent'. But as we shall see, this is a freedom that serves only the autonomous individual. It effectively denies freedom to those who find themselves in a state of neediness.

Being counted: the moral auditing of poverty

What is clear in the specification of contracts is that the *mechanisms of audit* have become essential to the tasks of monitoring. More particularly, they mediate 'the inherent controversy and undecidability of . . . [welfare clients'] truth claims' (Parton, 1996: 112). Audits and the whole panoply of numbers, and therefore accountabilities, are not value-discrete. They do not refer solely to the simple process of counting. Various systems of auditing are revealed, at least in the welfare area, as value-laden. They actively contribute to the 'blaming system', as we have seen in Castel's thesis, by creating classifications and categories of deviance (see also Procacci, 1994).

Foucault's depictions of the private space of the clinic, and how it is transposed into the public space where issues of social risk are salient, can now be associated with the very important work of Hacking. Chance is 'tamed' by the politics of counting and enumeration. As he suggests:

> The systematic collection of data about people has affected not only the ways in which we conceive of a society, but the ways in which we describe our neighbour. It has profoundly transformed what we choose to do, who we try to be, and what we think of ourselves. Marx read the minutiae of official statistics, the reports from the factory inspectors and the like. One can ask: who had more effect on class consciousness, Marx or the authors of the official reports which created the classifications into which people came to recognise themselves? (1990: 3)

The previous privacy of professional trust, which exemplified social casework, has been replaced by the intrusion of management audit and accountability. It is not possible to isolate that privacy of professional trust from the processes of governance and social control. Social work is now caught in the almost irresolvable paradox of having 'transparently' to explain the efficacy of the former caring roles (Culpitt, 1992: 45–6). Ironically, as Parton argues, 'once risk becomes institutionalized the ability and willingness of [welfare] professionals to take risks – in the original sense of possible positive as well as negative outcomes – is curtailed' (1996: 113). The paradox is that a system of greater account-ability and scrutiny developed out of a neo-liberalism that espoused privacy, autonomy and individuality. As I argued in the previous chapter, this reliance on auditing, and an attack on the legitimacy of welfare need claims, cannot be seen as discrete to the process of those welfare claims. It is part of the 'disciplining technology' which, Foucault asserted, created the social mechanism for fashioning a welfare 'self'.

Disciplining technologies: making up 'welfare' peoples

The imaginative phrase 'making up people' is Hacking's. We have seen how the auditing function of statistical researches 'has profoundly transformed what we choose to do, who we try to be, and what we think of ourselves'. As he continues:

> enumeration requires categorization, and . . . defining new classes of people for the purposes of statistics has consequences for the ways in which we con-ceive of others and think of our own possibilities and potentialities. (1990: 6)

Developing links between the disciplinary technologies of Foucault and how this 'makes up' the welfare client is a necessary obverse to all of those arguments which seek to justify and support autonomous indi-vidualism. What Foucault was able to do was pose the possibility of a relationship of power/knowledge (a particular *savoir*) between how specific populations were to be governed and how the resources avail-able to governments could be most efficiently used. The political mechan-ism for achieving this was, Foucault argued, dependent on the ability of the state to form the individual as an object of knowledge. Governing through individuals and their complex patterns of individual allegiances (their solidarities) became the norm of these new aspects of political control. The forms of political coercion became personal.

The great benefit of Foucault's analysis is to relate the meaning of any current set of political assumptions to how they are constructed and 'known'. Similarly, we can apply this analysis to social policy. As Hewitt has suggested:

> The subjects of social policy, e.g. dependency and social needs, are not caused merely by social forces and do not exist as pure facts. They are constructed within the discourse of social policy as categories, classification systems and forms of knowledge by individuals and groups within the political, administrative and economic spheres. (1983: 67–8)

It was the processes of categorization and measurement which established social policy as the 'social arena' within which the issues of social problems were to be debated. Hewitt goes on to argue that social policy 'in particular becomes one of the apparatuses of the state for harnessing and circulating power' (1983: 68). Similarly, Dean argues that:

> in displacing attention from both the constitutional state and the analysis of ideology, the analytic of government reveal the complex and irreducible domain of practices that form the conditions of social policy. Such an analysis thus directs our attention to the need for the analysis and description of the practical rationalities and minor 'arts of government' that are the conditions of existence of a social security system. (1995: 571–2)

An important question is the degree of reflexivity built into this process. While the facts of need were attested and obvious, it is also the mechanisms for responding to them which created the separate arena of 'welfare'. This is an arena which by its very difference and distinctiveness became the mechanism of governance, one which would increasingly measure, sort and differentiate the 'problematic'. What is being constructed under the guise of arguing the need for accurate information are the patterns of how the welfare recipient is to be moralized into the role of client – what Hacking (1986c) calls 'making up people'. This reflects all the manifold ways in which the state will intersect with welfare recipients to demand obedience to an agreed lesser status. For Foucault this internalization of a moral demand arose out of the subordinate role required of those undergoing any aspect of the 'professional gaze'. How this 'gaze' is translated into a pattern of 'surveillance' is germane to this overall discussion of risk.

Social policy: an apparatus of the state?

The new politics of governance required an internalized acceptance (in the general population) of the legitimacy of professional differentiation; it also required that we be counted! As Hacking argues, 'the very notion of an exact population is one which has little sense until there are institutions for establishing and defining what "population" means' (1990: 6). Statistical analysis stands as the new 'grand inquisitor' and the critical 'evidence' was to be found in numbers, carefully arranged. Statistical analysis gave 'scientific authority to the construction of reified categories which lead to the objectification of oppressed, subjugated groups' (Hughes, 1995: 401).

To conclude this chapter, which has explored some further aspects of governance, I want to engage in a slight digression – but one with purpose. Has social policy itself become, or has it always been, part of the coercive arm of governance policies, and thus is it a risky activity? Squires' position on this question is clear. Various 'punitive and coercive forms of social policy [are] frequently deployed under the mantle of "welfare" ' (1990: 1). So much so that he argues that social policy has become 'anti-social' policy. Megill, on the other hand, accepting that disciplinary power is a 'source of tyranny', suggests that the issue is not whether we are free but rather 'how are we modern individuals, imbued with and sustained by systems of discipline and surveillance to be free' (1997: 75)? The distinction between *are* and *be* is immense.

For Squires, 'anti-social refers to a kind of absolute individualism' (1990: 6) – the power or opportunity, in effect, to create policies that 'create avarice and discontent'. He suggests that one of the major problems facing social policy is that 'the expulsion from "the social" of any autonomy or spontaneity that would allow us to see it in anything other than the effects of a successful domination' is crippling (1990: 12). Breaking open the social, to use his phrase, is the intent of this volume. Foucault has established a theoretical rigorousness, if you accept his analysis about the ubiquity of power, which seems to admit of nothing but pessimism. However, seeking to explode the pervasiveness of risk is a constant thread in the rhetoric of 'domination'.

One of the intriguing questions at the heart of this exploration of social policy and risk is why the previous political accommodations, that the welfare state represented some sort of 'sensible pragmatism', have changed. The coming to fruition of a defensive politics based upon risk, which increasingly needed to depict the welfare 'other' as threatening, has contributed to this hegemonic 'certainty'. The conjunction of ancient 'welfare fears' with Beck's ubiquitous 'risk society' has ratcheted up the rhetoric. One of the political questions that arises out of these apocalyptic, Armageddon-like assumptions about welfare risk is why there is no longer room for pragmatism and compromise. Why has the new right decided to 'take no prisoners', so to speak? In seeking an answer to this, Squires' distinction between the social as *site or space* and *mode* is important. Is the attack on welfare dependency an attack on the space or the site of welfare? Or does it reap such hostility because it is a particular 'rationality' which imputes a collective moral order?

What this raises is the question of what constitutes the 'good'. For neo-liberalism it is an article of faith that the 'good' cannot be acquainted with the 'social'. If such disputations are successful then welfare, having lost its legitimacy, 'is just a subsidiary project for the management of discontents' (Squires, 1990: 43). What I think Squires fails to understand is how his analysis of social policy and all its 'enemies' does not adequately deal with Foucault's insights about governance. Yes, what Squires details, patiently and comprehensively, are the consequences of governance. He is persuasive indeed about how social policy has not been able to avoid being 'tarred with a compliant brush'. But in maintaining his analysis at an ideological level Squires does not take into account how Foucault was trying to establish an analysis of power that was not ideological. Nor was he overly preoccupied with the rationality of governments *per se*. What he sought was an analysis of an autonomous rationality of governance that Squires evidentially provides, but does not claim for his work. Having established his argument for an 'anti-social' social policy Squires still wants (and understandably so) to argue that 'new solidarities can . . . form themselves in the midst of the disciplinary society and in the face of the coercive state' (1990: 209). Squires suggests that we need to understand how such hegemonies are structured in order that we may, yet again, challenge those who speak of the 'truth' and will not yet admit to their perspective of the 'social' any contradictory 'evidence'. So perhaps social policy defined as 'the intended actions promoting welfare' (Hewitt, 1983: 75) is not so risky after all? In the next chapter the nature of how citizenship theory has been altered by these neo-liberal politics will be further discussed. We have seen previously how a new theory of governance argued that we order our politics not so much through normative appeals to the greater good of society but through the rational, calculating, private choices of individuals. The antecedents of this lie in how welfare was, quintessentially, the supreme disciplining social technology.

Notes

1 The fear of the 'future', which this entails, often involves some hybridization of a general theme about the 'problems' of single-parent families. The canard is that the welfare state has facilitated the break-up of families and allowed young women to 'retire' from the workforce into state-supported motherhood – all the worst excesses of dependency (cf. Fraser, 1989a; Fraser and Gordon, 1994a; 1994b). It is interesting, on two counts, to note that such 'modern' issues have a historical antecedent. The first is about the usage of risk and the second the application of morality to these fears. Donzelot argues that in the nineteenth century philanthropists assumed that 'the excessive fecundity of the lower classes constituted the chief cause of their misery' (1979: 175). The change in the 'modern version', in which the personal issues become 'social problems', is how ubiquitous is the theme of risk. In the past, as Donzelot says, it was *'their misery'* (my italics). Now it is *our misery*! The shift is significant and marks the modern discourse about welfare. It is, however, interesting to note that the contemporary 'attack' on the welfare mother betrays an ancient fear. Donzelot argues that such 'irresponsible fecundity' indicated a 'lack of foresight in the labouring masses' and that this 'placed a strain on public finances in the form of the rising costs of welfare procedures' (1979: 175).

The historical endurability of these themes about the risks occasioned by the welfare 'other' challenges the fundamental rhetoric of neo-liberalism. The issues of welfare dependency do, obviously, have a modern cast in the growth of the costs of maintaining welfare provision. But the stretch of these themes, historic-ally, should give us pause to reflect on a different aspect of the 'disciplinary state'. It is not new! One further point from Donzelot: he suggested that colonial economic expansion, and the massive growth in profits this provided, overcame these fears about the fecundity of the 'labouring classes'. Again we can hear similar 'echoes' in the contemporary political rhetoric about the requirement for private investment to create a strong economic base for 'social expansion'. The periodic re-emergence of these anti-welfare themes is no accident of history. There is a systemic linking of these themes with cycles of economic expansion. Morality, in this regard, serves a political master!

2 Procacci argued that such a society emphasized moral reform: 'the inclusion of the poor turned into a disciplinary action aimed at restoring a "normal" relation between wealth and poverty' (1994: 212).

3 My usage of clinical 'gaze' is restricted to its function, within this wider analysis of the origin of contract, as a mechanism of governance. A lucid exposition of the use of Foucault in relation to theories of medicalization and the sociology of the body is provided by Lupton. In a wide-ranging analysis she identifies a conceptual flaw in using Foucault in such a way as to 'neglect examination of the ways that hegemonic medical discourses and practices are variously taken up, negotiated or transformed by members of the lay population in their quest to maximise their health status and avoid physical distress or pain' (1997: 94–5).

4 See the Afterword for some further comments on the new threat to manage-rialism posed by the 'doctors'!

5 What the insurance contract also did was to dispense with the necessity for continuous surveillance (cf. Gordon, 1991). Some aspects of the 'gaze' could be relinquished into the licensing of a contract with indemnity for loss. As Ewald argued, to be able to 'calculate a risk is to master time, to discipline the future' (1991: 207).

6 Given the range of aporias surrounding the modernity/post-modernity debate I agree with Dumm that these questions will not easily be resolved by removing the hyphen, thus asserting 'that the modern age has ended' (1988: 224).

7 Foucault called this aspect of power the function of *dispositifs* – the 'specific assemblages of actors, knowledges, practices and techniques' that together translated the rationality of government into specific 'realized effects' (Garland, 1997: 176).

8 This new technology of prison management was very significant to Foucault who wove so much of his analysis of power around the physical implication of a centralized watchtower. It became a metaphor for the 'watchful' growth of professional and political power. See Hewitt (1983: 71–2) for a thorough examina-tion of this theme in Foucault's *oeuvre*.

9 Foucault's depiction of the history of the growth of the asylum has been criticized for failing to be an accurate history (cf, Hewitt, 1983). However, the 'picture' that he paints of the growth of the rationality of governing powers, and how they became autonomous and set up systems to 'remove' the deviant from ordinary commerce, is still vital.

10 This is an important aspect of contemporary welfare discourse (cf. Fraser, 1993; Fraser and Gordon, 1992).

11 In a brilliant essay Procacci shows how poverty in eighteenth and nineteenth century France emerged, from being an opportunity for private charity, to assume the status of a 'social question'. The intent was to moralize the poor, and so the 'category' of poverty was a reified construct integral to the development of liberal politics (1994: 207). She argues that the 'organization of wealth' can be seen to require a definition of 'social poverty', akin to Foucault's analysis of madness to reveal the nature of reason. The poor are always with us but definitions of poverty change according to political purpose!

12 Honneth, having argued the significance of Machiavelli in postulating a theory of human interaction based upon 'fearful mistrust', suggests that the 'negative consequences of a perpetual situation of struggle . . . of permanent fear, and of mutual distrust' requires that subjects be contractually related to a 'sovereign ruling power'. Contract then is an 'instrumentally rational weighing of interests' (1995b: 9–10). Contracts are essentially protective devices, as well as guarantors of professional privilege. They indicate some aspect of the seeking of order against a background of presumed chaos.

13 See especially Chapter 9 for a fuller discussion of how the notion of 'gaze' and the power of 'surveillance' became reified into the self of those labelled as welfare dependants.

14 For another perspective on the function of expertise see Castel (1991) where he discusses the transformation from care to expert diagnosis as part of a structural shift for professionals. They gained a new power by focusing less on the subject of their investigations and more on the generation of diagnoses that located their subject within a risk class or category.

15 'Family' in this sense means both the foci of social and public policy on the family unit *per se* and also how the family is reified into a symbol of early modern governance.

16 A small digression: such coherences are reflected in popular assumptions of Thatcher's that 'society', as such, does not exist and that really Britain was a 'nation of shopkeepers'. She had 'good company' in Foucault who, Gordon argued, thought the state had no 'inherent propensities' and no 'essence' (1991: 4). More significantly, Foucault's position was that the institution of the state was formed by governance practices and not vice versa. For another 'view' on this question about the 'social' see Donzelot (1988) and Squires (1990: 5ff).

17 Hindess (1997a: 270) does suggest that such definitions of sovereignty, associated only with the power of the prince, do not adequately encompass that which inheres in the 'king', which expressed not only sovereign power as action, but sovereign power as the embodiment of all the citizens under his rule.

18 Hewitt's claim that the shift in political power 'from sovereign to bio-power, involved for example, the deployment of sexuality for enhancement rather than repression', is instructive (1983: 81).

19 Foucault always expressed reservations about the use of *ideology* either to confirm or to deny the legitimacy of sets of belief. He had three objections. The first was that ideology 'stands in virtual opposition to something else which is supposed to count as truth . . . the effects of truth are produced within discourses, which in themselves are neither true nor false'. His second objection was that ideology referred not to itself but to 'the order of a subject'. His third point, relating to the second, is that 'ideology stands in a secondary position relative to something which functions as its infrastructure, as its material economic determinant' (1984b: 60).

20 Interpreters of Foucault sometimes use his 'toolbox of spanners' (see Mottier, 1995) too logically, it seems. His thinking about power/knowledge, and the 'protection of the self' from the juggernaut of modern governance, is sometimes better understood as a 'word-picture'. Or, perhaps, with an open appreciation for what White (1988b: 191) called Foucault's sense of *responsibility to otherness*.

21 Hewitt outlines a significant argument that 'rather than fade into the background, law operates more and more as a norm, so that the judiciary is gradually incorporated into a continuum of apparatuses (medical, administrative, etc.) whose functions are regulatory' (1983: 69).

22 The mechanism for how the state was 'cut loose from the infernal circle of the metaphysics of sovereignty' (Donzelot, 1991: 171).

23 Deleuze, in his introduction to Donzelot's *The Policing of Families*, notes how 'the appeal to saving' altered the previous structure of dependency between rich and poor. An individual 'model' of charity was now 'replaced by direct interventions whereby *the industrial system*, itself, would remedy defects for which it would make the family responsible'. The change was from the altruism of charity to a new philanthropy that regarded aid as an investment. The state, as Deleuze argues, justified intervention through a welfare state on the basis of 'civilizing mores' (1979: xiii). The welfare state is now blamed for weakening the *traditional* family. The style of philanthropy, which saw aid as an investment, is no longer so dominant. We are more likely to hear talk, not of the investment aspect of welfare fiscal transfers, but that welfare has become a 'bottomless pit'. This change in the moral policing function of an interventionist welfare state is one explanation for neo-liberals seeking to return the burdens of welfare to the family.

24 See Rabinow (1996: 31ff) for a discussion of Hacking's thesis that different styles of reasoning were necessary to counter the potential 'falsehoods' of deduction and induction.

25 The Charity Organization Society (formed in 1869) had set the early patterns for this in isolating the 'deserving' from the 'undeserving' by means of a personal relationship. The rudimentary casework had established the principle of a 'determining' relationship as the means for winnowing out who would be helped. What is significant is how this personalizing of a needs discourse is generated into widespread governance of the welfare 'group' as distinct from the welfare 'individual'. Charity had indeed been an antidote to Bolshevism!

26 It is important not to conflate contract too closely with a legal connotation. The intent is to highlight the institutionalization of a 'regularity', an expectation, and not a legally sanctioned contract.

5

THE RISK ARENA: CITIZENSHIP, RIGHTS AND THE MARKETPLACE

> Although strategies of welfare sought to govern *through society*, 'advanced' liberal strategies of rule ask whether it is possible to govern without governing *society*, that is to say, to govern through the regulated and accountable choices of autonomous agents – citizens, consumers, parents, employees, managers, investors.
>
> (Rose, 1996b: 61)

These new 'liberal strategies of rule' have individualized the 'public sphere' (the phrase, of course, belongs to Habermas) and challenged the former rationales for governing 'through society'. In the previous two chapters we have seen how comprehensively neo-liberalism has fashioned the discourse about risk and that this has severely circumscribed the 'public sphere'. These dominant 'strategies' have eviscerated the notion that there might be some social 'space' uncontaminated by market forces. The concept of the public sphere implied 'the minimal, necessary conditions for a discursive realm free of coercion or manipulation' (Johnson, 1994: 427). I want to make some brief comments on the continuing debate between Habermas and Foucault in order to highlight some aspects of the disputes about the current possibility of normative critical theory.[1] Baldly, and provocatively, Nielsen summed up their differences: 'Habermas believes in progress. Foucault, by contrast, does not' (1997: 11).[2] We might well assume in the light of Beck's thesis of risk society that his analysis forecloses such a debate. This chapter also provides an opportunity to comment on citizenship theory and the possible decay of the public sphere.

Normative theory: what possibility?

The controversy between Foucault and Habermas goes to the heart of some of the problems that critical theory has had in establishing any basis for normative deliberation in the present climate. Habermas was concerned about the decay in any workable 'exemplary models'. Without them modernity could not stand 'outside itself' and be critically reflective. The problem, as Habermas argued, was that modernity 'sees itself as entirely on its own' (1986: 1). Simply put, the issue facing critical theory is how to gain leverage within a milieu of obvious common-sense individualism. Philosophical legitimization of the social, 'what [does] it mean to create some legitimate commonality . . . with "legitimate" here carrying the sense of reciprocity and mutual respect' (White, 1988a: 154), is vital for critical reflection.

Paradoxically, articulating the commonsensical within neo-liberal policy does not include commonality – only that which may be expected in allegiance to specific self-referent groups. The constriction or contraction of the public sphere happens when 'existence is carved and comes to appear as if it were written in stone' (Pavlich, 1995: 554). Such is the power of anti-utopian discourse. Habermas was seen as an ally in the protection of a public sphere uncontaminated by the 'stones' of masculine marketplace reasoning (Fraser, 1992). Foucault's genealogical project, on the other hand, challenges critical theory to elaborate specific discourses that give 'expression to those voices that have been marginalized by specific power–knowledge arrangements'; more specifically to 'revitalise lost discursive events' and facilitate the 'insurrection of subjugated knowledges' (Pavlich, 1995: 556).

Foucault's requirement that there is no 'neutral rationality' and that 'social practices condition cognitive discourse' (Nielsen, 1997) does not remove the possibility that 'subjugated knowledges' can be used to challenge current hegemonies. Indeed he argued that it was through the re-emergence of 'disqualified knowledges' that 'criticism performs its work' (1980: 82). Specific constrictions of the public sphere can be challenged, applying Foucault's genealogical critique. Being critical, as Foucault argued, reflects an attitude, a process, and never a project to be completed (see the Afterword in this volume). However, while he might explicitly reject any emancipatory ethic that seeks normative closure, his work can nonetheless be aligned with Habermas in seeking to 'ground' our social hurts within a 'discursive realm free of coercion or manipulation'. He would have rejected this possibility of a non-coercive world and seen all calls for such 'freedoms' as false 'siren calls'.

What seems obvious, nevertheless, about Foucault's *oeuvre* is that he *did* see 'the struggle for interpretative dominance as a defining feature of the genealogical method' (O'Malley et al., 1997: 506). In the light of this understanding of Foucault, Nielsen has passionately argued:

All analysis and criticism must work from within some distinctive cluster of social practices, and, if as genealogists we are to do critical history, we should recognise and acknowledge right at the start our polemical interests motivating our investigation and critique of the emergence of contemporary social power. We should not seek to disguise from ourselves that we are political

animals in the midst of political struggle. Our intent as political animals is to
rectify the malignancies in our social practices. To do that effectively we must
understand them in a genealogical manner. (1997: 13)

Nielsen's valuable insight is to see how important it is to set such
genealogical searches within a diachronic and not a synchronic perspective. It is part of the power of neo-liberalism's incorporation of risk
into its anti-welfare rhetoric to depict welfare beneficiaries as part of a
synchronic reality. While it is clear (from within a neo-liberal perspective)
that a historical overview can be made about the structural problems of
institutional welfare, that verification of *personal* history is not granted to
the welfare recipient.[3] The implicit 'stone' of social stigmatism is that the
welfare 'other' will be accorded no 'historical' or precursive reality. To do
that would be to ground their experience within some description or
understanding of a legitimacy *extending over time*. The implication of this
for critical theory is clear. Revealing 'subjugated knowledges' requires
that they be studied and argued diachronically. Those who fall outside
the brave new world of the marketplace become 'impotent, indolent
players' (Bauman, 1997). Consequently, they are simply relegated to
some current stigmatized class or grouping by a synchronic constriction
of their experience. They are excluded from the market 'game' and thus
have no 'right' to their history.[4] The depiction of risk as a marketplace
'reality' is, quintessentially, a masculine view of the world. The 'bourgeois
public sphere was not only restricted to educated and propertied elites,
but was also predominantly a *male* preserve' (Thompson, 1993: 181). As
Fraser has trenchantly argued, a 'new societal role, the welfare client'
was intrinsic to the welfare state and women were its 'original and
paradigmatic subjects' (1987: 104–6).[5]

Any critical reflective task that would reveal these 'subjugated knowledges' must also demonstrate that the post-modern culture of neo-
liberalism has 'continuously excluded "otherness" in its one-way history
of modernism'. Successfully revealing that otherness gives some hope
that we might yet create 'a postmodernism of resistance to the series of
exclusions that that modernism was based on' (Richters, 1988: 630). This
concept of otherness is significant in Foucault's *oeuvre* and has some
correspondence to the importance of the 'silences of social policy'
discussed previously.[6] We have seen that part of Foucault's 'unsettling
effect' comes from his 'moral-aesthetic' focus on what 'one might call a
sense of *responsibility to otherness*' (White, 1988b: 191). White argues that
this sense of otherness not only is neglected but is actively 'shunted aside
in modern life'. Such a shift in imagination is discomfiting to a 'logo-
centric style of thinking' which cannot easily tolerate such intentional
voiding of rationality. It certainly is not commonsensical! What this
notion of otherness indicates is the same elusive awareness that preoccupied Katznelson who enjoined us to 'develop a taste for thinking
about possible worlds that are not very far away, but seem to be just

beyond our grasp' (1986: 325). Foucault's somewhat infamous aim to make an ethics of the self, 'to create ourselves as a work of art' (1984d: 351), makes more sense when seen in this light.[7] The potential to recognize fully the diachronic reality of the welfare 'other' is clearly 'there' in Foucault's commitment to the making of personal histories. What is not always so clear is how these histories might be used in the 'realm of contestation and struggle' (McNay, 1992: 190). That is still the key question for critical theory.

The moral-aesthetic force of such thinking which led Foucault to pose a 'responsibility to otherness' is counter-posed by White with the obverse, currently dominant in Western political thought, which seeks to develop 'a sense of responsibility to act in the world in a justifiable way' (1988b: 191). He argues that the language of politics must embrace both the practical aspects of co-ordinating action and the 'world opening' otherness of Foucault. Acting responsibly to otherness 'means inevitably . . . treating people as alike for the purposes of making consistent and defensible decisions about alternative courses of action' (1988b: 192). It represents a different aspect of common-sense that we certainly require if we are to mount any effective challenge to the rejection and stigmatizing of welfare recipients.

Bringing the future into the present: the new citizenship of risk

My intent here is to examine how successfully neo-liberalism has under-cut the old arguments about citizenship claim rights.[8] Neo-liberalism explicitly limits 'the recognition of – and indeed, toleration of – differ-ence' (Cooke, 1997: 280). Neo-liberalism has denied otherness within its 'one-way history of modernism' (and the politics of common-sense) and this has led to a greater intolerance of difference. It is a 'fighting creed' as Taylor (1992: 62) asserted. I am aware that these debates are still polarizing and that some considerable effort has been made by neo-liberal theorists to consign citizenship to their political 'dustbins'![9] There it keeps good company with 'socialist goals of egalitarianism and the defence of collectivist social and political arrangements' (Saunders, 1993: 57).

While these issues are vigorously contested at a philosophical level there is, nevertheless, some empirical evidence that these 'clashes by night' have not entirely dismissed the relevance of citizenship theorizing. This is not to argue that the communitarians have surreptitiously won. Rather it is to point to very interesting work done by Saunders who, accepting that the socialist mode of citizenship has indeed withered, nevertheless makes an argument for the emergence of a 'privatized mode' of citizenship. His contention is that the growth of the prevailing privatized nature of consumption 'enhances rather than diminishes citizenship' (1993: 62). His thesis is a significant one, further discussion of which lies outside my focus on risk. However, the empirical evidence, he adduces, does suggest some possibility of a bending back, if not a convergence, in the classical standoff between the one and the many.[10] As he says:

> The privatized society which is slowly emerging out of the ruins of the collectivist welfare system holds out the prospect not of social and moral disintegration, but of new and active forms of citizenship based on individual competence and the development of genuinely collective forms of association and sociability springing up from below. (1993: 88)

This 'springing up from below' as the focus of new politics is discussed later. What is at issue is how such new models of a privatized citizenry still articulate the reason for their own privatizations on some basis of exclusion where equal political recognition is denied to groups who can be defined out of, or excluded from, the contractual consensual state.

Honneth argues that 'motives for rebellion, protest and resistance have generally been transformed into categories of "interest" ' (1995b: 161). The former expressive feelings of 'indignation' are not accorded the same validity. They cannot easily be reified into anything other than what they are. Rebellious protest and resistance can, however, be transformed into rational arguments for bureaucratic deregulation and the supremacy of contract as a governance mechanism. Indignation at lack of recognition is thus redefined as 'competition for scarce goods' rather than being 'a struggle over the intersubjective conditions for personal integrity'. The implication for this in denying legitimacy to welfare claimants is obvious, since 'the moral grammar of social struggles has to remain hidden' (1995b: 165). The complex way in which risk is used to justify these exclusionary tactics, which morally stigmatize whole groups of people, who have fallen outside the contractual arena, is the major subtext of this book.

Cooke interestingly analyses the debate within political theory about the struggle inside neo-liberalism to defend the ineluctable ideals of individual autonomy and yet assume moral responsibility for those excluded groups. The nature of this debate is not one that I can give full attention to here.[11] There is the potential, as Cooke describes, for further structural stigmatization. As she says, the concern is

> whether in denying equal political recognition to certain social groups on the basis of their lack of commitment to the ideal of individual autonomy, it is desirable to *distinguish further between such groups* and the degree of political recognition allowable in each case. (1997: 288)

The possibility of a spectrum of acceptability, in relation to excluded groups, equally raises other vital questions, especially 'the (normative or pragmatic) reasons that might justify varying degrees of political recognition'. That this is not just a speculative debate will become clearer below in the discussion about whether it is correct to assume that neo-liberal politics have actually ushered in the 'death of the social' (cf. Baudrillard, 1993).

The death of the 'social': the shape of the new politics

For many theorists the 'death of the social' is no longer a proposition but established fact (cf. Hindess, 1997a; 1997b; Reddy, 1996; Rose, 1996a). Evidence of this 'death' is demonstrated in the ways this new consensual contractual world has altered the focus of government. No longer does the state see the 'subjects of government' as some generalized or reified coherence of *all citizens within a social fabric*. The proper subject of government is no longer 'the social' but the complex networks of interaction, bargaining and compromise which interpose and counter-pose interlocking, but separate, networks of individual obligation. Rose elegantly summarizes the effects of these changes:

> The human beings who were to be governed – men and women, rich and poor – were now conceived as individuals who are to be *active* in their own government. And their responsibility was no longer to be understood as a relation of obligation between citizen and society enacted and regulated through the mediating party of the State: rather, it was to be a relation of allegiance and responsibility to those one cared about the most and to whom one's destiny was linked. (1996a: 330)

Citizenship rights and obligations, which were the natural expression of civil society, can no longer be articulated. Whether such theorizing about citizenship is now really possible is significant (cf. Hindess, 1997a). Certainly if it is feasible it will increasingly be seen to represent 'claims' against a self-referent 'community' and not the state. Rose has summarized this 'mutation' in political language whereby the social is transmuted into community 'as a new territory for the administration of individual and collective existence'. The essence of Rose's argument is that there has been a 'complex reconfiguration of the territory of government' (see also Garland, 1997). This territory, Rose suggests, embodies radically different 'political languages' which 'problematize' issues not on the basis of the nation-state but

> *in terms of* features of communities and their strengths, cultures, pathologies. They shape the strategies and programmes that address such problems by seeking to *act upon* the dynamics of communities. (1996a: 331)

Society as the pre-eminent focus of politics is voided by the assumptions that support such 'collectivities' – what Hindess describes as 'the rationality of faction' (1997a: 263–4). Bauman has also suggested that this new focus of governance occurred because the 'nation-state proved to be the incubator of a modern society ruled not so much by the unity of feelings as by the diversity of unemotional market interests' (1997: 192). What concerns many defenders of citizenship entitlements and rights is that these newly self-referent 'communities'[12] appear to indicate 'that there is no longer a representing or representative consciousness in politics' and therefore no way to recognize the legitimacy of a 'pluralization of social victims' (McNay, 1992: 190). As privileged groups, their 'conduct' shaped by consumption and markets, these new political groupings can now comfortably stand outside the political struggles of the 'excluded' or the 'dispossessed'. They seek to govern through their newly found sense of freedom and not through any sense of civil society, imprisoned with the 'baggage of obligation'. The 'social', in this view, cannot really be postulated.

The articulation of a more particular 'community', as the proper focus of political administration, also reflects how social critique is voided and 'overcome' by expertise. Expert professional 'gaze' deconstructs the social into more specific areas of appropriate investigation. Bauman suggests that the deconstruction of national identity, explicit in such political transformations, appears to be a 'site-clearing operation for the market-led confidence game of quickly assembled and even faster dis-mantled modes of self-description' (1997: 192). We can hear 'echoes' here of the major thrust of Hacking's arguments about 'making up peoples'. The depiction of a self-referent community as a 'legitimate' focus of concern, in a deregulated neo-liberal world, suggests the importance of risk as a key fact in that 'mutation' of political thought.[13] Beck's depiction of the diffused and potentially apocalyptic nature of risk society seem-ingly creates a frozen response to the whole. Popular assumptions about the overwhelming character of globalized risk may equally have con-tributed to this 'mutation' in political rhetoric. His notion of 'sub-politics' is relevant here (see following chapter). Personal imperatives to act upon the world, to find some way to interpret experience, lead into justifica-tions for self-referent 'communities' and away from the state as having any significance. The notion reflects what we can call a 'tribalization' of social knowledges, a particularizing which is necessary in order to recover a sense of possible freedom, defined as the ability and oppor-tunity to act independently in the face of risk.

The possibility of the public sphere?

Habermas' attempt to maintain the possibility of a normative discourse depended on being able to achieve 'an institutional location for practical reason in public affairs, and for the accompanying valid, if often deceptive, claims of formal democracy' (Calhoun, 1992: 1). The justification of this inquiry merits some respect but the overarching question, in all of the arguments about 'formal democracy', is *whether it still exists in the manner in which critical theorists presume that it does.*[14] It seems to me that the governmentality literature has raised serious questions about the viability of formal democracy. As the defenders of the welfare state were forced to concede, post-modernism might have also effectively undermined the justifications for those expressions of formal democracy that might sustain normative discourse. The issue is whether Habermas' theory of communicative action 'can possibly make sense of intuitions it presents as contradictory'. Perhaps the cursory question is whether Habermas' elegant synthesis is too late! Perhaps, indeed, the structure of that argument about 'the intuitions of discourse participants [already] excludes certain types of intuitions' (Fleming, 1996: 177). With neo-liberalism the 'horse has bolted'!

Habermas assumed that reasoned argument, not entrenched status or tradition, was the decisive aspect of the public sphere. However, all of the suggestions about how 'community' is a newly mutated aspect of a political language call this into question. These newly fashioned 'communities', which Rose describes, express a valorization of tradition and status that makes such reasoned discourse problematic. If 'a public sphere adequate to a democratic polity depends upon both quality of discourse and quantity of participation' (Calhoun, 1992: 2) then surely those are not the signifiers of a neo-liberal contractual society? We need to develop an 'expanded concept of reason that . . . is essential for rethinking modernity's critical resources' (Fleming, 1996: 177).

Political discourse has become ritualized and is marketed for effect not dialogue. The arbiters of common-sense have become deaf. There are no clear ways in which to compel general allegiance to an ideal of normative social progress: certainly not if that means privileging such social aims over against the power of the new self-referent 'communities', and particularly not if critical theory harks back to an 'unsupportable objective teleology of history' (White, 1988a: 153). This is not a counsel of despair. It is however to accept the limitations now imposed on the complexity of Habermas' model of communicative action. I agree with White that effective deconstruction of the implicit common-sense of these core concepts must start with a recognition, from critical theory, that the former background conditions of tradition and civility must be rethought. We should not make too much of the idiosyncratic disputes between Habermas, Derrida and Foucault. This has all the hallmarks of a 'family squabble'. Fleming maintains, in opposition to Habermas, that the principles of deconstruction can be 'made from within the tradition of rational argumentation' (1996: 169). My hope is that a more thorough analysis of the epistemological politics of risk might reveal an aspect of that much needed process. What this implies is that critical theory must 'draw attention to its own limits; in short, [critical theorists] must at least signal their own incapacity to account for or illuminate certain kinds of otherness' (White, 1988b: 203). To seek, by implication for public sublimity, a 'larger, more thrilling communal goal', is simply not possible since such sublimity which involves the 'breaking out of some particular [constraining] inheritance' (Rorty, 1995: 457) is always essentially private.

That Habermas relied too heavily on a bourgeois ideal of the public sphere is correct (Fraser, 1992). Such a model of 'an institutionalized arena of discursive interaction' bears little resemblance to our present patterns of governance. Fraser seems to interrupt her argument by 'resting' at the 'emergence of welfare-state mass democracy'. In her definition of this we see an intertwined state and society, all now manoeuvred by various forms of 'mass-mediated staged displays and the manufacture and manipulation of public opinion' (1992: 113). We have, seemingly, in a very rapid fashion, moved considerably past this definition of the current state of affairs. Labelling the arguments for a neo-liberal deregulated and contractual state as 'ballyhoo' simply will not do. It has assumed much more menacing proportions than that. The efforts to decouple the traditional intertwining of state and society have been breathtaking. Again I refer you to the substance of Rose's (1996a; 1996b) analysis. While we still see the 'mass-mediated displays' it is arguable that *public* opinion now encompasses the same sets of meaning that Fraser intended.

Critical theory faces an altogether more difficult task. To argue that the official bourgeois public sphere is the 'institutional vehicle' for changes in political rule, from those based on domination to those in which the dominated acquiesce through some form of repression, accords with much of the new governmentality thesis. Certainly one can hear echoes here of Foucault's theories on power/knowledge. My cavil, however, is with the assumption that the official public sphere 'defines the new, hegemonic mode of domination' (Fraser, 1992: 117). Such assumptions still privilege the public sphere as an arena of manipulation and control. The origin of the hegemony of neo-liberalism was not essentially in its dominance of the public sphere *per se* but in its reification of 'forensic' risk as an indispensable part of individual privacy. This concept of 'forensic' risk implies that (in respect of universal risk) someone must be held to account – that blame be laid and protection from further risk obtained. The control of all others, the hegemony of the one against the many, if you will, arises out of this securing of the self against danger. There are manifold ways in which risk is woven into the heart of neo-liberalism's rhetoric. To see hegemonies strictly in terms of *public* power ignores the source of their real power, which is derived from these *private* discourses.

Agitating for the 'opening up of the public sphere', its greater democratization, misses the point. Expressed differently, arguing for more access to the 'institutionalized arena of discursive interaction' ignores the fact that such *public* discourses are either ritualized or vapid. Fraser takes issue with the notions of private and public. As she says:

In general, critical theory needs to take a harder, more critical look at the terms 'private' and 'public'. These terms, after all, are not simply straightforward designations of societal spheres; they are cultural classifications and rhetorical labels . . . they are powerful terms frequently deployed to delegitimate some interests, views, and topics and to valorize others. (1992: 131)

While it is hard to gainsay the moral-ethical position that informs such analysis, the processes of delegitimation have gone much further than Fraser proposes. A false nostalgia for a public sphere 'in which inter-locutors can deliberate as peers' has no weight in the nature of the critical analysis that is needed to challenge neo-liberal rejection of the legitimacy of oppositional discourse. Neither do arguments that depend upon analyses of 'participatory parity'. I do agree with Fraser that bourgeois discourses were 'governed by protocols of style and decorum that were themselves markers of status inequality' (1992: 119). It is these protocols which have become institutionalized into particular, and not general (or social), forms of government. They are much more powerful. These protocols are increasingly ritually codified discourses that brook no interference and seek no response other than formal agreement. They undermine critical theory, and the 'thematizing' of 'subjugated know-ledges', by redefining such knowledges as excluded. Or, as I have argued earlier, denied the accolade of common-sense!

Fraser clearly acknowledges the fact of these new self-referent com-munities but she still sees them as abstractions of the social.[15] She sees them as 'publics [which] are differentially empowered or segmented' or as ones that 'are involuntarily enclaved and subordinated to others' (1992: 137). Positing arguments about 'systemic relations of inequality' or 'structural relations of dominance and subordination' have a moral but no practical *gravitas*. These communities of difference – 'individuals *active* in their own government' – have articulated a new sense of responsibility, which, as Rose argued, 'was no longer to be understood as a relation of obligation between citizen and society enacted and regu-lated through the mediating party of the State' (1996a: 330). The issue for critical theory is how to *breach the ramparts of this privacy*. It is this *privacy* which is so strenuously defended and is represented by the mutation of political discourse such that community now no longer means the generalized but the particular social. These *private* reifications cannot be easily countered by *public* rhetoric no matter how sophisticated or trenchant it may be. The new critique of governance has raised the spectre that politics is no longer about the nation-state but about these congeries of self-referent 'communities'.

This may be the post-modern 'nightmare' but we cannot easily abstract from its reified decoupling into false nostalgia for a vanished social. What is possible may be better revealed to us in understanding Foucault's challenge not to seek for alternatives and resolve problems but to delineate a 'genealogy' of problems. A more profound analysis of risk may yet breach these private ramparts. As he says:

> My point is not that everything is bad, but that everything is dangerous, which is not exactly the same as bad. If everything is dangerous, then we always have something to do. (1984d: 343)

The 'doing', of course, did involve the hard work of genealogical research into the nature of the disciplinary power of the state, particularly in respect of welfare claimants. Habermas did accord Foucault respect in this area of his investigations. He acknowledged the significance of Foucault's work in outlining how the 'legal and administrative means for the implementation of social welfare state programmes' involved a 'reifying and subjectivating power' (1986: 9). These 'subtle distortions' revealed, as Habermas argues, the irresolvable conflict of institutionalized welfare. His argument is that 'inherent in the project of the social state is a contradiction between goal and method' (1986: 9). Establishing structures that allow for egalitarianism conflict with 'individual self-fulfilment and spontaneity'. It is this contradiction which neo-liberalism has so elegantly exploited in advancing its 'solution' to this flawed utopian project.

Habermas on welfare: thoughts for a future debate

In this final section I want to return to some aspects of Habermas' depiction of the issues of the welfare state. For him the whole enterprise of welfare reveals aspects of the 'dark side' of modernity. Habermas set out his explicit concerns about the general issues of the welfare state as follows:

> the *new obscurity* is part of a situation in which the program of the social welfare state, which still feeds on the utopian image of a laboring society, is losing its capacity to project future possibilities for a collectively better and less endangered way of life. (1986: 5)

Any attempt to respond to the profound challenges that neo-liberalism has mounted against the welfare state will be better informed by understanding something of Habermas' criticism where he argues that 'it is now the very means of guaranteeing freedom that endangers the freedom of beneficiaries' (1987: 362). For Habermas, as Hewitt (1992) summarizes, the real crisis of the welfare state arises because there is an internal conflict about the 'compensatory functions, geared to the distribution of use values to satisfy human needs that are vital to the lifeworld'. These efforts to compensate for loss or distortion of needs conflict with the welfare state's 'reification functions that promote forms of system domination and abstraction inimical to the lifeworld' (1992:

108). It is the idea of retraction that is significant since it is risk that has been used to justify this further collapse of the 'lifeworld'.

This internal conflict sheds further light on Foucault's analysis of disciplining technologies and the ways that welfare claimants internalize such reifications. There is an urgent requirement, for those who would seek to defend the legitimacy of the welfare state, to come to terms with this overarching criticism. As Habermas stated:

> In the area of *public welfare policy* . . . [and] social welfare law, it has been shown repeatedly that although legal entitlements to monetary income . . . definitely signify historical progress when compared with the traditional care of the poor, this juridification of life-risks exacts a noteworthy price in the form of *restructuring interventions in the lifeworlds* of those who are so entitled. (1987: 362)

The consequence of these interventions, as Habermas outlines, is to embed a whole constellation of administrative regulations *vis-à-vis* entitlement into the 'context of a life history and a concrete form of life'. That very process, he suggests, subjects the 'other' of the welfare claimant to a 'violent abstraction' because of the juridification demands of administration.[16] A new analysis of 'legal' welfare is important in this discussion (cf. Le Grand, 1997). The professional 'gaze' of the medical specialists (see Chapters 4 and 9) who reinforced a 'clinical' perspective in social work has been superseded by a contractual legal 'gaze'. The personal and contractual 'gaze' of medicine has been recast in the legal/moral 'gaze' of juridification.

Risk in all its forms has shaped this transformation of 'surveillance'. An increasing requirement to define the 'other', those excluded from the safety of the contract, as forensically dangerous is significant (cf. Bauman, 1997; Castel, 1991; Douglas, 1990). What informed the medical 'gaze' was the necessity to create an arena for the exercise of professional power. What now informs all the processes of juridification is the necessity to protect those enclaves of professional and contracted power. The political ground of governance has shifted from 'surveillance' to risk management. The crisis now is how to protect the possibility of the social and not specifically how to protect professional 'space': neo-liberal contractural policies have done that 'job' exceedingly well.[17] Various administrative processes escalate more precise juridification requirements. This, paradoxically, collapses options for social transformation and change while increasing the demand for it. Juridification depends on the maintenance of a distinction about what is really at risk! Neo-liberalism collapses the individual complexity of welfare discourses into the relative simplicities of risk and scarcity. These reflect various 'mantra-like' discourses: the welfare state, for example, cannot sustain such high levels of expenditure; or people would rather accept welfare than work. Security is no longer about the social, about the satisfaction of an 'infinite' range of hopes and fears, but is about the protection of privilege. It is here that the notion of 'subjugated knowledges' has its sharpest relevance, and Foucault's genealogies, which explicate these 'knowledges', have their ethical grounding. Post-modernism may sit uncomfortably with acknowledging the 'violence' of such abstractions and has little patience with trying to draft these personal histories into 'meta-narratives' but, as Foucault argued, if 'everything is dangerous, then we always have something to do'! It is how we articulate that danger and the means we find to enlarge the arena of this discursive debate that is significant.

The source of our conceptual problem about the welfare state was, Habermas thought, consequent upon the 'deceptive symbiosis' that juridification and administrative reality forged with 'the rational domination of nature and the mobilzation of social energies'. The nexus of social and political power, formed by this symbiosis, was the ground for the rhetoric of the practical 'can-do': the epistemologies of common-sense that 'there is no alternative'. Habermas coined the word 'therapeutocracy' to refer to the application of this administrative 'violence'. As he goes on to argue:

> while the welfare-state guarantees are intended to serve the goal of social integration, they nevertheless promote the disintegration of life-relations when these are separated, through legalized social intervention, from the consensual mechanisms that coordinate action and are transferred over to media such as power and money. (1987: 364)

The interesting dilemma is that in validating, for welfare claimants, 'areas of private discretion' in counter-reaction to the violence of juridification through the 'therapeutocracy', Habermas, like all critical theorists, is caught by his own argument. We cannot easily privilege *privacy* for the beneficiary without seemingly laying the ground for the articulation of a multiplicity of self-referent 'communities' under post-modernism. Political power is now couched in terms of individual, not social, obligation. It is this that has added weight to the calls for the whole range of deregulated privatization of health and welfare. For example:

> social insurance, as a principle of solidarity, gives way to a kind of privatization of risk management. In this new prudentialism, insurance against the future possibilities of unemployment, ill-health, old age and the like becomes a private obligation. (Rose, 1996b: 58)

The 'variegated array of groups' that had been relegated to the periphery of the 'economic-administrative complex' has come to dine at the power-table! As Habermas argues, the 'bond that unites these heterogeneous groups is the critique of growth' – as well as their articulation of a politics of risk. Explanations for the power of these groups (Rose's 'communities') cannot be found in the histories of 'bourgeois emancipation movements [or in] the struggles of the organized labor movement'

(1987: 393). Habermas locates these heterogeneous groups more within a 'populist middle class', or in various expressions of former 'escapist' movements. It is interesting to note how relatively unprepared Habermas has been to accord the consensual contractual politics of neo-liberalism any real historical significance. It is as if his theorizing of the 'whole' has not made it easy to accommodate the post-modern power of communities, as subcultures within the whole. While he theorizes about the fact of these emergent subcultures he seems still to see the proper 'subjects' of government as intrinsically citizens of the nation-state.

The valorization of risk, the pejorative rejection of the welfare 'other', the denial that government should take place '*through society*', have indeed come to pass. As Rose suggested, the neo-liberal 'strategies of rule' are establishing a new politics in which governing 'without governing *society*, that is to say, to govern through the regulated and accountable choices of autonomous agents – citizens, consumers, parents, employees, managers, investors', is the reality (1996b: 61). How that politics used and fashioned risk will be the underlying focus of the next chapter. We turn now to an analysis of Beck's risk society thesis in order to develop further our understanding of the interrelationship of social policy and risk.

Notes

1 That there may be more correspondence than difference between Foucault and Habermas is explored by White (1988a: Chapter 6, especially 144ff).

2 This discussion of the important debate between Habermas and Foucault is intentionally limited to my more immediate focus on risk in relation to welfare state justifications and restructuring. It is not an easy debate to resolve but the attendant 'heat' and 'noise' throw up valuable commentary on the wider modernity/post-modernity question. There are excellent discussions of this debate in Fleming (1996), Fraser (1989b; 1992; 1995a), Landes (1992), Nielsen (1997), Pavlich (1995), Richters (1988), Rorty (1995), White (1988a).

3 See Chapter 8 for a consideration of Honneth's critical challenge to the denial of recognition. For Honneth 'the normative ideal of a just society is empirically confirmed by historical struggles for recognition' (1995b: xii). His ethical question (after Hegel) is: how can we claim the morality of individual uniqueness, as a political ideal, while denying it to others?

4 It is an interesting point to note that in developing such public outcry about welfare dependency, neo-liberalism is not doing what classical stigmatization of the poor and the insane did – which was to remove the stigmatized from sight. As Douglas has suggested, in the past the 'alleviation of wrong, removing stigma could only make the privileged members of the community feel more comfortable' (1990: 15). These are no longer moral questions, if indeed they ever were! They are political, about power and governance issues. The current stigmatizing of welfare, in a climate of risk society, is essential to the heart of neo-liberal assertions of the individualized self, as I have argued elsewhere in this volume.

5 Feminist analysis (cf. Fraser, 1987; 1989a; 1989b; Fraser and Gordon, 1994a; 1994b; McNay, 1992; Mills, 1994; Mouffe, 1995; Sawicki, 1991) amply demonstrates the 'masculine' depiction of risk as a marketplace 'reality' and how such discourse attempts to close down or limit the public sphere.

6 White indicates why Habermas had such trouble in accommodating the notion of a 'pre-rational, embodied otherness'. The maintenance of a 'rational, self-reflective, self-mastering subject of the humanist tradition' was essential to Habermas' defence of normative argument (White, 1988a: 145).

7 Wain, defending Foucault, suggests that Foucault's argument 'is not to be regarded as Cartesian self-absorption but as a kind of activity *on and within the world*' (1996: 359, my italics).

8 For a summary of some of the most recent debates about citizenship (which has spawned a vast literature) see Bader (1995).

9 Squires, for example, argues that there is a paradox at the heart of citizenship theorizing in that the evolution of citizenship criteria went hand-in-hand with strict eligibility criteria for limiting rights (1990: 142).

10 *Omnes et singulatim* was the title of one of Foucault's lectures in his last series which had the overall title of 'The government of one's self and others' (Burchell et al., 1991: 2–3; see Foucault, 1981b).

11 However, some aspects of the politics of recognition will be discussed in Chapter 8.

12 I will apply this term 'self-referent community' to refer to the wide range of these political collectivities. The term can refer to commercial groupings (the 'organization'), groups with a common purpose both practical and ideological, and also communities of origin. It is from the last that we get the idea of tribalization. The singular importance is that while I think it is a clumsy and grab-bag term it does refer to those groups who seek to govern below an allegiance to the nation-state and citizenship rights.

13 Rose's use of the word 'mutation' may well be suggestive of the irregular and unnatural change that may occur from the mutation consequent upon the misuse of nuclear weapons. This may be drawing too long a bow but the idea of the negative aspects of mutation is important.

14 Certainly Habermas was less hopeful, and presumed that the 'exhaustion of utopian energies' was not a 'passing mood' and maybe there was 'a fundamental change of modern time-consciousness in general' that vitiated the normative foci of critical theorists (1986: 3).

15 In a later revision of her earlier paper Fraser (1995b) does accord the 'multivalent, contested categories of privacy and publicity' more salience. She also argues that post-modernism does theorize about the 'multiplicity of public spheres' and that the search for egalitarianism and democracy involves some acceptance of their respective differences.

16 By 'juridification' Habermas means the complex legalizing of social life.

17 White argues that juridification 'exerts a *reifying* influence on the lifeworld, which, when combined with the enhanced claims to *expertise* of social workers and other administrators in the newly redefined categories of life, produces an insidiously expanding domain of dependency' (1988a: 113).

6

AVOIDANCE OF BADS:
BECK'S NEW UBIQUITY OF RISK?

The attempt to submit chance to thought implies in the first place an interest in the *experience* . . . of that which happens unexpectedly . . . Indeed there are those of us who are inclined to think that unexpectability conditions the very structure of an event.

(Derrida, 1984: 5)

Beck's *Risk Society: Towards a New Modernity* has had a remarkable impact, not only within sociology, but more generally in capturing something of the 'fears and paradoxes of modern society' (Goldblatt, 1996: 154).[1] Prior to Beck's 'arrival' the major theorist about risk was Mary Douglas (see below). Part of the impact of Beck's book was that it arrived in a world 'ready for it', so to speak. It is clever, mordant, and written in a metaphorical style designed to offend those social theorists whose analyses were grounded in reflections on the progress of modernity *per se*.

Theorizing about risk marks an important shift in the debate about the complex definitional and descriptive issues surrounding the possible decay of modernity, the validity of risk society, high modernity and/or the transition to post-modernism (cf. Bauman, 1992; 1997). Such conjectures are often fraught, representing various theoretical lures within social theory 'to impose some overbearing, melancholy singularity upon our present' (Barry et al., 1993: 265). Whether Beck's thesis about risk society does mark a major 'rupture' with modernity (towards reflexive modernization) or whether it is only one more 'melancholy singularity' to be avoided is the focus of the next two chapters. What is not in question is that his book did present an important goad to social theory (Draper, 1993; Goldblatt, 1996; Turner, 1994; 1995; 1997). While Beck's development of risk theory is so obviously striking, we cannot ignore the contributions made by Giddens (1991; 1994a; 1994b; 1994c; 1995) and earlier by Douglas (1986; 1990; 1992).

Mary Douglas: acculturation – the meaning and knowledge of risk

Douglas argued for a 'cultural theory of risk' in order to explain why blame figured so highly when humans, confronted by risk, sought to make sense out of it. She suggests that the notion of risk has become a 'central cultural construct' situated between 'private, subjective opinion and public physical science' (1982: 194). Formerly risk had been an aspect of the analysis of probability – what she called the 'hedonic calculus'. As it has become increasingly politicized within modernity, risk 'has weakened its old connection with technical calculations of probability' (1990: 2). She argues that the new political construction of risk is less involved with probabilities than with danger. This construct reflects one of my premises, that neo-liberal attacks on the viability of an interventionist state are not about risk probabilities so much as they are about 'welfare dangers'. The rhetoric of blame is struck. Effectively, Douglas premises this urge to apportion blame on the underlying structural function of cultural belief systems to create and maintain social order. These patterns involve the particular, and symbolic, processes by which 'being made safe', and 'securing a just society', come to dominate discourses about risk. For Douglas, 'all human societies construct elaborate cosmologies which attempt to make social relations meaningful and predictable against the background of inevitable uncertainty and anxiety' (Turner, 1994: 173).

Douglas saw risk as a social mechanism that enables cultures to determine principles of accountability.[2] Discourses about risk also serve to locate and identify the dominant and determining 'political stakes' inherent in a particular society. A mechanism is thus provided for individuals to assess their relation to these political markers. Thus fears of risk are ways in which 'social groups use beliefs about disease risks to place blame, reinforce power relations, define their cultural project, and control their boundaries' (Draper, 1993: 643). Risk becomes part of the social resolution of authority, how that authority is validated and the cultural processes of social support that surround it. The 'neutral vocabulary of risk is all we have for making a bridge between the known facts of existence and the construction of a moral community' (Douglas, 1990: 5).

These assumptions about culturally different and distinct attitudes towards authority led Douglas to conclude that since risk perception is essentially political, public debates about risk are inevitably debates about politics. What fundamentally distinguishes Beck's new paradigm of *risk society* from Douglas' theory of risk is that he denies the relevance of such cultural perspectives. Beck, initially, had no concept of risk as neutral.[3] He argues that risks become 'a political issue only when people are generally aware of them'. He did later define risks as 'social constructs which are strategically defined, covered up or dramatized in the public sphere with the help of scientific material supplied for the purpose' (1996a: 4). Nevertheless, despite a nod in the cultural direction he argues that previous generations did not have the kind of technological 'lurking demons' with which we must now contend. These 'lurking demons' of the past 'did not have the same political dynamic as the man-made hazards of ecological self-destruction' (1996a: 4).

Essentially, Beck is concerned to dramatically alter our understanding of risk. He is not content to rest in Douglas' assumption that risks are intrinsically part of the fulcrum of change in societies, where 'concepts of liability and tort are continuously at stake, always in process of revision' (1990: 4). His concept of risk involves a heightened sense of threat and danger: risk society is epochal and cannot be regarded as a typical process of cultural transition. Ewald (1991), discussing prudentialism, suggests that risks can be defined in two ways: those that arise out of 'probability, hazard, eventuality or randomness on the one hand, and those that occur as a result of loss or damage on the other'. The first set of descriptors of risk follows the classic Kantian assumption that 'risk is a category of the understanding; it cannot be given in sensibility or intuition' (1991: 199). It is the second aspect of risk that Beck generates into an apocalyptic risk society, where risk is not a 'category of under-standing' but is rather a social 'fact' from which there is no exit.

Ulrich Beck: the harbinger of a new threat?

For Beck, risk is a category of fear – the imminent rupture of what might be. His theoretical explication of risk society is one of those signal pieces of social analysis that have the capacity to alter the structure of our theoretical thinking about the world. The three essential aspects of his complex argument about risk society incorporate the contemporary debate about the 'individualization of politics' – his assumptions about reflexive modernization and his analysis of apocalyptic ecological threats arising out of unbridled technology (cf. Bronner, 1995).[4] Turner argues that:

> Beck's theory is primarily concerned with the impact of globalization and deregulation within the broader process of the modernization of society. In sociology it is clear that globalization as a theory of change has brought about an interest in the nature of risk, which in turn is connected with the process of postmodernization . . . Beck draws a distinction between the incomplete modernization project of industrial society and the radicalized modernity of the present world to which he gives the title 'reflexive modernity'. (1994: 168–9)

It is the first aspect of Beck's analysis, specifically focused on the indi-vidualization of politics, which most obviously relates to the relationship of risk within social policy. What is expressed in the full *oeuvre* of Beck's about risk is not always consistent. Nevertheless, the imaginative power of the original conception is incontrovertible. Beck's notion that the 'contours of the risk society' represent a 'new twilight of opportunities and hazards' (1992: 15) dovetails with Foucault's assumptions that modernity represented a series of 'exclusions and silencings'. Similarly for Beck, modernity was not an inevitable process of rational emancipation from the 'seductions' of prior immanent beliefs about the 'social'.

'Hierarchical poverty and democratic smog'

This subtitle is a reworking of one of Beck's most frequently quoted epithets – which captures the essence of his argument (1992: 36). Particularly relevant to this analysis of neo-liberal anti-welfare discourse is his conclusion that 'the risk society contains an inherent tendency to become a *scapegoat* society' (1992: 75). As he says:

> problems of the system are lessened politically and transformed into personal failure. In the detraditionalized modes of living, a *new immediacy* for *individual and society* arises, the immediacy of *crisis and sickness*, in the sense that social crises appear to be of individual origin, and are perceived as social only indirectly and to a very limited extent. (1992: 89)

We have seen earlier, particularly in Chapters 2 and 3, how neo-liberalism employed a 'semiology of catastrophe' as part of a rhetorical push to attack welfare dependency. This attack is not discrete: the pejorative nature of it serves a wider purpose. Disentangling 'security' from 'welfare' was necessary to sustain the overall rhetoric about risk, independence and the responsibilities of autonomous individuals (cf. Foucault, 1988a: 160–1). It was important to link security with independence in order to reinforce the push towards individualization and marketization. Economic efficiency, security and independence became synonymous. Those techniques of macroeconomic management that had previously associated security with dependence were disdained (cf. Hindess, 1997b). Similarly to Foucault, Beck assumes that the problems of such macroeconomic systems were lessened politically through complex discourses about risk as threat. They were transformed into personal failure. The new solidarity was framed around risk and anxiety and not rights and needs: hence the avoidance of bads, not the distribution of goods. As Beck argued, the arrival of a risk society means that 'the economy becomes *self-referential*, independent of its context of satisfying need' (1992: 56). The object was to undermine the former 'welfarist' presumption that the state ought to provide adequate services to meet obvious social need. Neo-liberalism did attempt to drain the 'swamp of need'!

Denying the social legitimacy of the welfare 'other' is an intrinsic aspect of neo-liberalism, so dependent on the rationality of modernity.

Beck used the phrases 'non-guidance' and 'non-liability' (1995a: 67) to refer to the absorption of technology within the dominant rationality of modernity. Technology, he argued, was so compromised that it had lost its critical acumen and comprehensively denied the importance of risk. Similarly, neo-liberalism is redrafting the rhetoric of welfare support on a basis of 'non-liability'. Beck suggests that the dominant motif of this era of risk society is our dependence on rationality. However, this rationality has not proven a reliable guide to understanding the magnitude of the change attributed to risk society. As he argues:

> One cannot impute a hierarchy of credibility and rationality, but must ask how, in the example of risk perception, 'rationality' *arises socially,* that is how it is believed, becomes dubious, is defined, redefined, acquired and frittered away. (1992: 59)

The utopia of the risk society: the solidarity of anxiety

Beck declares that the neo-liberal depiction of a welfare society, which depends upon a new *solidarity of anxiety,* has replaced the former *solidarity of need* typical of welfare states. The reasons for this are clear to Beck. His concern is to demonstrate that 'whereas poverty (the main problem of class society) is hierarchical, in that it is confined to a well-bounded subordinate class, risk is egalitarian' (Dryzek, 1995: 236). As Beck argues:

> The place of the value system of the 'unequal' society is taken by the value system of the 'unsafe' society. Whereas the utopia of equality contains a wealth of substantial and *positive* goals of social change, the utopia of the risk society remains peculiarly *negative* and *defensive.* Basically one is no longer concerned with attaining something 'good', but rather with *preventing* the worst; self-limitation is the goal that emerges. The dream of class society is that everyone wants and ought to have a *share* of the pie. The utopia of the risk society is that everyone should be *spared* from poisoning. (1992: 49)

How communication about risk became 'intricately entwined with the culture of the middle classes' will be discussed further in the next chapter (Eder, 1993: 182). The complex of middle class fears, and the changes in the economy which valorize risk and competition over co-operation, have made more explicit the neo-liberal alignment of the individual with the 'practices' of governance. Risk not only is part of the rituals of communication, which separate the successful from the 'others', but is intrinsic to governance! Various perceptions about the apparent insolubility of problems associated with global risk were refracted into the demand for welfare reform. Focusing this more specifically on the issues of risk and welfare, Beck argues that the concept of industrial society rests upon a *contradiction* between the *universal* principles of modernity – civil rights, equality, functional differentiation, methods of argumentation and skepticism – and the exclusive structure of its institutions, in which these principles can only be realized on a *partial*, *sectorial* and *selective* basis. The consequence of this is that industrial society *destabilizes itself through its very establishment*. (1992: 14)

This is the flaw at the heart of neo-liberalism in its pejorative analysis of welfare states and the projection of apocalyptic fears about welfare dependency. It is the very mechanisms of contractual monitoring of welfare, the patterns of its establishment, which create a potential for instability. Beck makes the further observation that:

> There is no place in the jungle of corporatist society for such global risks that span groups. Here every organization has its clientele and its social milieu, consisting of opponents and allies, who are to be activated and played off against one another. The commonality of dangers confronts the pluralistic structure of interest group organizations with almost insoluble problems. (1992: 48)

The vision of public choice theory that seeks to create and maintain a collectivity of autonomous agents who in 'moving out from their private needs and sufferings . . . create a public world where each can appear before the others in his or her specificity' (Young, 1996: 479) is laudable. However, such grand visions fail because, as Beck argues, 'the market fundamentalism they idolize is a form of democratic illiteracy' (1997a: 53). They do not understand the elusiveness of Derrida's (1994) epithet that 'an event worthy of . . . [democracy's] name cannot be foretold'. What always remain are those unexpected *experiences* that define the lived reality of individuals. The neo-liberal vision of individual emergence and growth may not be part of 'that which happens unexpectedly' for those who must survive as welfare beneficiaries. As Beck suggests, one reason for this inability to really see the legitimacy of the welfare claimant is that 'immediate need competes with the known element of risk' (1992: 44). The question is whether they can be 'seen' as the *subjects of risk* and not merely as part of the *objectification of welfare dependency*. Bauman has concluded that such objectifications are intrinsic to his analysis of post-modernity. As he says:

> The disarming, disempowering and suppressing of unfulfilled players is therefore an indispensable supplement of the integration-through-seduction in a market-led society of consumers. The impotent, indolent players are to be *kept outside the game*. They are the waste-product of the game. (1997: 41)

The possibility of a politics of recognition might, in the light of such pessimism, be deemed impossible. It is a 'game of seduction' that depends on a social matrix of *'pour encourager les autres'* defined as 'flawed welfare consumers'. Nevertheless, despite the force and reality of such structural criticisms, which validly tie neo-liberal politics about welfare together with the fundament of individual responsibility, a politics of recognition is still possible.

Beck's paradoxes of individual freedom in the risk society

Beck suggested that modernity was always 'half-finished'. What he meant by this is that the state of being 'half-finished' occurs because the 'either/or' of previous welfare state economic arrangements has been substituted with the 'and' of neo-liberalism. What this implies is that the 'and' of accumulation has no ethic, no weighing of costs and benefits against risks beyond that of maximizing possessive and purposive individualism. What this implies is the need to reconsider the legitimacy of the 'either/or' of policy deliberation. In a later book Beck clarifies his use of these terms and makes it clear that, from his perspective, the 'institutions of industrial society and their claims to exercise control and provide security are being refuted by the global risk society' (1997b: 2). The sense of 'either/or' when applied to the implementation of welfare policies does express some aspects of the 'control' of welfare, which Beck now depicts as out of control. However, the concept of welfare as judgement, as assessment, is still valid and can be counter-posed against a notion of welfare as out of control. It is this reawakening of the necessity to reapply the policy of 'either/or' which lies behind a re-vamped politics of obligation through new systems of recognition. It is the 'and' of current neo-liberal policy which removes the essence of ethical judgement, and denies the full weighing of alternatives beyond the purview of narrow individualism. Certainly this is an aspect of that singular perception which denies the legitimacy of the welfare 'other'.

In some senses both Beck's and Foucault's emancipatory power comes from their ability to 'disturb' considered reflection, not through patient and 'careful' scholarship, as 'servants' of an obvious tradition of historical explication (cf. Said, 1991). Their particular intellectual style raises the possibility that it might indeed be possible to consider Derrida's 'unforeseeable'. The notion that 'unexpectability conditions the very structure of an event' is at the core of Beck's analysis, and I agree with Bronner that 'Beck's notion of "organized irresponsibility" and the new implications of risk for decision-making can only prove seminal for any future form of emancipatory thinking' (1995: 85). The 'making up' of welfare peoples, through the disciplining technologies of neo-liberal governance, can be interposed with a counter-technology of rebellion. What Beck is counter-posing is the 'simultaneity of individualization and standardization'. He argues that these two aspects of risk society

> span the separated areas of the private sphere and the various aspects of the public sphere. They are no longer merely private situations, but also always institutional. They have the contradictory double face of institutionally dependent

individual situations. The apparent outside of the institutions becomes the inside of individual biography. (1992: 130)

The purposive individualism of the neo-liberal project, he concludes, which depended on 'specialization' and 'differentiation', has seen these props to their position collapse and disappear in the global hazards of risk society. 'Progress is [as Beck concluded] a blank cheque to be honoured *beyond* consent and legitimization' (1992: 203).

Giddens' 'hopefulness': against post-modern excesses

Giddens departs from Beck in his analysis of the sociology of risk on two counts. He is more hopeful of risk resolution (or reduction) and proffers a different history of risk. His discussion of risk is couched within a presumption, about basic life security, that 'the risk-reducing elements seem substantially to outweigh the new array of risks' (1991: 116). Elsewhere he expressed this as 'opportunity and danger are balanced in equal measure' (1994c: 58). Giddens' viewpoint has less room for any perspective that would define risk in the language of eschatology or extreme crisis. As he says, the 'world is not seen as a directionless swirl of events . . . but as having intrinsic form' (1991: 109). His analysis represents a more measured opinion of risk than that proposed in Beck's apocalyptic risk society (with its imputation of a radical rupture in modernity). Giddens argues, against this, that the 'intrusion of manufactured uncertainty into our lives does not mean that our existence on an individual or collective level, is more risky than it used to be' (1994a: 21).

Giddens prefers to describe risk as 'manufactured uncertainty'. By this he implies that the 'sources, and scope of risk, have altered. Manufactured risk is a result of human intervention into the conditions of social life and into nature' (1994b: 4). Giddens' view focuses our attention on the problems that have arisen from the forceful attempts within modernity to order the world rationally: those that do not now respond to the old remedies, and those that are not amenable to the application of more knowledge and control. They reflect more the questions of 'damage control and repair', as he says, rather than achieving a 'perfected mastery'. The political consequences then of manufactured risks are that

> liberal democracy, based on an electoral party system, operating at the level of the nation-state, is not well equipped to meet the demands of a reflexive citizenry in a globalizing world; and the combination of capitalism and liberal democracy provides only limited means of generating social solidarity. (1994b: 10)

Giddens acknowledges that risks are generated out of a rogue technology, but there are aspects of his analysis which hark back to a more cultural view of risk, similar to Douglas (see above).[5] Giddens casts his analysis within 'notions of fate and destiny'. He argues that fate 'typically involves a moral conception of destiny and an esoteric view of daily events – here "esoteric" means that events are experienced not just in terms of their casual relation to one another, but in terms of their cosmic meaning' (1991: 110). He reflects Douglas' assumption that risks are part of the fulcrum of change. Certainly in his earlier writings Giddens (1991) seems to be in agreement with Turner's critique of Beck that mainstream sociological theory is more suggestive of the *decline* of risk rather than its *increase* within capitalist development (1994: 173). Giddens argues that the heightened focus on risk 'in modern life has *nothing directly to do with the actual prevalence of life-threatening dangers*' (1991: 115, my italics). This does not accord with the substance of Beck's arguments. Giddens also argued (pre-Beck) that 'in terms of life expectation and degree of freedom from serious disease, people in the developed societies are in a much more secure position than most were in previous ages' (1991: 115). Certainly in his concept of 'manufactured uncertainty', his presentation of risk within modernity shifts markedly towards aspects of Beck's radical rupture (hence his notion of high modernity) – but not entirely.

Giddens is preoccupied with the 'sites' and tangibility of risk – those that are mundane, those that are more serious and those that are of 'high consequence'. Giddens also discusses the sociological implication of risk seeking and its relation to expressions of self-identity within modernity. This is an aspect of risk that Beck ignores. Giddens' theory of 'disembedding processes' provides a valuable tool to understand the development of the self. While this is only tangentially relevant to my concern about social policy and risk, his ideas about how 'abstract systems' intrude into personal identity echo (unintentionally) something of Foucault's analysis of power/knowledge. Giddens sees the penetration of these 'abstract systems' as more intrusive because they are presented as 'expert systems': perhaps they do reflect aspects of an expert's 'gaze'? These disembedding processes are 'processes of loss' and 'the advent of abstract systems sets up modes of social influence which no one directly controls' (1991: 138).

Modernity, he suggests, eviscerates the previous socialist view of the state. Any notion of a 'directive intelligence' is denied. Giddens argues that modernity, as a complex political and economic system, requires the 'supply' of a vast amount of 'low-level input data' – none of it explicitly, individually, directive. His use of cybernetic concepts is instructive: a multiplicity of 'low-level inputs' is necessary to produce 'effective neural integration' (1994a: 25–6).[6] The diffused 'intelligence' that modernity requires to operate the complexity of an information society also implies an analysis of risk that offers some explanation for how neo-liberalism 'diffuses' risks and their resolution – away from the state and towards the multiplicity of individual 'intelligences'. Social policy, which harks back to the relative homogeneity of the welfare state, can offer little normative easement in Giddens' vastly heterodoxical world. As I have commented earlier, any left-wing analysis of risk which appeared socially radical in the inception of the welfare state has been linguistic-ally routed. It is the left that is now conservative. The right, 'stimulated by the incessant expansion [and play] of markets', has assumed the radical mantle (1994a: 26). This notion that old radicals are the new conservatives, while the old conservatives now embrace a radical politics, has assumed the status of sociological canard.

Giddens does not see this political reversal as value-free. Such conflicts have not been transmuted into the 'bits' and 'bytes' of a cybernetic model of social change and risk. It has been neo-liberalism's strength to claim 'radicalism' as its own epithet! This is yet one more example of the extraordinary 'make-over' of political discourse which neo-liberalism has achieved. Nevertheless, Giddens argues that neo-liberalism is caught in a contradiction of its own making:

> Having no proper theoretical rationale . . . [neo-liberalism's] defence of tradition . . . normally takes the form of fundamentalism. The debate over 'family values' provides a good example. Liberal individualism is supposed to reign in the marketplace – and the purview of markets becomes greatly extended. The wholesale expansion of a market society, however, is a prime force promoting those very disintegrative forces affecting family life which neo-liberalism, wearing its fundamentalist hat, diagnoses and so vigorously opposes. This is an unstable mix indeed. (1994a: 26)

True, but such 'unstable mixes' have had enormous power to compel in the past. Seeking to weaken the driving force of neo-liberalism by assuming that it has 'no proper theoretical rationale' may have a conceptual 'edge' but has no practical 'bite'. Assuming that contradiction exists in the heart of an effective ideology is often only to state the obvious.[7]

Politics is a strategic 'conversation' about power. Despite the ideals of the Enlightenment, liberal reason needs a compulsion other than logic to alter its presuppositions. Privileging the usage of risk as a way to challenge these neo-liberal contradictions does not assume that such ideological contradictions will necessarily 'go away'. In fact Giddens' own analysis attempts to show how disparate elements of the 'contra-dictory' are held together systemically. Giddens' analysis of risk is 'measured' through his basic analytic which developed the idea of the individual as a 'creative rule-follower in possession of tacit knowledge' (Pleasants, 1997: 37). Giddens (1994b) does not confront his 'own tacit knowing' which supports his arguments for the 'impossibility of social-ism'. Pleasants' important critique of Giddens is that he misapplies Wittgenstein and looks for explanations instead of seeing 'facts' as

'primary phenomena' (1997: 35). Seeking to 'understand' these contradictions of ideology is, of course, what theorists like Foucault have set as
their pre-eminent task. Will exposing the contradiction of contradictions
lead us any further? The presence of the illogical in political ideologies
does not allow us to be too sanguine, but we are compelled to try!

Giddens' analysis of risk and how individuals 'seek to colonize the
future' gives practical expression to how public choice theories operate.
He is clearly right to argue that 'risk assessment proceeds on the level of
practical consciousness and . . . the protective cocoon of basic trust blocks
off most otherwise potentially disturbing happenings which impinge on
the individual's life circumstances' (1991: 126). Giddens' is a descriptive
sociological exposition but it doesn't penetrate below the level of the
commonly observed. What Giddens argues is that 'abstract systems
of modernity create large areas of relative security for the continuance of
day-to-day life' (1991: 133). The notion of security, havens, the defence of
private space, 'landscape' and 'nature' as symbol systems merit much
greater analysis than I have time for here (cf. Baudrillard, 1993). Certainly
Giddens' work is suggestive of how such investigations might proceed,
although an uncritical acceptance of tacit patterning and rule following
falls foul of Wittgenstein's attack on the 'myth of symbolism' (Pleasants,
1997: 36).

Foucault: Giddens' 'parrot'

Giddens' consideration of Foucault is cursory and somewhat dismissive
(1991: 57; 1995: 262ff).[8] Lash and Urry (1994) make the assumption that
this hostility occurs because he regards Foucault's ideas as 'a threat to
ontological security'.[9] It is certainly true that they differed markedly
about the human subject. Gordon suggests 'that Foucault's representation of society as a network of omnipresent relations of subjugating
power seemed to preclude the possibility of meaningful individual
freedom' (1991: 1). The implicit assumption of ontology, that the human
subject was to be the 'fount of meaning' and social relationships are one
consequence of that prior subjective knowing, was anathema to Foucault.
He insisted on 'the efficacy and logical priority of social relations in the
analysis of knowledge and social practice' (Cousins and Hussain, 1984:
252). Modernity, for Foucault, is an 'attitude' not a valid 'period of
history': it is a 'vertigo in the face of the passing moment' (1984a: 39).
Foucault offers the ascetic visions of the stoic observer: an obvious
grotesquerie for Giddens!

Clearly such ideas are an affront to Giddens, who presents a theory of
'structuration' which maintains that humans 'are always and everywhere
regarded as knowledgeable agents, although acting within historically
specific bounds of the unacknowledged conditions and unintended
consequences of their acts' (1995: 265). He presents a view of tacit

knowledge which is inherently static and ignores Wittgenstein's assumption that the 'important thing about knowledge . . . is that it is always potentially open to challenge' (Pleasants, 1997: 32). The obvious consequences of such ontological reasoning dovetails well with the neo-liberalism that Giddens is at pains to criticize! Deconstructing these categories of explanation is vital if we are to recognize the manifold ways in which risk has structured neo-liberal politics. It is a mistake not to see that risk is fundamental to neo-liberal discourse and it cannot simply be aligned with risk society and reflexive modernization. Foucault's privileging of 'social relations in an analysis of knowledge' is useful in allowing us to stand back from the dominance of neo-liberal thought. Giddens' theorizing of risk does not make this possible. Giddens appears to see the self as heroic and ultimately triumphing in the battle 'against ontological security' so apparently typical of the 'high modern self' (Lash and Urry, 1994: 42). It is a 'warrior' narrative in which the 'fight' is against real, rather than imagined hurts. Imaginatively, Giddens battles against 'principalities and powers' while Foucault undermines the legitimacy of the 'battle'!

More pointedly, Giddens' elementary discussion of Foucault's thesis about the 'body' 'will not do', to use his words of dismissal in rejecting Foucault's theory of the 'carceral society'. Giddens makes this extraordinary statement in rejecting Foucault's disciplinary theory:

> Foucault is wrong to trace [a similarity between prisons and asylums] to discipline as such . . . What they share in common with the broader frameworks of modernity is the attempt to develop reflexive self-control even among minorities who might seem intrinsically recalcitrant . . . incarceration serves at least to protect those in the outside world from unalterable irregularities in the behaviour of the minority. (1991: 160)

This is instructively revealing of a range of prejudices about Foucault's intellectual 'grotesqueries', involving his ideas about freedom, discipline and governmentality. Giddens wants to restrict the notion of 'discipline' to that which occurs *within* prisons and asylums, not to that which *created* them. This is a perfectly rational and reasonable assumption but it is one driven by an excessive reliance on 'things-as-they-are'. The argumentation is self-referring and cannot be extended beyond itself. It compartmentalizes and reifies social analysis within the 'units of observation' themselves.

This is *precisely* what Foucault was trying *not to do*! Foucault sought to challenge the certainties that came from 'within' and to explode internally logical arguments. His, too, is a reasonable question: is the irregular 'behaviour of the minority' intrinsically the result of their recalcitrance? The governance thesis (the 'Foucault effect' in social policy) confounds 'the logic of sociological concepts which oppose state to civil society [the classic Marxist project], the public to the private, the coercive to the consensual and so on' (Garland, 1997: 183). Giddens fails to appreciate this new debate about power. He wishes to discuss deviance as an aspect of 'internally referential systems of [control within] modernity' (1991: 160). It is not hard, given a nodding acquaintance with Foucault, to see why Giddens should have been so cavalierly dismissive. Yes, prisons and asylums do serve to protect, but that we are so quick to 'lock away' deviance is something which Giddens cannot address within the nature of his analysis. He shows no awareness of the significance of Hewitt's (1983) classic exposition of Foucault's bio-power and its relevance to social policy. Giddens' abrupt dismissal of Foucault's justifiably famous treatise *Madness and Civilization* is cavalier to say the least (cf. Giddens, 1991: 156). Giddens' argumentation about internally referential systems betrays no relationship to his previous usage of cybernetic concepts where social integration within modernity needed *dispersed* reflexive processes and a 'greater autonomy of action'.

His analysis is not a 'genealogy' of risk (not that he sets out to present one) in the Foucauldian sense. Foucault was interested in analysing not the state *per se* but the *practices* of governing the state. Giddens' aim is to present an analysis of the tangible onset of risk factors, their amelioration or their endurability and persistence. He is more interested to detail aspects of risk profiling, to develop the sociological explication of stock market risk, to set out complex aspects of health risk analysis, and to locate the functions of 'institutionally structured risk environments'. Criticizing him because he does not apply the argumentation of another social theorist (whom he apparently disdains) is not 'reasonable', but that he fails to see risk in governance terms restricts the usefulness of his analysis. In some senses it restricts it to the notions of practicality and the presumed tangible – all the hallmarks of neo-liberal rhetoric. While this is valuable, I have argued that an archaeology and a genealogy of risk is necessary within social policy to make a theoretical and rhetorical challenge to the neo-liberal stranglehold on the 'realities' of common-sense.

Reflexiveness and risk: do we construct our own biographies?

Critics seeking to illuminate just what it is that Beck intends in his thesis of 'reflexive modernization' often pose this question of 'autobiography'. Framed another way, the question is what empirical evidence Beck adduces for his thesis that 'for modernization to advance successfully, people must actively free themselves from the social control mechanisms that frame modern society' (cf. Draper, 1993: 642). The general conclusion of these criticisms is that Beck's assertions are basically exhortatory, betraying a phenomenological intent rather than an empirical possibility (cf. Braun, 1996: 756; Goldblatt, 1996: 187).

Such empirical/critical approaches to Beck's work have their own internal sets of validation but they, similarly, rarely have the power to alter dominant political epistemologies. As I outlined in the first chapter, the empirical tradition in social policy has produced many valid objective data, but that in itself has not been able to hold much sway against the dominance of a neo-liberal politic. As Beck has imaginatively argued, ethics by itself is rarely helpful: 'it comes along too late, trailing behind, its point of view that of an alien world. It has no more effect than a bicycle brake on an intercontinental aircraft' (1995b: 504). If we do dare to confront such intellectual hegemonies then perhaps the presumed 'phenomenology' of Beck has some leverage. To dismiss Beck too easily, to condemn him as sociologically outlandish, is to abandon a set of ideas that may have quite profound emancipatory power.

The alteration in risk consciousness, from the individual fear of happenstance to the consciousness born out of a forensic fear of threat, that there should be an accounting for such fears, does have a profound effect on our view of the world. It reinforces Foucault's theorizing about governmentality, and the manifold ways in which we are required to author our private responses in the face of universal threat. The paradox inheres in the fact that the very exhortation to be self-reliant inflates the possibility of risk and a distorted sense of individual identity. Globalized potential threat undermines a trust in the authenticity of the present. For example, Beck has said that:

> The center of risk consciousness lies not in the present, but *in the future*. In the risk society, the past loses the power to determine the present. Its place is taken by the future, thus, something non-existent, invented, fictive as the 'cause' of current experience and action. (1992: 34)

It is the inauthenticity of the fictive, the future 'might-be', that is significant in relating these concepts of risk society and reflexive modernization to the concerns of social policy. Beck's point is that perception of an 'eschatological eco-fatalism allows the pendulum of private and political moods to swing in *any* direction. The *risk society* shifts from hysteria to indifference and vice versa' (1992: 37). We must take seriously Beck's vital assumption that 'it is precisely individualized private existence which becomes more and more obviously and emphatically dependent on situations and conditions that completely escape its reach' (1992: 131). Simply to consign such extraordinary and potentially liberating thinking to an 'empirical wastebasket' is to miss the point.

Some final questions of risk society

Can we reassociate Beck's strictures against the evils of technocracy, which is not as perfect and assured as it presumes, with the neo-liberal anti-welfare project? What are the points of stress in the implacable façade of an anti-welfare rhetoric? Is it, as Beck argues of technocracy, that in respect of welfare risk neo-liberalism is 'only a loosely concealed collection of contradictions, which ossifies in its claim to perfection' (1995a: 172)? Neo-liberalism represents a political expression about the need to maintain an individual responsibility for certain risks. Challenging that may well involve arguing that such an apparent political symbiosis of political 'truth' is 'rife with contradictions of safety'.

Social policy faces a significant problem in that it needs to find a new theoretical exposition of risk and its relationship to welfare. We might well start by articulating what Beck termed a 'dramaturgy of safety' and how that might be used to challenge neo-liberalism. Fears about the organized power of a dispossessed underclass are relatively weak. How the earlier apocalyptic fears of the potential for revolutionary change, arising from that underclass, have been overcome may reveal why the present ethos of market liberalization has such power. As I have been arguing, one of the levers of such control has depended on the various rhetorics of risk. How it has been able to silence critics of its policy is significant. How the normative concerns of social policy have been 'washed away on a diet of bread and water' (Beck, 1995a: 177) may allow us to refashion the debate. Neo-liberalism must be attacked from *within* its presumptions – which are varied reifications and valorizations of risk. All forms of 'external' attack have been easily dismissed. However, the reifications can be opposed on the ground that risk is a universal reality and cannot simply be used to construe one aspect of a political debate.

The turbulence of reflexive modernization: an aspect of the welfare debate?

For Beck, the crises of capitalism could no longer be encapsulated in the class struggle, which marked a change in modernity. On the contrary, he argued, they develop out of their entrenched successes (cf. Beck et al., 1994: 2). It was modernity constantly being modified *within* modernity that typified current society. Within his concept of risk society, exemplifying this process of constant reflexiveness, the notion of *post*-modernism had little meaning. He wished to prove that there was no 'tacit equation of latency and immanence in social change', the constant focus of much sociological theory. He argued against the preoccupations of mainstream sociologists, that 'reflexive modernization of industrial society occurs on cats' paws, as it were, unnoticed by sociologists' (1994: 3). For Beck there could be no latent change process because of his assertion that we are beset by 'factional struggles on all levels'.

Beck establishes a new epistemology of change – one that circumvents analyses of social change predicated on crises, social transformations or the fading possibility of revolution. While he sees these conventional analyses of social change intersecting with his new critique of risk society, his view of the ubiquity and anonymity of risk is that it 'escapes' from the best efforts of modernity to calculate risk. Metaphorically, it is like the hydra-headed 'monster' that lurks and overwhelms even when we seek to defend against its power. There is a hidden quality, an aspect of uncontrollability to reflexive modernization. Echoes again of Foucault!

While Beck's paradigm is particularly influenced by ecological theory it is not too fanciful to apply this to the debates about social policy and welfare provision. The 'attack' on the validity and social legitimacy of welfare may yet release consequences that are similarly hidden and uncontrollable, and that will seriously damage our ability to construct a workable society. If reflexive modernization 'means self-confrontation with the effects of *risk society*' then perhaps *welfare reflexiveness* can mean a self-confrontation with the profound damage we continue to do each other. That would expose the rhetoric of bitter normality, which relies on winnowing out and condemning those who require welfare assistance to survive. In the same fashion that Beck argues overwhelming risks elude our perception and 'exceed our imaginative abilities', so do the hazards of our current pejorative preoccupation with welfare dependency. Neo-liberalism has established a baseline argument about welfare cheats, bludgers and dependants. Its proponents must equally be challenged to confront the inherent biases and 'limits of their own model to precisely the degree they do not change, do not reflect on their effects and continue a policy of more of the same' (Beck et al., 1994: 6–7).

We can see how conveniently *within* the frame of neo-liberal rhetoric falls the attempt to make welfare personal and individual. To see welfare issues as global, in the sense of a structural element that confronts this individualized discourse, is almost impossible. This rhetoric does not allow for challenge, nor does it wish to place its cherished assumptions 'at risk'! It is possible, therefore, to 'imagine' group-specific allegiances in respect of radical individualism, but clearly not when the group-specific experience is the need of welfare assistance. The 'worm' in the comfort of neo-liberalism is that not only has the 'unequivocal self . . . become fragmented into contradictory discourses of the self' but individuals 'are now expected to master these "risky opportunities" privately' (1994: 8).

The 'worm' is revealed in that there is no analysis of the consequences of such possessive individualism beyond an internal reference to personal security and satisfaction. The dichotomy 'safe/unsafe', which drives this rhetoric, expresses that empty reliance on rationality that Beck funda-mentally challenged. It is its own self-referent, and stands in no relation-ship to anything other than itself. This is the callous fallacy of 'unaware technology' which Beck so persuasively details. As Hacking argued considerably earlier, 'in a world of accelerating new technologies that interact in unforeseen ways, we require endlessly proliferating border sects which can force new dangers into our consciousness before we are destroyed' (1982b: 41). It is also the obdurate and unimaginative self-absorption of a bankrupt human politics that denies the 'otherness' of anyone not perceived to be independently self-responsible. It is the last 'gasp' of a linear social policy that must become reflexive if we are to accept and understand social ambivalence that has the potential to alter the basis of our social analysis and action. To accomplish this requires, as Beck et al. argue, that we consider how the

> crisis of industrial society's security fictions implies that opportunities and compulsions for action open up, between which one must permanently decide, without any claim to definitive solutions – a requirement through which living and acting in uncertainty becomes a kind of basic experience. (1994: 12)

Beck makes a distinction between risks defined as 'issues of order' and risks as expressive of a 'form' within which a 'dynamism *ad absurdum*' operates. Risk society is therefore not just reflective of the sequencing of problems in modernity but must be understood as the form of a social dynamism driven by a false trust in rationality. This distinction is useful in my analysis of risk and social policy. Observably, neo-liberalism considers the questions of welfare dependency within an interpretation of risk that is about order and sequence. My purpose here is to remind us that the manifold epistemologies of welfare risks reflect issues other than the 'form' of risk, and that the 'dynamism *ad absurdum*' of these assumptions has its own internal and uncontrollable danger. Focusing solely on order and sequence restricts the debate to one of control: how to make the disordered nature of welfare policies 'tidy' and amenable. As Beck et al. argue so well:

> in risk society the unforeseeable side and after-effects of this demand for control, in turn, lead to what has been considered overcome, the realm of the uncertain, of ambivalence, in short, of alienation. (1994: 10)

Significantly, considering the risks of welfare as solely 'issues of order' invalidates their organizational forms and patterns. If we follow Beck's argumentation about risk society and reflexive modernization, we call into question not only the patterns of how welfare systems operate, but also the whole structure of ethics, legal principles and categories that are fundamental to neo-liberalism. Pre-eminent assumptions such as self-responsibility and 'user pays' are 'not suited to comprehend or legitimate this return of uncertainty and uncontrollability'. Current anti-welfare rhetoric espouses an unambiguous sense of modernity, hence its trust in solving 'issues of order'. Understanding what Beck is alluding to, in his depiction of a risk society, requires us to see that unambiguous policy-making must find ways to tolerate and articulate an 'ambivalent modernity'. Beck is not playing with words here. Beck et al. observe the growth in the 'political vacuity of institutions' while there is a corresponding evolution of the 'non-institutional renaissance of the political' (1994: 17). That requires the emergence of all the non-institutional forms of politics that can respect difference, acknowledge the need for recognition and tolerate ambivalence. The issues of welfare are not just those of establishing order. What the welfare debate must encompass is a critical self-reflectiveness that allows the biases and 'mentalities of rule' to be examined. Attempting to argue anew for a gentle politics of recognition and respect may seem ludicrously inept within a rhetorical frame that sees only the harsh and crude 'disorder' of welfare, and the consequent need to control it. However, if we can sustain an argument that anti-welfare rhetoric is a potentially destructive reflexive 'form' – that it contains the hidden seeds of its own destruction, as Beck argues – a new welfare politic can be fashioned.[10]

The arrival of subpolitics: Beck's sociological crystal ball?

In his discussion of globalization Beck distinguishes between the potential of new international treaties and coalitions, formed in response to global risk (what he terms 'globalization *from above*'), and new risk coalitions which occur outside the usual systems of parliamentary democracy ('globalization *from below*'). The substance of his paradigm of risk society depends upon the validity of his assertion that industrial modernity is typified by the dominance of a 'purposive-rational system of politics'. That reflects the hegemony of neo-liberal commitment to marketization and radical individualism. Beck is at pains to argue that the 'process of sub-politicization should not be considered as irrational, because it has all the marks of republican modernity in contrast to the representative, national-parliamentary democracy of parties' (1996a: 21).

His concern is to prove that such rationality, typical of modernity, which seeks the 'obviousness' of social control, has, in its co-opting of technology, undeniably created the global inexorableness of risks out of control. This is what he means by the unintentional way that hegemonic policy, caught up in the flow-back of global risks, is inescapably challenged by these 'side effects' so that society is forced to look for trustworthy options and possibilities that lie outside the usual gamut of politics. It is this process that informs his concept of reflexive modernization where self-transformation will not occur unless we look away from mainstream politics, which evince a 'loss of legitimacy and a vacuum of power'. When the system is found wanting, then disobeying and the 'refusal' becomes the expressive norm of subpolitics.[11]

> The concept of 'subpolitics' refers to politics outside and beyond the representative institutions of the political system of nation-states. It focuses attention on signs of an (ultimately global) self-organization of politics, which tends to set all areas of society in motion. Subpolitics means *'direct'* politics – which is *ad hoc* individual participation in political decisions, bypassing the institutions of representative opinion-formation (political parties, parliaments) and often even lacking the protection of the law. In other words subpolitics means

the shaping of society from below. Economy, science, career, everyday existence, private life, all become caught up in the storms of political debate.
(1996a: 18)

Beck, interestingly, argues that the site of political resistance has
changed. Previously, the site of resistance was the 'street'. However, the
new political site of a globalized 'risk society is not the street but
television'. Globalization has forever changed the locale of resistance
such that the previous cultural symbols of rebellion (the old pictures of
street 'refusal' – protest marches) have no compelling power. Effective
alliances with union resistance and the 'working class' have been
replaced with the complex of cultural *symbols 'staged in the mass media,*
where the accumulated bad conscience of the actors and consumers of
industrial society can be off-loaded' (1996a: 22). He argues that these new
cultural symbols, controlled by the media, are so dominant because they
have become the only sites for resistance, the only means to search for
the substantial in a 'forest of symbols'. The screen (not the street) dictates
'symbolic politics' and, as Beck suggests, this is made especially true by
'the abstractness and omnipresence of destruction that keep the world
risk society going'. As he continues:

> Tangible, simplifying symbols, in which cultural nerve fibres are touched and
> alarmed, here acquire a key political significance. These symbols must be
> produced or concocted, in the open fire of conflict provocation, before the
> strained-terrified television eyes of the public. The decisive question is: who
> discovers (or invents), and how, symbols that disclose or demonstrate the
> structural character of the problems, as well as creating the capacity for action?
> (1996a: 22)

What is to be done?

Beck's challenge to technology leads him to propose the creation of new
political or, more appropriately to his overall thesis, trans-political
organizations. As he argues, it 'is the reification that cries out to be
overcome. This is the admittedly tiny chance for global subpolitics in the
world *risk society* . . . Our fate is that we have to invent the political anew'
(1996a: 24). One of his imaginative ideas was to propose an 'Upper
House of Technology' that would attempt to release the regenerative
autonomy of technology, so that the counter-'art' of a 'reflexive and self-
skeptical technology' could, similarly, be released. Such a body would
have quasi-parliamentary and quasi-judicial powers. Searching for how
the complicity of technology might be overturned, Beck acknowledges
that no one involved knows how this might be done. He alludes to
Arendt's famous dictum that technological policy exemplifies the principle of 'nobody's rule'. Having posed the difficulty he then 'leaps' to a
possible solution:

> If we liberate technology from the yoke of economic necessity, we will also
> have to reorganize its application. We must establish an autonomous process
> in which ethicists, politicians, the public, lay-people, and, in this chorus, of
> course, technological experts play their parts. (1995b: 506)

Another of his concepts revives the notion of public or 'social' work.
This, he argues, requires 'active compassion', 'practical critique' and
'active democracy' (1997a: 54). By active compassion he means some
form of 'public work' – 'an odd blend of politics, care for others, and
everyday co-operation'. By practical critique he means the deliberative
decision of a range of professionals to use their specific skills in some
socially useful way and to be rewarded by some form of public recognition. Finally, by active democracy he means citizen participation – the
possibility of citizens' juries.[12] He argues that it is important to 'reveal'
the practices of social self-help and grassroots political organizations
that operate unseen. He wanted to give 'economic, organizational and
political weight' to those 'lay knowledges' which Wynne (1996) described
so well. Beck's final plea was to develop a 'citizen–state alliance for civil
society, if need be, in opposition to work and capital' (1997a: 56). The
fundamental difficulty in this reasoning is that it presupposes a recentral-
ization of power 'when the needs of a *risk society* require the greatest
devolution of power and resources to the sites of risk creation and
exposure to threats' (Goldblatt, 1996: 171). We can bring this survey of
Beck's ideas to an end with the gentle pessimism of Rustin that:

> The forms of mobilization that Beck proposes are undoubtedly good things,
> but whether they are a match for the capitalist penetration of the world is
> another matter entirely. If the nation-state has become too weak to contain
> globalised capital, it may be that we need co-operation between states or
> supranational states, and that nothing else will do. (1994: 400)

In the next chapter other criticisms of Beck's thesis will be described in
order, among other things, to see whether the pessimism of Rustin is
indeed justified. Nonetheless, Beck's originality has established examination of risk at the centre of contemporary sociological debate. His great
achievement is that he has made understanding the concept of risk
fundamental to an assessment of modernity. And, for my purposes,
he has provided valuable ways to lever the neo-liberal hegemony of
common-sense.

Notes

1 The phrase 'avoidance of bads' in the chapter title is evocative: Beck's risk
society effectively sought an avoidance of 'bads' rather than a distribution of
'goods'. See also Goldblatt (1996: 176).
2 Douglas' view of risk as neutral is significant in establishing a cultural
framework of universal ethics. She sees that sin and taboo (the powerful social

control sanctions of former cultures) can have no place in modernity. It is to the 'neutral' discussion of risk that she would turn to seek for a way 'to build a homogeneous culture using a uniform vocabulary for moralizing and politicizing the dangers around'. Her hope is that the 'neutral vocabulary of risk is all we have for making a bridge between the known facts of existence and the construction of a moral community' (1990: 5).

3 There are some interesting conjunctions between Douglas (1992) and Donzelot (1979). Douglas' concepts about purity and danger dovetail well with Donzelot's depiction of how the development of the social control function of medicine was allied with the 'hygiene' movement. Beck's sense of the rupture of risk precludes such cultural associations.

4 See Goldblatt (1996) for an excellent survey of Beck's risk society thesis. It is one that Beck, himself, acknowledges as 'stimulating' (1998: 22).

5 Braun (1996: 756) also depicts Giddens' consideration of risk as a topic of cultural change.

6 It is an age-old descriptive habit to extrapolate from the body to explain social complexity. Nevertheless, Giddens' cybernetic metaphors are useful, not the least in pointing to the power of the Internet!

7 Foucault respected neo-liberalism as a powerful and 'novel set of notions about the art of government' which posed, he assumed, a vibrant challenge to the left since 'socialism itself does not possess and has never possessed its own distinctive art of governing' (Gordon, 1991: 6).

8 The play on words in the section heading refers, of course, to Julian Barnes' novel *Flaubert's Parrot* where Barnes writes that 'parrots and Holy Ghosts can speak, whereas doves cannot . . . the parrot is a perfect and controlled example of the Flaubertian [Foucauldian?] grotesque'.

9 This may not be an unreasonable assumption given Foucault's statement that the 'purpose of history, guided by genealogy, is not to discover the roots of our identity, but to commit itself to its dissipation' (1984c: 95)!

10 Axel Honneth's excursus into a potential new theory of social recognition will be discussed in Chapter 8.

11 Foucault's usage of 'refusal' in his depiction of bio-politics as 'counter-politics' is interesting. Foucault did not deny the legitimacy of 'dissenting counter-conduct' as a means to seek for a strategic 'reversibility' of power relations (cf. Gordon, 1991).

12 See Coote (1998).

7

THE RADICAL RUPTURE OF
RISK SOCIETY: A CRITICAL REVIEW

The overwhelming feature of the age is not physical – the threat of annihilation – but social: the fundamental and scandalous way in which the institutions, almost without exception, fail it.

(Beck, 1995a: 69)

Statistical information leads to the discovery of statistical laws. We who collect the information change the boundary conditions and thereby change the laws of society. Such control of a human population seems to diminish its freedom.

(Hacking, 1990: 115)

Naturally enough, Beck has faced substantial criticism of his risk society thesis – the fate awaiting any iconoclast or 'unwelcome prophet'! Can he be typecast as a modern-day anti-technological 'Luddite', who runs the risk of being demonized because he is the conveyor of 'unpleasant truths'? Perhaps he revealed his real intent when he posed the 'question of questions . . . how can one entice, from the force of compulsive progress, the contrary power of liberation' (1995a: 169)? Is he not rather better located within that proud and rebellious tradition of the 'grand refusal'? Given the florid prose about the ineluctable power of risk society, he can appear to be an apocalyptic visionary of the 'fictive' possibility of total social and technological collapse. However, Beck argues that modern, so-called Luddites are 'not enemies of technology . . . but specialists who know their way around and have courage' (1995a: 112).[1]

Whatever our critical view of Beck's *oeuvre*, his thesis is important. It has altered our worldview: no subsequent analysis of risk can ignore the enormous contribution that he has made. My overall criticism is that his thesis is somewhat limited because it is so focused on the *consequences* of modernity, the *toxins* of industrialization, and the *arguments* for risk society that it doesn't fully deal with *the origins of risk discourse*. The overwhelming nature of risk in society does exist; there is no escaping that. However, *some of the discourses about risk are socially constructed narratives*. Neo-liberalism constructed the discourses about welfare risk for its own hegemonic purposes (cf. Bauman, 1997). Their 'collapse' cannot simply be aligned with the consequences of risk society. In that sense neo-liberalism has *used* the anxiety about risk society for its own political ends. But its use of risk *per se* is antecedent. Analysis of its use within neo-liberal discourse must go back further – into the analyses of Foucault about governmentality, the 'birth of the clinic' and the surveillance aspects of the professional 'gaze'. This wider or contextual reading of discourse is not fully developed in Beck. He sees the potential *end* rather better than the *beginning*!

Typically, criticism runs the gamut from the argument that he presents an inadequate analysis of the past (thus failing to acknowledge his indebtedness to classical sociology) to the argument that risk society is really only a 'selective projection of present trends into the future'. Dryzek contends that this theory of risk only amounts to 'an appreciation of how these trends might combine to produce altogether novel states of affairs' (1995: 237). Lidskog, similarly, thinks that Beck seems unaware of the ambiguity he creates in identifying an 'oscillation between a definition of risk as a purely social construct and as an objective entity which *de facto* affects humankind and nature' (1993: 403). Another strand of critical opinion holds that Beck displays no awareness that risks may be willingly chosen for personal reasons. He does not seem to factor into his analysis any understanding of 'economic change that is premised on the necessity of risk-taking and innovation' (Goldblatt, 1996: 175). On a different tack, Dryzek thinks that Beck doesn't really acknowledge the massive constraints on environmental policy-making and viable political discourse resulting from globalization. He argues that Beck does not deal with how 'these constraints might be confronted', and whether the less developed nations 'have any path to an ecological modernity that does not repeat the same issues'. Without discovering such paths Dryzek assumes that 'the global ecological outlook is bleak' (1995: 241).

Metaphors of risk society and governmentality: Turner's counter-critique

Within the current sociological literature Bryan Turner has articulated the clearest set of objections to Beck's risk society paradigm, associated with a comparative analysis of Foucault's governmentality thesis (1994; 1995; especially, 1997: ix). Turner interprets risk, within Beck's paradigm, to mean risks 'are no longer observable, local and personal. They are unobservable, global and impersonal' (1995: 177). The general substance of Turner's critique, briefly described in the previous chapter, is that in mainstream sociological theory risk '*declines* rather than *increases* with the development of capitalism' (1994: 173, my italics). Previous political commitments to social security facilitated the development of social service organizations (and a welfare bureaucracy) that were 'a cushion against the uncertainties and insecurities of the market-place' (1994: 168). Social institutions were hedges against risk and social welfare was specifically designed to preclude risk. Representing the welfare state as ameliorating the social risks of capitalism was associated with the complementary theory that 'human beings, either individually or collectively, cannot tolerate a high level of uncertainty and unpredictability in social relations' (1994: 168). These observations led Turner to his first major criticism, that Beck 'failed to take into account earlier analyses of risk and uncertainty', thus allowing him to present his ideas as if they were a incisive new social critique which marks a major rupture from the traditions of sociological analysis.[2]

Turner's focus is on the elaboration of theory and so he is predisposed to criticize any new theory that does not reveal a developmental coherence with the traditions of previous intellectual struggles. He says of both Beck and Giddens that they deny 'their dependence on more conventional sociological paradigms'. Perhaps the lure of 'grand explanations' still holds! Presenting these 'new conditions in risk society' within 'a context of high modernity' inevitably meant asserting 'the irrelevance of much classical sociology' (1995: 224). To digress slightly, Beck responds to the general criticism of his original paradigm in a trenchantly flamboyant way. While Turner poses a valid sociological critique, this doesn't concern Beck who sought no appeal to classical sociology (1995a: 82–4). On the contrary, he portrayed himself as a quasi-sociological 'prophet', not wanting to be seen as one of the articulate sociological 'priests' of the classical tradition. His rejection was almost brutal. He asked how it could ever be 'possible to champion and vindicate historical appearance, of all things the most ridiculous and ragged of excuses, against a hydra-headed social science armed to the teeth with expensive theories and figures?' More explicitly, he argues that sociology 'with its excessive partiality to institutional objectivity has condemned action. The tradition of intervention and resistance has wasted away, and is decaying into conceptual ruins such as "class struggle", "revolutionary subject", "subjective factor", "critical public opinion" ' (1995a: 7). This was the first flurry of many shots to come, no doubt!

To return to the substance of Turner's critique, he reproves Beck for ignoring the work of Mary Douglas.[3] Douglas argued, as we have seen in the previous chapter, that a popular cultural expectation about risk was that blame might be laid against some real or imagined perpetrator. Equally, protection against further risk might be obtained from a real, or imagined, magical figure. The visionary in Beck did not initially pay specific attention to the work of Mary Douglas. His arguments about the potential of globalized threat moved past the narrower understanding of risk that Douglas represents. For Douglas the 'idea of risk in itself was neutral; it took account of the probability of losses and gains' (1990: 2).

Beck was more interested in a concept of risk that demonstrates '*fabricated uncertainty* within our civilization: risk, danger, side effects, insurability, individualization and globalization' (1996a: 1). His depiction of risk is not neutral! This sense of risk as rupture meant that Beck was less able to take an overall historicist perspective. He doesn't really deal with Douglas' relatively simple, but important, argument that while technological risks have increased 'other risks have decreased' (1990: 1; see also Goldblatt, 1996). Beck does not take into account her argument that the 'line between man-made and natural causes is a social construct, often used to mask some political or personal purpose' (Lidskog, 1993: 403). Both Beck and Douglas

> miss something important about equality and justice. Beck argues that safety is
> the ideal in risk societies, just as equality had been the ideal in class societies.
> But this theoretical framework overlooks a significant fact about politics and
> society: safety claims have typically become more powerful when cast in terms
> of equality . . . Douglas, like Beck, does not acknowledge the centrality of
> egalitarian ideals and collective claims of environmental justice in risk rhetoric.
> (Draper, 1993: 643)

Nevertheless, Beck attacks the collusive silence of the technological experts who denied culpability. In an early article on this debate, which reflects Turner's substantive criticisms about Beck's neglect of Douglas, Rustin agrees that 'the litany of "risks" cited by Beck – global warming, chemical toxicity, the extinction of species, radiation, genetic engineering' are compelling. However, it is still valid to criticize Beck as being obviously 'less sensitive to the cultural and even quasi-religious shaping of this "risk agenda" than he might be' (1994: 397). While Beck saw that modernism did arise out of a rational critique of pre-modern beliefs he is only implicitly able to consider historical aspects of belief and their social construction. His theory of reflexive modernity (part of a new 'Enlightenment of risk'?) echoes the liberating claims of rationality against the modern *beliefs* of science. Beck does understand, so well, the 'prisons' of expertise that defend these belief systems but not their discursive origins.

Globalization: welfare state and risk society

What Beck doesn't understand, Turner argues, is the historical nature of welfare state development and change. Within welfare discourses Beck's apocalyptic focus is less persuasive – ironically so in respect of his own country![4] Turner observed, in his review of governmentality and risk, that increasing globalization, particularly of financial markets, has markedly increased 'political and economic uncertainty between nation states' (1997: xviii; see also Dryzek, 1995; Goldblatt, 1996). While neo-liberalism encouraged external competitiveness, and the freeing up of international trading regulations, it paradoxically increased the internal sets of micro-surveillance and disciplinary controls. There is an important linkage between globalization and internal state surveillance. As Turner argues:

> the importance of a carceral society has increased with the growth of extern-alised macro-risk. As the global economy develops into a culture of risk, the nation state is forced to invest more and more in internal systems of govern-mentality. (1997: xviii)

There is surely a major disjunction in neo-liberal political theory when external economic and political 'freedoms' are placed alongside the growth in a supposedly internal state commitment to privatization and deregulation. As Pleasants argues, the 'attribution of privileged tacit knowledge to producers and investors has . . . undemocratic conse-quences: it serves to shield their activities from public accountability, and it thereby becomes impossible to question their competence or ration-ality' (1997: 39). An increasingly globalized risk society has expanded the demand for individual accountabilities and responsibility while allowing for an increase in micro-surveillance techniques. It is incontrovertible that privatization and the contracting out of welfare provision have been allied with much more intense governmental surveillance.

Turner also argues that the pattern of social 'micro-surveillance', which has arisen out of commitments to deregulation and devolution, is reflected in greater controls over 'systems of quality control where public utilities have been privatised'. Most importantly he argues that:

> financial deregulation increases the scale of economic risk. Where major companies and public institutions fall into debt and bankruptcy, governments typically intervene, despite their ideological commitment to privatisation and deregulation, to save such institutions. (1997: xviii)

With the emergence of the Asian financial crisis in late 1997 we similarly see governments and the international banking system intervene despite the various state ideological commitments to privatization and deregula-tion. The irony is that in relationship to individual or community need, the perverse cycle of anti-welfare rhetoric is complete. However, in respect of international monetary threat, where there is the possibility of state default, 'welfare' exists and is writ large! Colloquially, one cannot help thinking that the bigger the risk and threat, the more 'welfare' becomes possible. This poses an interesting digression on how welfare beneficiaries can ratchet up their possible threat-value! It does, however, lend credence to the assertion that the drive to refashion welfare systems, at least at the individual, familial and community levels, reflects aspects of financial surveillance and control.

The sequestration of the welfare claimant within a pejorative frame of dependency is *necessary* for the maintenance of a neo-liberal political epistemology. Attacking welfare dependency is not a discrete part of such political objectives but is intrinsic to them. Neo-liberalism creates the climate of risk in order to justify its overall politic. The attack on the welfare state is a secondary consequence of a more fundamental purpose, which is to maintain the hegemony of its political stance. It is true, as Turner argues, that risk 'for the great majority of citizens, particularly those who are in some respects socially dependent, is a function of the transformation of welfare capitalism' (1994: 180). So in that narrower sense it is possible to argue that such risks, generally perceived, do not mark a *sudden irruption* of the traditions of social power and privilege. However, it is not accurate to suggest, as Turner does, that 'the debate about risk should . . . be located within these quite specific political struggles over the nature of the welfare state' (1994: 180). It is that, but as I have argued earlier, it cannot be associated with the welfare debate *per se*. It serves a much wider political purpose. Beck's apocalyptic notion of the globalized and universal nature of risk, the possibility of radical 'rupture', is not reducible to a critique of welfare state perspectives. Bronner interestingly notes that Beck's rejection of the current 'failure' of politics in risk society did not involve an adequate consideration of his paradigm of risk in relation to changes in welfare state discourse. The question about the individualization of risk perception and protection might well relate to the 'institutional conquest of the *political*' rather than to the concerted power of 'individuals engaged in a "turning back to society" '. As Bronner argues, welfare state 'decline' 'was the product of a *concerted institutional assault* by various interests and it disastrously impacted on political participation from below and the various attempts to liberate everyday life' (1995: 84).

Of somewhat more moment is Turner's argument that 'risk has not changed so profoundly and significantly over the last three centuries'. He argues for the historical reality of apocalyptic risk: 'the devastating plagues of earlier centuries were certainly global, democratic and general' (1994: 181). However, the fact of apocalyptic risk is not the essential criterion of a risk society alone. Beck also associates it with his notion of reflexive modernization, with the essential technocratic aspects of modern deregulated markets and individualization. In this respect Beck has managed to associate a radically new political perspective about radical individualism with the apocalyptic nature of risk. Turner's simple but powerful question 'has life become more risky?' must always remain open. However, the radical nature of Beck's thesis does not solely depend on his apocalyptic depiction of nuclear, biochemical and other potential catastrophes.

Turner can legitimately, within the frame of his specific analysis, argue that 'risk has to be seen as merely an illustration of the more general notion of contingency in human and social life' (1994: 181). Here his reliance on Douglas' ideas that the 'line between man-made and natural causes is a social construct' can clearly be seen. However, he can equally be charged with attempting to reduce the significance of Beck's ideas to

a predetermined historicist perspective. Turner's criticisms about the
endurable historical reality of apocalyptic risk events which shape the
discourse about risk are important, and reflect the fact that further work
is required to establish a fuller perspective on this specific aspect of the
debate.[5] However, Cohen has put a new perspective on this question
when he argues:

> These threats are fundamentally different from those that existed in earlier eras
> for three reasons: (1) they are undetectable by direct human sensory percep-
> tion; (2) they are capable of transcending generations; and (3) they exceed the
> capacity of current mechanisms for compensating victims. (1997: 107)

The sets of risks that Beck is describing arise not from nature, what might
be called natural apocalyptic disasters, plagues or tempests, but politically
and technologically. They are the consequence of our own deliberative
decisions. Turner questions, as we have seen, whether 'the epidemics of
syphilis and bubonic plague in earlier periods [were] any different from
the modern environmental illnesses to which Beck draws our attention'
(1994: 180–1)? Perhaps not at the specific level of disease. However,
Beck's warnings of potential ecological catastrophe are not empty
threats. Turner's historicist arguments are significant, but only as far as
they can go. It is possible that something more destructive than plagues
does exist (Chernobyl for example). At least in this respect, Beck's
warnings do represent a disjunction and not a thread of history.

Post-modernism: strangers in our own society?

The phrase is Turner's. He locates the emergence of post-modernism
within the wider perspective of globalization. Effectively he considers
post-modernism to be 'an intellectual movement in social thought and
. . . a cultural criticism of modernism'. He suggests that:

> the global diversity of cultures creates an alien environment in which all
> cultures appear strange. The counterpart of course for postmodern cultural
> alienation is nostalgia, that is, the nostalgic quest for real communication, real
> experience and real culture. Postmodernisation produces a profound sense of
> the artificial and constructed nature of both social arrangements and cultural
> forms. All cultural artefacts appear, therefore, to be mere artefacts. (1994: 185)

Turner's concluding point, reviewing Beck's risk society thesis, is
that there are two contradictory processes that structure modernity:
'the growth of risk cultures and the McDonaldisation of society'. By
'McDonaldisation' Turner means how the universal predictability of
similarity and quality in McDonald's foods represents an attempt to
reduce uncertainty. As he says, 'McDonaldisation removes surprises
from everyday life by an extension of instrumental rationality to production, distribution and consumption' (1994: 180–1). Turner sees that such

expressions of instrumental rationality are being reflected in welfare and health systems which seek to remove the former public reliance on ease and universality of access. The 'new doctrine of obligation', in respect of access to health and welfare, is an explicit attack on the older notion of citizenship rights and entitlements. As Turner suggested, the 'traditional notions of citizenship rights (to health and social welfare) are being questioned by a liberal ideology of individual obligation (to save and create personal bases of security)' (1997: xix). It is in effect a different form of disciplinary action, which is at the core of Foucault's theory of governmentality. Turner argues that the processes and 'policies of privatisation, "out-sourcing", "down-sizing", internal markets, managerialism and de-institutionalisation' are not 'easily described or explained within Foucault's paradigm of the disciplinary society, panopticism and governmentality' (1997: xix). The assumption that these 'new' political and social realities (the substance of Beck's risk society) undermine the validity of Foucault's arguments needs some further reflection.

Aspects of Turner's theoretical criticism of Beck were also addressed to Giddens' work on risk and reflexivity. Turner has argued that their theorizing about reflexive modernization does not undermine the substantive arguments for post-modernism. Turner states that Beck's and Giddens' 'account of high modernity and risk society depends heavily on a particular view which they develop of the modern self, namely of the self as a project'. The conjunction of this expression of the self with the 'self-politicisation' of neo-liberalism is clear. As Turner continues, 'the reflexive self is a core feature of the general progress of detraditionalisation in high modernity' (1994: 187). Much of the future debate within sociology will pivot around the resolution of this major theoretical argument. The discussion about the 'self as project' seems to me the most significant because it is closer to my previous critical discussion about the autonomous individualism so beloved of neo-liberalism. Concentrating on the differences between these theorists on the question of individualization is most useful to my overall debate about risk and social policy.

Giddens: risk and detraditionalization

Do the claims of Beck and Giddens mark a radical new shift in theory? Giddens' notion of 'social reflexivity' is valuable but flawed. By social reflexivity he means how the individual, in a 'detraditionalized' society, winnows out and filters 'all sorts of information relevant to his or her life situation, and routinely acts on the basis of that filtering process' (1994a: 24). As he says, the 'growth of social reflexivity is a major factor introducing a dislocation between knowledge and control – a prime source of manufactured uncertainty' (1994a: 24). Consequently, he argues that these reflexive processes lead to a 'greater autonomy of action' and by extrapolation are part of the implicit governance structures.

He may be right that the 'pauper' can now 'cock a snook', so to speak, but Wynne (1996) raises an interesting and serious question about the usefulness of this concept of reflexivity. Wynne argues that there never was a previous condition where 'unqualified trust' typified the relations between experts and 'lay publics'. Adducing reflexivity to mark a disjunction between a traditional and a detraditional (read 'high modernity') society is not historically valid. The notion of opposition, or 'pervasive public scepticism', Wynne argues, cannot be attributed solely to the disjunctions of modernity. Modernity did not create the notion of an oppositional consciousness: the solitary individual faced with overwhelming risk can never be a valid icon of modernity. In that sense, Wynne argues, 'situations of reflexivity' always existed. Giddens is overdramatizing present disjunctions. The notion of a traditional 'idyll' may simply reflect the fact that the pauper had no effective 'sling-shot'!

Giddens' notion of reflexivity is too rational (too dependent on 'rational-choice models of the social') and thus too focused on the centrality of social change situated in descriptions of the 'interpersonal and the intimate' to be useful. It is easy to see how such sociological preoccupations have the capacity to underscore the neo-liberal project. They do pose the common-sense of the solitary individual (the self as project) as the fundamental 'bearer' and 'driver' of change. That there might be other alternative sources of knowledge, other discourses; that a paradigm of recognition might take these wider cultural processes into account; is denied in Giddens' model of the reflexive self. As Pleasants contends, Giddens takes no account of Wittgenstein's argument 'that "knowledge" and "doubt" are not "names" for states of, or processes, in individuals. Knowing and doubting are *practices* in which people engage' (1997: 32). His failure to understand Foucault's arguments about disciplinary 'practices' weakens his overall theory of structuration. The creation of the self is problematic in isolation from the cultural ground, which gives not only physical birth but also the birth of context – the social constructivist position. As Wynne states, 'Giddens has reproduced what is a widespread confusion between unreflective trust, and reflexive dependency and reflexive ambivalence' (1996: 48ff).

The notion in reflexive modernization that trust is *invested* (rather than simply given) leads Wynne to the conclusion that such arguments empty out the possibility of any universal 'moral talk'. Wynne would rather contrast what he called an 'authority of universals' instead of the tyranny of the solitary individual.[6] The question then emerges: have we lost so much in modernity that we cannot validly transcend the loneliness of individual consciousness, or argue for any universal truths in postmodernity? The post-modern denial that we can have no universal ethical categories, however, is still a belief. Those 'truths' that obtain between myriads of experts and lay publics only refract that part of the 'whole' which 'our' reflexive imagination will allow! By attacking an over-reliance on expert 'knowledges' and 'expert systems' as the fundamental drivers of modernity, Wynne finds:

> The potentialities for new forms of political, moral and epistemic order – one's enjoying greater public identification, and reinvigorated democratic grounding – are significantly broadened by introducing the problematization of 'expert knowledge'. (1996: 73)

Postscript: risk and the eclipse of class?

Can we assume that Beck's analysis does usher in a new social world in which class, social stratification and capital accumulation are no longer feasible? Perhaps his most articulate expression of his argument about class contradictions is that these contradictions now mark the 'ranks of capital' as well.[7] They cannot simply be associated with poverty and wealth. As he says:

> The transverse differentiation of the social structure, the fact that the structure of industrial conflict melts and is recast in the heat of hazards, is the most menacing and inflammatory problem from the point of view of the social structure and the economy. (1995a: 137)

Not unexpectedly, Beck's fundamental assumption that the ubiquitous risk society has made the classical issue of class analysis redundant has met with a range of counter-opinion.[8] His successful articulation of a globalized risk (the democratic smog) does not fully consider that resources and risks are not entirely distributed 'democratically'. Certainly, while it is an interesting point of view 'that risk positions have become entirely detached from class positions', the conclusion is not yet sustainable (Goldblatt, 1996: 178). Dryzek (1995) also argues that Beck's distinction between industrial society and risk society is overdone. He argues, persuasively, that class 'politics may be waning in importance, but unemployment and inequality attendant upon deindustrialization and economic globalization mean that class divisions are actually increasing in developed societies' (1995: 237). The same sets of issues which led to the decline of the working class are 'responsible for the immiseration and isolation of its members, making them as unlikely participants in risk democracy as they are in class-based political action' (1995: 237). Beck falls into the same trap as the neo-liberalism he criticizes in that an emergent individualism is not always possible or part of that which the working class welfare dependant might seek or want.

Draper makes the trenchant point that 'Toxic waste dumps are seldom found beneath the green estates of the wealthy.' In fact she goes on to argue that environmental 'hazards present the greatest threat to the poor and racial minorities' and that 'suspect and dangerous goods find more willing buyers within less developed countries and impoverished communities' (1993: 642). This argument is also substantiated by Marske who uses empirical US-based research to argue that the 'poor risk more' (1991: 171–2). In sum, Draper argues that Beck overstates the importance of the universalization of risk and pays insufficient attention to empirical studies about the specific allocation and distribution of hazards. She agrees that his analysis does substantiate the fact of new 'communities of threat' but also contends that these new 'communities' have been shaped in the past by class divisions and by those of gender, race and ethnicity as well.

Despite Turner's strictures, Beck's paradigm of a risk society does mark a radical new shift in theory. I see an important relationship between Beck and Foucault that does have the elements of a 'rupture' in theoretical tradition. In some senses both are intellectual *enragés* whose mutual *oeuvre* was premised on rethinking the whole structure and pattern of social thought. Yes, there is an unbroken almost universal thread to our typical understanding of risk, but the change from happenstance to threat, from dangerousness to risk (Castel, 1991), I submit, is different and must be seen in that light. Cohen (1997), in support of this conclusion, argues that Beck's assumptions about risk society have dissolved social class and the accumulation of wealth as the major arbiters of social stratification. With the advent of the risk society the rhetoric of 'I am hungry' has now become 'I am afraid'. Bronner is typical of Beck's critics in arguing that:

> Struggles in the future will not simply transcend conflicts between the privileged and the underprivileged. New traditions will, in the same vein, not mechanically divorce themselves from those of the past . . . Abstractly seeking to move 'beyond' the designation of the 'left' and 'right' will only lead back into Hegel's night in which all cows are black. And there we cannot remain. (1995: 85)

Honneth, whose work we shall consider in the next chapter, is one of the more articulate defenders of the position that we cannot so easily do away with class issues. Perhaps it is not accurate or subtle enough, as Beck does, to counter-pose being 'hungry' and being 'afraid'. It is possible that those two states are common aspects of human experience. It seems reasonable, before considering Honneth (who makes no mention of Beck), to give the last word to Beck himself. His point is that in the risk society capital is turned against capital and 'occupational group against occupational group'. This leads to a drastic change in class analysis such that the key question in the struggle for economic survival is not co-operation and acquiescence in social obligation but 'how to win and exercise power, in order to foist on others the consequences of social definitions of risk' (1995a: 10). This argument may be 'speculative', as Beck himself allows, but the question that he raises is crucial.

How to effect the result of Beck's ideas?

In the final analysis such radical reinterpretations of our social world must respond to the common-sense question of what now. What is to be done? Political 'action can no longer take the form of merely *intervening* in the capitalist economy. It must increasingly take the form of *detaching* material life from the logic of capitalism' (Wood, 1997: 558). Must we be as pessimistic as Rustin argues?

> Whether it is possible, in a postscarcity society, to bring this juggernaut of transformation under control, when the agencies that previously resisted it are so weakened, is the great unanswered question for contemporary radicals. Ulrich Beck formulates this problem in a new and challenging way. But he does not offer a convincing solution to it. (1994: 400)

It is difficult, given the ecological 'weight' of Beck's thesis about risk, not to accept the legitimacy of such views. Posing the issues of 'knowledge' in modernity as struggles between various forms of expert knowledge, and lay publics, has led to the current hegemony of neo-liberalism. Giddens' overly dependent use of expertise as a pivoting factor has radically delimited 'our understanding of the sense of risk' and seriously constrained the 'imagination of new forms of order and of how their social legitimation may be better founded' (Wynne, 1996: 45). Being an 'expert' or functioning within a definition of 'good science' are not distinct from the cultural and intellectual processes that validated them.[9] The debate, as Wynne suggests, becomes a debate of experts and counter-experts fighting on a 'darkling plain' of their own imagination.

It is, of course, a debate that has only just begun. The elements of a revamped social responsibility model are only just appearing. Such 'green' tendrils of an objection to the dominance of neo-liberal rationality will need careful nurturing but we need not fear the power of the idea. What is ultimately hopeful about human social life is the inevitably of change, and that present political orthodoxies, no matter how powerful, will eventually be transmuted. Beck's aim, as Bronner concluded, was 'less a confrontation with the present than an analysis of how the present is giving rise to a new future' (1995: 86). One of these 'green tendrils' is the thinking about the politics of recognition reflected in Honneth's reworking of Habermas. It is to this that we now turn to explore its relevance to the overall debate.

Notes

1 This criticism however has been weakened by Beck's more recent comments on global risk factors. See previous chapter and Beck (1996a).

2 An interesting variant on this specific point has been made by Reddy who argues that one way to challenge contemporary political hegemonies is not to

lose sight, in the ubiquity of Beck's risk society, of risk as uncertainty. While uncertainty is there in Beck's formulation, uncertainty by its very definition reflects a 'softer' perspective on risk. It is softer in the sense that it returns the discourse about risk to possibilities not probabilities. Reddy argues that such bracketing of risk with uncertainty can broaden the bases of the rationality of modernity. As Reddy concludes:

> The rehabilitation of the idea of 'uncertainty', of radical, irreducible indeterminacy, not amenable to authoritative or authoritarian 'expert' definition and measurement, is a necessary step with which to open to contestation this new and necessary public domain. (1996: 248)

3 Turner's criticism is accurate in respect of Beck's original *Risk Society: Towards a New Modernity*. However, in a more recent article Beck (1996a: 4) addresses this oversight. He acknowledges that some dangers are socially constructed, and that Douglas and Wildavsky (1982) do set out a valid argument that present danger is similar to that posed in early history. However, Beck is still adamant that modern ecological catastrophes are potentially qualitatively different.

4 Refer back to Chapter 1 for the full description of these concerns within social policy about risk society.

5 See Goldblatt (1996: 175) for confirmation of this critique.

6 Wynne's argument is that debates about 'universal knowledge and values' are not exhausted. On the contrary, these new debates about risk society are 'quintessentially tied up with larger crises of legitimacy' (1996: 78).

7 For a detailed discussion of Beck's perspective see Beck (1995a: 146–52). See also Goldblatt (1996: 154–87).

8 The core aspect of this from critical theorists is that middle class obsession with 'personal aggrandizement, autonomy and competition' developed a style of communication which separated them from the lower class. The vehicle for an exclusive and separating middle class discourse was risk communication. Eder argues that preoccupation with risk 'seems to be the newest version of a rise in middle class culture in protest and collective mobilization' (1993: 181–2). Within this version of critical opinion Beck's theorizing serves the hegemony of the middle class. Colloquially, if risk didn't exist then it would have had to be invented. Perhaps Beck is just a middle class apologist!

9 This is the fundamental point of my debate with neo-liberalism. No matter how powerful and hegemonic it might be it is only an aspect of the possible. The autonomous solitary individual is a socially derived being. These beliefs about individual reality are socially constructed beliefs.

8

RISK AND RECOGNITION: A VIEW FORWARD?

The 'struggle for recognition' is fast becoming the paradigmatic form of political conflict in the late twentieth century. Demands for 'recognition of difference' fuel struggles of groups mobilized under the banners of nationality, ethnicity, 'race', gender and sexuality. In these 'post-socialist' conflicts, group identity supplants class interest as the chief medium of political mobilization.

(Fraser, 1995b: 68)

Honneth's basic theory is that 'the moral force within lived social reality that is responsible for development and progress is a struggle for recognition' (1995b: 143). Such struggles are set within an obviously 'fragmented world' which, he nonetheless contends, is irreducibly social. Honneth's thinking about the moral logic of this presumed 'inter-subjectivity' takes the form of a 'grand narrative': seeking out the different ways that such contentions can be philosophically grounded. His ethical aim is well expressed in Forster's famous literary injunction:

Only connect the prose and the passion, and both will be exalted, and human love will be seen at its height. Live in fragments no longer. Only connect, and the beast and the monk, robbed of the isolation that is life to either, will die. (1965: 197)

Honneth's purpose is to find an incontrovertible means to re-establish the *logic of the social*, a 'moral grammar' of our human connectedness that has normative force. More expressively, he does intend to find a theoretical way to link the 'beast' and the 'monk'! His explorations reflect a search for a universal and compelling language of respect. He contends, *inter alia*, that 'normative demands . . . are, structurally speaking, internal to the relationship of mutual recognition' (1995b: 92). Whether such a *grand* and morally valuable assumption can be sustained remains to be seen.[1] Nonetheless, the effort to articulate the possibility arouses a welcome 'leap of faith' in a world so obviously riven with risk and denial of recognition.[2]

What Honneth 'emphasizes [in his theory] is not the struggle for self-preservation but rather the struggle for the establishment of relations of mutual recognition' (1995b: x). It is this that distinguishes his argument from neo-liberalism, which, he argues, is preoccupied with preservation of personal autonomy, not recognition of legitimate difference. As I discussed in Chapter 5, neo-liberalism transformed the 'passions' of rebellion, protest and resistance into more manageable 'categories of "interest" ' (Honneth, 1995b: 161). His reworking of Hegel's 'politics of recognition' poses the kind of paradox that can challenge the common-sense rhetoric of neo-liberalism. For example, Honneth (1992) argues that the achievement of autonomy (the irreducible ideal of individualism) requires self-confidence, self-respect and self-esteem. This places the neo-liberal moral attack about welfare dependency in a double-bind. Demanding autonomy and self-responsibility of stigmatized welfare recipients requires the admission that these moral injunctions presuppose the existence of those very qualities they are now presumed to lack. Typical processes of labelling and 'name-calling' deny these attributes to welfare recipients. A perverse social 'double-bind' is struck!

Recognition: the exigencies of risk and class?

This brief review of Honneth's work gives us an opportunity to 'draw breath', so to speak, and consider the radical nature of Beck's paradigm of risk in relation to other perspectives about the nature and 'reality' of social experience. Beck's (1996a) assumption that risk society has swept away the possibility of class consciousness as a lever for political mobilization is central to his analysis. The apparent 'triumph' of neo-liberal politics, that has seen a concomitant diminution of the strength and political clout of unions, would seem to prove his point. However, the stimulating question is: does Honneth more accurately portray the current situation when he suggests that class is still important, but now controlled by these forces of risk that we have been discussing? Honneth's analysis of class and risk reveals the possibility that we might yet consider the politics of recognition within a 'moral grammar of social conflicts'. His thinking serves as welcome counterpoint to Beck's apocalyptic 'certainties' about the difficulty of such a task.

Finding a context for the grand narratives of critical theory has never been easy. They are even less persuasive since 'denunciations of the welfare state . . . [have fallen] on fertile ground, thereby setting in motion a political mechanism of self-fulfilling predictions and interpretations' (Offe, 1996: 179). Attempting to remake the traditional links between 'normative theoretical intention and historically situated morality' (Honneth, 1995a: 205) is fraught. Critical theory did appear to have found an empirically effective way to assert the normative morality of its arguments, in identifying 'a class of the impoverished, excluded, hopeless, alienated and marginalized' (Offe, 1996: 261). This 'welfare class' still exists but has lost its edge of scandal. Honneth's reworking of the politics of recognition gives some hope that a new social grammar of neglect might reawaken our previous sense of outrage about such structured disadvantage. He sets out to reimagine the nature of an empirically effective morality 'which arises from socio-cultural conflicts' (1995a: 206). He reintroduces the grammar and 'possibility' of scandal. For Honneth, it is Habermas who best achieves the laudable aim of articulating the empirical force of such a moral consciousness. Peering into the 'entrails' of the structural conflicts, which impel such massive social disadvantage, might reveal 'the signs of an historical movement in which the moral learning process of the species persistently achieves expression' (1995a: 206).

In his reflections on Habermas' massive 'project' Honneth suggests that a new form of recognition has been articulated. He shows how Habermas argues that a new avant-garde is carrying the 'moral learning process'. The struggle for recognition of the dispossessed has now found new expression and allegiance in those who, while satiated, are unsatisfied with their economic wellbeing. As Honneth interprets Habermas:

> it is no longer experiences of economic dependence and social deprivation, but rather the sensitivity to socially unrealized claims to justice, which in turn is linked with a well organized process of socialization, which have now become the presupposition for a moral-practical critique of society. (1995a: 206)

Recognition of disadvantage, Honneth argues, is complicated by two factors. The first is that 'the authentic social ethic of the lower strata', constructed out of their real experience, is used as a 'cognitive filter' with which to comment on the 'hegemonial or dominance-critical systems of norms'. Specific hurts are reified into aspects of power: they are no longer recognized as such, but serve a wider political purpose.[3] The second difficulty is that such reifications do serve to create 'self-consistent and logically connected ideas of right and wrong' but they arise out of 'the fictive perspective of an observer outside experience'. The actual experience of the dispossessed is obviously less systematic and rather reflects 'an uncoordinated complex of reactive demands for justice' (1995a: 209).

Consequently, attempting to provide a coherent and morally persuasive requirement for the empirical verification of these needs runs 'smack into' an 'unwritten morality' which condemns the raggedness of the 'reactive demands'. This 'unwritten morality' sees no need to accord recognition but applies, instead, a stringent framework of individual risk. In this way Habermas' attempts to structure an 'outer morality' which would empirically verify the legitimacy of need stumbles over an 'inner morality' that is framed around risk and self-preservation. For both protagonists, the 'successful' and the 'excluded', this results in the valorization of 'injustice'.[4] It does not lead into any formulation of 'ethically grounded goals'. However, as I have argued throughout this book, applying aspects of Foucault's radical analysis to 'unmask' the hidden normativeness of these valorizations offers the hope of making some progress.[5]

Honneth, similarly, seeks to set out a socio-structural analysis for the validation of the 'moral consciousness of socially suppressed groups'. In order to do this it is necessary to validate that consciousness, without applying the institutional and informal demands for consistency (1995a: 210). There are, however, some important observations about socially mandated legitimizations that do qualify any possibility of recognizing the legitimacy of socially suppressed groups. These legitimizations constitute the acceptable discourses that construe the 'divide' between the subjugated and the successful. Honneth highlights two. The first is that only those from the 'societally dominant class are required to normatively justify themselves'. However, it is a 'reckoning' that is intrinsically flawed. While it appears to be a personal 'audit', the required justifications really represent reifications of the whole. Personal account is automatically reified into a 'social audit' of welfare. It is *privilege* that has been required to give an account of itself and not *disadvantage*. However, in the increasing moral arguments about welfare dependency we can discern attempts to redress this imbalance. These remoralizations do, increasingly, require welfare recipients to 'give account of themselves'. While there are explicit and implicit requirements to explain privileges laid on the 'socially dominant', the systems of cultural explanation that are applied are increasingly less motivated by principles of justice. Various valorizations of risk have contributed to the defence of privilege and increased the demand that welfare be radically reconstructed.

Honneth's second point concerns the internal logic of the 'socially suppressed'. He suggests that they are under no normative pressure to challenge or decode the symbolic embedding of their own norms. The dominant internal rhetoric is a discourse about injustice, and rarely considers the means for participating in generalized systems of social justice.[6] Such groups are not required to 'reach beyond [their] specific situations'. They are more inclined to 'treat the moral problems of their own environment in a normatively secure and ethically mature manner, but fall back helplessly upon standard normative clichés when they are asked to deal with questions about the possible value principles of social orders in general' (1995a: 211). The relative 'comfort' of these 'embedded norms' raises the issues of what can be termed the problem of regenerating struggle. As Honneth said, 'the experience of a particular form of recognition was shown to be bound up with the disclosing of new possibilities with regard to identity, which necessarily result in a struggle for the social recognition of these new forms of identity' (1995b: 162).

Patterns of normative dominance

Honneth argues that normative class dominance involves two inter-locking processes: that surrounding the creation of 'cultural exclusion', and that supporting the institutionalization of individualism. He suggests that these joint processes of social control serve to limit the 'symbolic and semantic expression' of perceived injustice, and to deny any 'spatial' or 'socio-cultural conditions of class-specific experiences of deprivation and injustice'. This semantic and spatial constraint or limitation reinforces individual experience as the only validly discussible reality, or socio-cultural condition. He shows that the processes of 'cultural exclusion' are achieved by a systematic 'desymbolization'.[7] That is to argue that radical protest and 'talk of injustice' is made reflexive only to the protesting group. It cannot therefore, by definition, be generalized. Similarly, by reducing the power of its symbols it cannot 'reach the threshold of proposals for a just society'.

We have seen how constraining discussion about issues of social injustice, and escalating fears about welfare dependency, have been explicitly used as processes of 'desymbolization'. They set out to eviscerate the claims of injustice or deprivation by denying the validity of the symbols used to depict that injustice or deprivation. The second powerful process of normative class dominance, outlined by Honneth, achieves this. Not only are the symbols of hurt and deprivation denied but the spatial or experienced ground of that hurt, deprivation or injustice is similarly circumscribed. Attempts to discuss this as one aspect of a 'class-specific consciousness of injustice' are considered vapid. The hegemonic thrust of institutionalized individualism invades that social 'space' and undercuts the claims for group or class consciousness. As Honneth has argued, the hurts occasioned by active disrespect can 'become the motivational basis for collective resistance only if subjects are able to articulate them within an intersubjective framework of interpretation that they can *show to be typical for an entire group*' (1995b: 163, my italics). This depends on being able to generalize a 'semantics of disappointment': the grounds for such a social generalization are exceedingly difficult to fashion.

In the 'world' of neo-liberal risk, disappointment can only be individual. Such semantics actively seek to refashion the discursive world. The real question is whether individuals who 'are *active* in their own government' have actually refashioned the 'relation of obligation between citizen and society' (Rose, 1996a: 330). That refashioning does not allow for the universalizing of a 'semantics of disappointment'. By 'institutionalized individualization' Honneth means all the strategies employed to deny legitimacy to group-specific experiences of claims – or, more specifically, group-specific claims that arises from various welfare communities. How this 'communicative infrastructure' (*pace* Habermas) is destroyed involves three complex and interlocking processes. The first, which relates to the theme of this book, is the complex matrix of 'social and political rewards for individualistic risk-taking'. The second relates to the devastation of local body politics and the 'destruction of neighbourhood living environments'. The third relates to all the supports for an individualized 'ideology of achievement', and the creation of competitive labour markets.

Honneth demonstrates how the power of such 'normative class dominance' works. He argues, against Habermas, that communicative action excludes those who define themselves as outside the dominant social discourse. He does this by suggesting that protest about class consciousness of injustice, no matter how valid, leads only to an awareness of that injustice. It cannot establish the grounds for a wider analysis or possible resolution. As he says:

> The standards governing moral disapproval of social processes are more reliable indicators of expectations for a just and good social order than the often conventionalistic value system of the lower strata, which is seldom ordered in a logically satisfying manner. If this consideration is correct, then there is a potential for expectations of justice, needs claims, and ideas of happiness preserved negatively in the consciousness of injustice in these social groups, which for social-structural reasons do not reach the threshold of proposals for a just society. (1995a: 212)

Justice arises out of the logic of the successful, not from the poor or excluded. The patterns and processes by which awareness of, and protest about, injustice 'do not reach the threshold of proposals for a just society' are vital to this analysis about risk and social policy. While Honneth's theorizing serves the wider purpose of an analysis of class conflict and injustice, within sociology it provides a structural analysis of how risk has become defined as invariably individual and not collective.

Recognition: tribal and specific or universal?

Honneth develops three models or levels of recognition. The first is where the individual desires and needs of one person are held in respect by another – leading to all the concepts of care or love.[8] The second, proceeding from the particular outwards, is where an individual is recognized and ascribed as having 'the same moral accountability as every other human being'. Where recognition was acquainted with love at the first level now, in the second, recognition is associated with 'moral respect'. The third level further develops this outwards movement from the self towards the social. There an 'individual is recognized as a person whose capabilities are of constitutive value to a concrete community'. The processes that surround this, Honneth argues, involve the ascription of 'solidarity' or 'loyalty' (1997: 29–30). That these three levels are sometimes held in tension is an obvious feature of our social debates.

Given this interrelationship between these three levels, Honneth contends that an empirical argument can be made where 'the tradition of an ethics of care as well as communitarian models may claim a legitimate place in a morality of recognition' (1997: 33).

Honneth attempts to resolve the strain of the public debate by arguing that 'the entire domain of the moral is pervaded by a tension that can be resolved only in individual responsibility' (1997: 33). On the face of it such a conclusion appears to underscore much of the neo-liberal rhetoric. There is nonetheless a 'bite' to this apparent agreement. His threefold model of individual recognition does raise how well such political rhetoric can respond to the subtlety of what moral recognition actually involves. The relevance of this to my discussion of risk is that the self-evident truths of neo-liberal individualism, which deny any relationship of the individual with the social (Honneth's third level), can now be challenged. They are a façade: they do not represent inalienable and unchangeable truths but are part of the structural and moral decisions necessary to frame them. They must be seen as a stance, a position, a particular and not universal set of beliefs about the world. Associated with this more developed paradigm of recognition we have seen the emergence of a new 'tribalism' of interest group identity.[9] How we are to be recognized, in our group or other identities, seems really significant. Honneth's examination of the 'hiddenness' of these assumptions echoes Katznelson's concept about the 'silences' of social policy and Foucault's 'otherness' – the knowledge that lies below speaking.

What we see in Honneth's arguments is a way to challenge the apparent normativeness of the supremacy of individual market choices about risk. Risks are not intrinsically individual. Engaged in by individual actors, yes; but in as much as they can be generalized, risks are not individual. Risks are collective; it is accidents which are irreducibly personal (cf. Ewald, 1991; O'Malley, 1996). They are taken within, and are a response to, a social context. If Beck is right and the state of reflexivity is a recognition that we now are caught up in a context of social risk over which we can have no control, then why should that not equally be conceived of as a legitimate social risk? Honneth has shed some light on the origins of an unacknowledged normative individualization.

Taylor argues that the explicit 'demand for recognition' results from the assumption that 'we are formed by recognition' (1992: 64). This is an assumption that Honneth (1995b) sets out to ground in his assertion that the full perception of individuality is always an intersubjective process. Thus, for both theorists, the hurt that can be wreaked on dispossessed groups, through an active lack of recognition, can be 'hardheadedly enumerated'. Taylor argues, against Foucault, that his philosophy of power/knowledge is 'bankrupt' because it misconstrues the 'politics of recognition' which is not about 'power and counterpower' but does, indeed, reflect 'the search for recognition and respect' (1992: 70).[10] Taylor goes on to argue that in the colonizing of the lifeworld of the 'other' there 'is a struggle for a changed self-image, which takes place both within the subjugated and against the dominator' (1992: 65). It is interesting to note how such 'violence' is grounded in a terrible fear that is driven by overwhelming risk.

A welfare paradox: redistribution or recognition?

In order to develop this argument about 'desymbolization' and how the validity of the former class-specific sets of injustices are denied, I want briefly to consider Fraser's (1995b) paradox. Discussing the politics of recognition she sketches out the core dilemma that redistributive modes of welfare collapse the distinctions and differences of groups (gender or racial for example) into the generalized citizen claimant.[11] On the other hand, she suggests, the attempts to recognize 'cultural-valuational injustice always enhance group differentiation' (1995b: 82). The question is how to create a politics that can redistribute and recognize at the same time. Fraser's 'valiant' attempt to construct a model that might overcome this dilemma stumbles over the realization that we remain 'stuck in the vicious circles of mutually reinforcing cultural and economic subordination' (1995b: 93). The conclusion is not really even polemical: it falls into the category of a 'longing for difference', an expression of a belief in normative political transcendence. But where do we go to find such an alternative? Where, to start, should a different politics of renewal be possible? All the rhetoric that we use to find a 'different way' has seemingly been deconstructed. For as Rorty (1995) has contended, the important question is whether, following Nietzsche, philosophy can have an emancipatory content. Honneth's paradigm of recognition merits our respect – if not always our recognition!

   Some aspects of this discussion will be pursued in the next chapter in relation to dependency and the welfare 'gaze'. Features of the imaginative claims made by Baudrillard will be used to see whether Fraser's dilemma might admit of some leverage. Baudrillard defines the 'real' normative struggle not on the 'plane of the real' but on the symbolic level. He argues that the hegemony of the present system is its ability to retain what he calls the 'exclusivity of the gift without the counter-gift' (1993: 36). If we accept Baudrillard's requirement that the hegemony of the 'real' can only really be challenged at the symbolic level, then Fraser's paradox may admit of some movement.[12] This analysis of symbol systems poses a potential alternative. Arguing normatively for the transformative or revolutionary claims for class consciousness does not deal with the fact that modernity has hidden the old working class debates. As Honneth suggests, the wage-earning class has been easily 'diverted onto the track of private consumption'. Consequently 'the normative potential of the working class seems to be dried up by state intervention' (1995a: 207). What we require is not a theory of traditional normative 'oughts' but intellectual tools to understand what 'is', and to find ways to challenge the hegemony of common-sense.

One of Honneth's most interesting suggestions is 'that a field of moral-political conflicts may lie hidden behind the façade of late-capitalist integration'. His analysis of how the obviousness of social injustice has been hidden reinforces his point that 'class conflicts continue to take place either in socially controlled or in highly individualized forms' (1995a: 207). It is this revamped individualism which has denied the subjectivity of the 'citizen-stranger', only acknowledging the subjectivity of the 'citizen-friend'.[13] If Honneth is correct, and we can argue a new paradigm of recognition, then a reconsideration of subjectivity becomes possible. As Rorty has argued:

> Since Nietzsche's time, the philosophy of subjectivity has been taken over by the ironists – by people who are interested in their own autonomy and individuality rather than in their social usefulness, and whose excursions into politics are incidental to their principal motives. (1995: 438)

Post-modernization, according to Turner, depends on the 'prevalence of certain stylistic devices in culture, such as simulation, parody and irony' (1994: 187). The use of ironic detachment as a rhetorical means to deny 'otherness' is not considered by Honneth but it does add strength to his analysis.[14]

While the theme of risk is used to create cultural and economic subordination, an examination of the symbols surrounding such usage can explode the practical certainties of the intractable that create and maintain Fraser's paradox. As Honneth suggests:

> The language system taught today by the agencies of socialization and spread by the mass media so strictly formalizes and depersonalizes group- and class-specific experiences of injustice that they remain completely external to the world of communication. (1995a: 213)

How that formalization of injustice and the depersonalization of the welfare 'other' are expressed is the focus of the next chapter on welfare dependency. We will examine this by returning to some aspects of Foucault's consideration that issues of surveillance are woven into the 'welfare gaze'.

In conclusion, Honneth set himself a *grand* task, thoroughly embedded within the critical theoretical tradition, which was to see if he could substitute a *paradigm of recognition* for the former Marxist *paradigm of labour*. Whether he did in fact achieve his aim requires an investigation independent of my theme of risk and social policy. However, in abstracting from his task the relevance of a theory of recognition to an analysis of the rhetoric against welfare I think he provides some fresh insight into the possibility of normative argument. I think that he is successful in revealing the 'norms by means of which capitalism can be criticized as a social relation of damaged recognition' (1995a: 14). We may, yet again, be able to generalize the 'semantics of disappointment' and risk as social as well as individual 'truths'.

Notes

1 Honneth readily acknowledges this. As he wrote in the published revision of his inaugural lecture:

> The principles of a morality construed in terms of a theory of recognition only have a meagre chance of being realized in the social life-world to the extent that human subjects are incapable of reacting with neutral feelings to social injury, such as physical abuse, underprivileging, and degradation . . . The admitted weakness of this practical pillar of morality within societal reality is evidenced by the fact that these emotional reactions do not automatically disclose the injustice which disrespect entails but only *bear the potential for doing so*. (1992: 199–200, my italics)

2 We need to find a way to translate the politics of the 'heart' into politics of the 'mind' so that our 'leaps of faith' are not vain. Asserting communal values and the morality of recognition (the 'heart' of Honneth's project) must deal with Foucault's assertion that placing ourselves within an initial 'we' can 'falsify' the arguments for the legitimacy of the 'we'. Perhaps, as he seems to be suggesting, we need political arguments that do not first take refuge in the defensive and alienating 'we', but are based in the possibility of an 'us'. A radical reinterpretation of our aloneness might allow for the 'sight' of the other again. Foucault argues that 'the "we" must not be previous to the question: it can only be the result – and the necessarily temporary result – of the question as it is posed in the new terms in which one formulates it' (1984e: 385).

3 I am reminded here of Hannah Arendt's famous observation about 'goodness' (in *The Human Condition*) that it can be done but never discussed. As she says:

> Only goodness must go into absolute hiding and flee all appearance if it is not to be destroyed . . . The man, however, who is in love with goodness can never afford to lead a solitary life, and yet his living with others must remain essentially without testimony . . . good deeds can never keep anyone company; they must be forgotten the moment they are done, because even memory will destroy their quality of being good. Moreover, thinking, because it can be remembered, can crystallize into thought, and thoughts, like all things that owe their existence to remembrance, can be transformed into tangible objects which, like the written page or the printed book, become part of the human artifice. Good works, because they must be forgotten instantly, can never become part of the world; they come and go, leaving no trace. (1959: 67–8)

4 It is the appropriation of a discourse of 'injustice' here which is significant. It is a discourse now of rights and not needs. The neo-liberal argument about unjust and unfair tax burdens is further evidence of the ease with which the

'right' has successfully 'absorbed' the moral language of the 'left'. The linguistic hegemony of such 'appropriations' is part of the rhetoric of governance.

5 Honneth is more considered than Taylor in his criticism of Foucault. However, he still argues that he can find 'no trace of an interpretative approach' in Foucault 'to the psychic suffering of subjects as being a last individual response to reconciliation' (1995a: 131). This rejection of Foucault is almost a wilful misreading of how his analyses can be used to achieve the very moral/ethical purposes that Honneth intends. Foucault is to be understood in the 'otherness' of his prose as well as its explicit content. It has elements of that ancient Zen observation that both the branches of the tree and the spaces they inhabit are part of its visual 'meaning'.

6 However, as I have argued elsewhere (Culpitt, 1992: 34), before we can argue validly for the moral logic of universal entitlement we will have to address the rhetoric of claimants' rights that has rationalized the validity only of their respective claims.

7 Honneth does acknowledge that 'Foucault's discourse analysis could aid the discussion' about the 'thematization of the consciousness of social injustice' (1995a: 213).

8 Honneth, quoting Hegel, defines love at this first level of recognition as 'being oneself in another' (1995b: 96).

9 See Chapter 5 for a discussion of tribalism in knowledge and how that intersects with the emergence within neo-liberalism of self-referent 'communities'.

10 It is perhaps an unreasonable cavil but Taylor's abject rejection of Foucault in this essay is remarkably peremptory, betraying no respect, and little recognition! Labelling Foucault as a 'Euro-centred' intellectual is, in one respect, only an acknowledgement of the 'truth' to which Foucault would offer no demur. To assert that Foucault has nothing to offer in analysing the politics of recognition is misguided at best.

11 We can see an echo here of the constriction of respect that Habermas argued was intrinsic to his theory of juridification.

12 However, as we have seen, critical theorists have a powerful resistance to this mode of speculative thinking.

13 See my previous book, *Welfare and Citizenship: Beyond the Crisis of the Welfare State* (1992), for an examination of these themes.

14 Parody for Foucault was the first of three platonic 'modalities' of history. The other two were dissociative and sacrificial.

- Parody attacked reality and opposed 'reminiscence or recognition'.
- Dissociation revealed a history of blows against identity.
- Sacrificial modalities attacked the possibility of truth.

The potential relevance of this to post-modern discourse was his suggestion that parody offers individuals the 'possibility of alternative identities, more individualized and substantial than his own' (1984c: 93). The importance of the potential destructiveness of parody to undermine Honneth's paradigm of recognition is clear.

9

THE WELFARE GAZE: RISK AND THE DILEMMAS OF DEPENDENCY

Words have profound memories that oil our shrill and squeaky rhetoric. The normal stands indifferently for what is typical, the unenthusiastic objective average, but it also stands for what has been, good health, and what shall be, our chosen destiny. That is why the benign and sterile-sounding word 'normal' has become one of the most powerful ideological tools of the twentieth century.

(Hacking, 1990: 169)

Throughout this examination of risk it has become clear that there are two transparent and interlocking palimpsests of risk.[1] These 'mental parchments' reflect attempts to create autonomous perspectives and understandings, where risks are again made manageable and solutions accessible. One is personal, shaped by our private assessments of potential danger. The other, a public inscription of the massive fears reflected in risk society, could be neither managed nor made easily accessible. These palimpsests are flung over each other, almost at random, as we try (like former shamans examining the entrails of the sacrificed) to discern from their random conjunction the shape of what is, or might be.

It is this intersection of public fears and private fears which is important. Any discussion of 'welfare dependency' must separate out the socio-structural use of dependency from its moral/pejorative usage. My focus is more specifically on the second usage of dependency, particularly, in the alignment of risk and dependency. Habermas' depiction of juridification and how that produced 'an insidiously expanding domain of dependency' (White, 1988a: 113) must be taken seriously. The new sets of social risk become overwhelming and terrorizing because of their very 'unmanageability', because they are no longer private. They are defined at a systemic level, are often invisible, seem only to be solved technically by 'experts', and inevitably, as Habermas has accurately said, they 'invade the lifeworld and at the same time burst its dimensions' (1994: 147).

Since the scale of the risks that have 'burst the lifeworld' are so potentially apocalyptic they can only be defended against – not easily resolved. The result of this is to alter the politics of responsibility so that, increasingly, individuals cannot be held responsible for the moral management of risks outside the area of the personal palimpsest. Consequently, as Habermas suggests, valid social protest is distorted. Faced with the massive encroachment of global risk we are forced to direct our resistance toward 'abstractions' of the lifeworld. These 'abstractions' are quirky, unique and singular. It is the idiosyncrasy of this that is important in understanding how dependency has been recast in risk society. The public palimpsest is so overwhelming that we are forced to return, almost atavistically, to inscribing the personal. This is one reason why depictions of welfare dependency have become so pejorative. The 'abstraction' from that which is publicly overwhelming, into managing a private sense of risk, has refashioned our perceptions about needs and rights. A new logic of moral responsibility has been created about work and success: a presumed public arena, within which some certainties about risk, rights and responsibility are forcefully negotiated. What it represents is an attempt to reinscribe the personal palimpsest over the public and seek a false harmony between them. Consequently, the reflexive modernization of risk society has created (within neo-liberal political discourse) a perspective about welfare dependency that is similarly reflexive.[2] We have seen previously how risk has been used to circumscribe the moral legitimacy of welfare protest, and the attempt to establish a rational legitimacy of needs. Honneth has demonstrated how social movements are drawn inexorably into debates about collectivized 'interests' rather than universal moral debates. As he says, these movements 'misidentify, as it were, the moral core of their resistance by explicating it in the inappropriate terms of mere interest categories' (1995b: 163).

This last chapter brings together all the threads of this book – which has been a 'reflection' on risk, recognition and obligation. I use reflection in the sense that we still need to spend time with the issues, without seeking an easy resolution, in order to see whether it is possible to 'revision the social'. Social theory ought more properly to be 'a specific kind of instrument of observation' (Luhmann, 1990: 238). It will be important to see whether there is any 'public sphere' left, or whether risk society has indeed evacuated the possibility of the 'public sphere'. The rhetorical and ideological nature of this debate is such that it still represents more a 'dialogue of the deaf'. It is the intersection of the private and public palimpsests of risk, and the inevitable 'abstraction' to the private, that adds a different dimension to an understanding of these genealogies of dependency. Bringing together all the threads of the previous discussion of risk further elucidates the already excellent work made to establish a genealogy of dependency (Fraser, 1996; Fraser and Gordon, 1994a; 1994b).

The 'remasking' of dependency: from social fact to private knowledge

The debate is clearly engaged between social theorists who argue normatively for social change and those who question the validity of such 'grand projects of the mind'. Opposing the injustices of social risk and dependency, as we have seen previously, informs the 'heart' of critical reason. However, this pattern of social thought must deal with the profound conundrum that it too is part of the problem. As Rorty argues, the 'frozen relations of dependence'

> become detectable only when somebody suggests concrete alternatives to them . . . We linguistic historicists think that there is no such thing as 'humanity' to be emancipated by being ushered from an age of 'distorted' to one of 'undistorted' communication – no common core to men and women of all ages and climes, other than their shared susceptibility to pain and humiliation . . . *every* form of social life is likely, sooner or later, to freeze over into something which the more imaginative and restless spirits of the time will see as 'repressive' and 'distorting'. What is wrong with these forms of life is not that they are 'ideological' but that they have been used to justify the systematic administration of pain and humiliation. (1995: 451–2)

This philosophical 'gauntlet' must be kept in mind as we ask whether we can still posit the reality of a common humanity that must be appealed to in order to undo the violent segregations we have established between the autonomously successful and the dependent.

So much of the debate about the crisis of the welfare state has 'turned on the spit' of a normative debate about needs and rights. There is both a practical moral observation to be made about social disadvantage, and an intellectual lure in wanting to fashion a normative argument about welfare. While it is important to continue to search for a 'robust' defence of welfare systems, the discourses about risk have altered the balance of that debate. Any discussion about progressive taxation and social obligation is *tout court*.[3] The 'crisis of the welfare state' has been subsumed into the more generalized debate about risk society, the function of which is to render immobile those former normative arguments about needs and rights. There is still an obvious place for critical theory in the 'burst lifeworld' of risk society. More work, however, needs to be done to establish its imperatives. Without it, we will remain caught in the 'abstracted world' of our own private concerns.

Ironic contingency: the hidden moral grammars of risk

Derrida has suggested that an 'abstracted' private world creates a new form of dogmatic discourse which 'is attempting to install its worldwide hegemony in paradoxical and suspect conditions' (1994: 51). The 'suspect conditions' of this hegemony involve risk. However, there are some more fundamental questions at work here. These 'suspect conditions' reflect the ways that neo-liberalism has voided any 'emancipatory content' in modernity. Talk of social justice has been discarded by a form of political theorizing that is fundamentally ironic, one that is interested only in 'its own contingency'. So extreme is this sense of autonomous contingency that Baudrillard can suggest, perhaps fancifully, that:

> There is a paradox of modern bourgeois rationality concerning death. To conceive of it as natural, profane and irreversible constitutes the sign of the 'Enlightenment' and Reason, but enters into sharp contradiction with the principles of bourgeois rationality, with its individual values, the unlimited progress of science, and its mastery of all nature in all things. Death, neutralised as a 'natural fact', gradually becomes a *scandal*. (1993: 160)

For our purposes, the question, somewhat less extreme but equally important, is how the natural fact of dependency has become such a scandal. Despite various attempts by critical theorists (cf. Fraser, 1996) to 'demystify the current common-sense about dependency', it is clear that such arguments have little public sway. The genealogical project about dependency is important but if it resorts only to an ideological analysis of power then it is weakened. The 'abyss between the present and the ideal is a feature which marks the work of all the critical theorists' (Miller, 1987: 218). The purpose of constructing such a Foucauldian genealogy is not just to argue about the relative rights and responsibilities that ought to obtain between the powerful and the weak, or to establish the basis for an alternative politics. That has been argued over and over again. The more vital question is whether critical theory actually establishes, and reflexively reinforces, the power of that which its adherents seek to change (cf. Rorty, 1995). We cannot, as Baudrillard argues, destroy hegemonic political systems 'by a direct, dialectical revolution of the economic or political infrastructure. Everything produced by contradiction, by the relation of forces, or by energy in general, will only feed back into the mechanism and give it impetus' (1993: 36).

The important struggle, as Baudrillard sees it, is not on the 'plane of the real' but on the symbolic level, where the power of the system is its ability to retain the 'exclusivity of the gift without the counter-gift'. This insight is especially significant. The underlying epistemology of welfare transactions involves the offering of a welfare 'gift' (whether social service or income maintenance) associated with the *refusal* of any 'counter-gift'. The denial of any sense of mutuality in the welfare exchange removes the debate to the symbolic. The welfare exchange is therefore defined as a one-way transaction of dependency. It is an exchange of monetary or other support, defined as a 'social gift', that has no reciprocal correspondence. The previous reciprocal ideals of citizenship obligation are destroyed so that there can be no 'counter-gift'. Such destruction of reciprocity, in the 'welfare exchange', is a prerequisite for reframing need as dependency. The pejorative response of neo-liberal politics requires this denial in order to sustain its critical rhetoric of welfare distribution.

What we must be concerned about is how the processes of 'mystification', which result from the sense of powerlessness in the face of global risk, reinforce the pre-eminence of the private lifeworld. It is the perception of the overwhelming fact of risk that has rendered immobile the public lifeworld. This has increased the prevalence of the private 'abstractions' which have so powerfully reconstructed risk and dependency. These private sets of 'abstractions' are reinforced by a discursive style of 'ironic contingency' that disdains any recognition of mutual subjectivity that might lead to social justice claims-making. The universal subjectivity of dependency is remasked in private discourses about risk, which serves the hegemonic aims of neo-liberal politics. The 'facts' of need have indeed become the 'politics of need interpretation' (Fraser, 1987). The obligation for the satisfaction of these needs has become, through the modern mechanism of governance, more a private than a public responsibility. It has also become an arena for the reintroduction of a male discourse of need and priority. The neo-liberal 'project' represents a 'remasculinization' of welfare. Such illiberal 'practices of moral government', Valverde argues, 'end up re-colonizing the white male adult's relation to himself' (1996: 359).

The critical point is how this remasking actually intersects with Foucault's work on governance and power. Fraser's aim may well have been to set out to identify 'a hegemonic complex of significations' (1996: 533) but this patterning of responses to risk has made the project of rendering the politics of significations more difficult – or if not more difficult, less able to be used. Part of the reason for this, Luhmann argues, is because establishing overall social legitimacy is one of the central issues in modernity. The classical hierarchies of power cannot be appealed to in fashioning political equity since the processes of legitimization refer no longer to the whole system but to Habermas' abstraction from it – or, similarly, to Rose's self-referent 'communities'. This occurs because governance really constrains political debate to issues about 'the representation of the system within the system'. The specific patterns of the significations that define neo-liberalism (the salience of the phrase 'there is no alternative' for example) construct a 'system within the system'. Contemporary post-modern politics really represents how powerful subsets have arrogated the imperative to legitimate only themselves. The hegemony comes out of the ability to circumscribe the system – to retain, for example, the 'exclusivity of the gift without the counter-gift'. Exposing the contradictions and the significations of how the notion of citizenship reciprocity is denied is important. However, critical theory must be concerned, not only to expose the occurrence of the paradoxical in the operations of social systems, but also to describe how such apparently paradoxical social systems are functional – how they elaborate and reproduce themselves (Luhmann, 1990: 15).

While constructing a genealogy of dependency is vital, the issues of governance, which Foucault also explicated, may well offer an explanation for the way that neo-liberal discourse sidetracked normative debate about welfare. The issue is how such systems became self-referential so that they could no longer stand outside their own internal certainties to experience the paradox of their own claims-making. As Foucault argues in one of his later commentaries:

> the failure of political theories is probably due neither to politics nor to theories but to the type of rationality in which they are rooted. The main characteristic of our modern rationality in this perspective is neither the constitution of the state, the coldest of all cold monsters, nor the rise of bourgeois individualism. I won't even say that it is a constant effort to integrate individuals into the political totality. I think that the main characteristic of our political rationality is the fact that this integration of the individuals in a community or in a totality results from a constant correlation between an increasing individualization and the reinforcement of this totality. (1988c: 161–2)

It is risk which has served to develop this perception of individualization, and it is the singular palimpsest of risk that reinforces the totality. However, as we have seen earlier, it is defined as a 'totality' but is really yet another 'abstraction'. The fact that it is an 'abstraction' serves our current political rationality that seeks to maintain a profound antinomy between the autonomous individual and the welfare 'other'. Actual social experiences, for Foucault, 'are not mere [individual] contingencies, they have complex contradictions of existence' (Cousins and Hussain, 1984: 262). This is the core of my argument that welfare policy reflects that notion of 'complex conditions' which occur *prior* to any one individual becoming a client. Welfare dependency is, therefore, a prior category of epistemological labelling and cannot, by definition, be associated solely with the individual claimant.

Draining the swamp of need

This is Young's (1996) colloquial definition of the intent of the neo-liberal project! It may well be fanciful to suggest any alternative to a competitive oppositional world, one driven by respective agency.[4] However, the simple question – what stops us from seeing the validity of 'common human needs' – doesn't completely disappear. Why is it that the welfare 'other' is so easily denied reasonable survival and social opportunity? Looking for answers to these questions takes us into the centre of Derrida's apparent conundrum – 'the establishing of relations between differences is also the promised complicity of a common element' (1982: 112). We have seen earlier how a defining aspect of neo-liberalism was the valorization of autonomous individualism. Respect may be shown the 'citizen-friend' but denied the 'citizen-stranger'. Constructing a pejorative 'relation of difference' between welfare dependency and autonomy reinforces 'the promised complicity of a common element'. Neo-liberalism requires a companionship of similarity – but only so far. It also depends upon the denial of that which it arrogates to itself.

It is this 'complicity' of the singular 'common element' that drives the reworking of dependency and risk. It destroys the legitimacy of social obligation that requires recognition of difference. What makes the neo-liberal denigration of dependency so apparently watertight is that adopting a rhetoric of crisis (Beck's apocalyptic risk society) makes any argument for commonality appear hollow, naïve and romantic. The leitmotiv of an individual battling self-responsibly against a risky and dangerous world now appears immutable. Assuming an inevitable cupidity in 'welfare-relevant situations' (cf. Le Grand, 1997) has become an essential part of the complicity of the successful. Directly opposing that complicity seems only to reinforce it. It is the nature of defensive individualism to thrive on opposition.

However, developing a genealogy of dependency and risk shows how both sides in the debate about welfare dependency are reflexively intertwined. Such analysis challenges both neo-liberal individualism and romantic communitarianism. We require a much clearer understanding of all the sets of arguments that go into the construction of 'story lines'[5] about welfare dependency. It requires an examination of the 'benign sterility' of how we construct the 'normal' autonomous individual who stands over against the increasingly visible 'social junk'.[6] How the fear and/or risk of dependency shapes the way welfare dependency has been framed is prototypically part of the new risk society. Similarly, we can examine the communitarian 'story lines' of welfare claim rights to see how they reflect the same issues of governance that has created the pejorative welfare 'other'.

Fraser's groundbreaking work on a genealogy of dependency, in contra-distinction to Foucault, explicitly welcomed locating this genealogical work within the context of normative discourse. As Fraser defines her intent, she had 'hoped precisely to enhance the potential for efficacious, intentional, oppositional agency' (1996: 533). It seems inevitable that the normative exposition of genealogy tends towards the oppositional areas of agency – what might be done to rectify specific disadvantages. This reflex response of opposition, towards 'refusal', cannot be disputed in terms of the politics of identity. However with respect to the politics of risk and dependency a normative focus on agency is delimiting. It is such a contested area that 'maintaining the fight' with our present 'weapons' seems to admit of no change; rather the reverse. It is all reified polemics, and Foucault's phrase is apt: 'polemics . . . is a parasitic figure on discussion and an obstacle to the search for truth' (1984e: 382). If public discourse about welfare depends on the polemics of agency and opposition (an acceptance that the public sphere can only be a primal arena of conflict) then the only possible system of governance is that predicated on domination.[7] The task is to see whether it might be possible to construct a genealogy of dependency that reaches beyond the validations of oppositional agency to a more fundamental critique of the norms that surround welfare dependency.

Beck's thesis about reflexive modernization, as we have seen, implies 'self-confrontation' – in the sense that the arrival of 'the risk epoch of modernity occurs *un*intentionally, *un*seen, compulsively, in the course of a dynamic of modernization which has made itself autonomous' (1996b: 28). Self-confrontation requires an acknowledgement that 'dispersed forms of critical knowledge partake in the formulation of new political interventions' (Hewitt, 1983: 76). The rhetorical dynamic against welfare dependency, central to the neo-liberal thesis of welfare, is powerful because it is similarly made to seem inevitable, compulsive and ineluctable. One significant difference is that the issues surrounding welfare dependency are not as apparently apocalyptic or unintentional and compulsive as the emergence of global risk and reflexive modernization.

We can, therefore, outline the 'shape' of a reflexive welfare dependency and see what relationship it has to the overarching theory of risk that Beck formulated. What might it mean to define dependency as reflexive and as having the same aspects of self-confrontation as risk society? The same critical scrutiny which is applied to the discourses about welfare dependency can equally be directed at the 'autonomous rational actor of modern discourse' (Petersen, 1997: 191). The rhetoric about the primacy of the solitary self has been vital to the maintenance of the polemic against welfare dependency. Whether we can still apply the tools of epistemology to establish the normative basis of so much of this neo-liberal depiction of welfare is an important and unresolved question.

Foucault and 'social security': the welfare 'gaze'

This investigation of risk has provided an opportunity to discuss the valuable contribution of Foucault to an analysis of welfare and social policy. The strength of Foucault's current appeal, in relation to social science analysis, is extraordinary. His whole *oeuvre* can sometimes stand like a 'reflection' outside the boundaries of our normal social policy discussions. Indeed it stands not only outside the boundaries of the categories of explanation that we seek to refine and to be clear about, but also against them. His depiction of the power of the 'professional gaze', an essential aspect of his analysis of normalizing power, can be turned back reflexively onto the 'certainties' of our social policy analyses.

In *The Birth of the Clinic* (1973) Foucault suggested that an essential aspect of the medical 'gaze' (or surveillance) was to be able to 'look with knowledge' upon another. The looking was not so much a discovery but a confirmation, an attempt to prove what was already known. For Foucault, the 'gaze' was 'master of its truth' (Miller, 1987: 147). Similarly, the 'welfare gaze' presupposes a knowledge that needs no looking – what Foucault importantly and elliptically called a 'speaking eye'. There is no discovery to be made. By virtue of being in a state of need the welfare claimant is already 'known' as dependent. The 'welfare gaze' therefore is contained within the process of how we define our response to need. To seek public support is to define yourself as needy, and by definition, to be dependent.

At times the manifold use of Foucault in the social sciences seems to have the character of an 'appeal', where the utilization of his writings approximates the search for 'proof texts' (cf. Mottier, 1995). Given the allusive character of his prose, that interpretation is understandable. As Goldstein has argued, there 'is something in Foucault's very unsettled nature – his famous changes of mind; his alterations between an icily cold, critical eye and shows of passion, between disdain for our old, self-deceptive liberal humanism and attachment to it – that fits the unsettled world' (1994: 15). However, we need to be cautious in searching for meanings not to parody what he has written, such that we fall into a vain polemical use of his ideas. The importance of Foucault is not only his relevance to an exegesis of the discourse about power/knowledge but also as knowingly misrepresenting the world as a counterfactual. He could, at one and the same time, say that his works were fundamentally fictional, that he'd 'never written anything but fictions', and yet still claim that his work would elucidate the 'truth' through his archaeological or genealogical project.

To take Foucault at face value, as Rorty does, and criticize him because of a 'false' or inadmissible contrast between truth and power, is to miss the point (1995: 440). What Foucault is trying to do is to 'induce effects of truth'. Whether the *Narrenschiff* (the ship of fools in *Madness and Civilization*) operated historically in the Middle Ages, exactly as Foucault argues, is not the issue. As Megill has suggested, it 'is not the [veracity] of the text but the *activity* that is central for Foucault, since he wants his texts to *change the world* by the power of their rhetoric' (1985: 184, my italics). The *Narrenschiff* depiction does, however, 'induce the effect of truth' in that it raises the validity of the process by which the so-called insane were removed from a frenetic and mad 'commerce' with the normal. The mad were increasingly isolated and locked away as public asylums emerged for that purpose, and so a distinction between the normal and the pathological had been institutionalized. Foucault's insights about the 'birth of the clinic', which are relevant to this discussion of welfare dependency and risk, are about the politicizing effects of the 'normal' (cf. Hacking, 1990; Miller, 1987). How that 'normal' has become part of the neo-liberal autonomous 'project' is also the great value of Fraser's work (see below).

Asylums of the mind: the isolation within the 'gaze'

The important aspect of Foucault's thought, for this study, is how in social security discourse the 'normal' no longer needs the 'asylum'. It is, as suggested earlier, the welfare dependent, themselves, who have internalized the 'gaze of surveillance'. The isolation is complete. The dependent are sequestered within their own minds; their own perception of disadvantage is therefore turned back upon themselves reflexively so that there is no possibility of a reciprocal 'gift' of citizenship.[8] In Foucault's terms, we can almost call this an 'asylum of the mind'. It is Foucault's 'effects of truth' that we must deal with (and use) to recognize how the issue is not just to articulate a genealogy of morals or dependency. What is at issue is the yawning gap we make between ourselves by distinguishing between the successful and the dependent. As Castel comments:

> Instead of segregating and eliminating undesirable elements from the social body, or reintegrating them more or less forcibly through corrective or therapeutic interventions, the emerging tendency is to assign different social destinies to individuals in line with their varying capacity to live up to the requirements of competitiveness and profitability. (1991: 294)

Again it is the issues surrounding the reflexiveness of risk which are important in this depiction of the 'dual society'. It is the complex associations of risk that can explain the nature of this huge gap. An analysis of risk may yet undo the certainty of our 'successful normality' and allow us to see how contingent it is, only marginally defensible as a quality of our autonomous selves. While the insane were separated out onto the 'ship of fools' they were not initially reified into the madness of the lonely, independently 'crazy' self. There was still the jeering and jousting of awkward communication. Only subsequently were the mad denied their subjectivity by incarceration. It was that which made them an object of medical or psychiatric 'knowledge', so that subsequently madness became a description of the object of knowledge and not the subject of knowing. They became a 'population', as welfare recipients have become, for neo-liberalism, a rejected 'population'. Subjective experiencing is reified into 'fact'.

Similarly, the welfare state created, within the notions of citizenship responsibility, the boundaries of the 'welfare gift'. Welfare recipients were expected to have some reciprocal responsibility (to get well, to look after themselves or their families better, to seek work etc.). Citizenship theory posed similar issues of a mutual knowing based upon an acknowledged intersubjectivity ('there but for the grace of God go I'). However, the nature of much anti-welfare, anti-dependency rhetoric does not assume the legitimacy of the need, let alone its unique subjectivity. The state of need (or lack) has become reified into the status of neediness. The 'social fact' has indeed become private risky knowledge. There can be no real exchange, therefore, between the autonomous and the dependent, except that of disdain. The only acceptable form of 'reciprocity' is not to be in a state of dependency. The double-bind of welfare is struck: *welfare recipients ought not to need that which demonstrably they do need*. The pendulum swings against the poor. As Johnson very interestingly suggests, Foucault deliberately adopted 'a rhetorical strategy of exaggeration aimed at establishing a critical perspective' (1997: 574). My task, throughout, has been to see how relevant Foucault's work on genealogies is to this discussion of risk and dependency.

Foucault established in his genealogical method a historical analysis of the limits that are imposed (the very structure of risk perception and analysis), and how we can go beyond them. Risks define the limits but also, in embracing them, provide a means of overcoming these limits: again he seems to be alluding to a belief that to fully experience risk is the way to 'truth' (cf. Miller, 1993). That Foucault does not seek, in his genealogical or historical analysis, any universalizing structures returns the question to the individual – to the particular and not to the general. For Foucault there is no ahistorical way to use 'language to represent reality or to use language as a vehicle for undistorted communication' (Nielsen, 1997: 6). On the face of it this reinforces a neo-liberal viewpoint about individualism. However, applying a genealogical analysis to welfare dependency 'in order to see the strangeness of our society's practices does not mean that . . . [Foucault] considers these practices meaningless'. These 'cultural practices' depend upon a social context, and 'since these practices have made us what we are, we have, perforce, some common footing from which to proceed, to understand, to act. But that foothold is no longer one which is universal, guaranteed, verified or grounded' (Dreyfus and Rabinow, 1986: 115).

Foucault's antipathy to the possibility of any universalizing structures cuts both ways. Anti-welfare cultural practices, which generalize and stigmatize welfare clients, represent an attempt to forge a 'common footing' (an identity of success) that is separated from the failure and risk encapsulated in the survival claims of welfare applicants. But if Foucault is correct, and welfare dependence is one of 'society's strange practices', then it must be understood as particular and contingent. There is no 'universal, guaranteed, verified or grounded' common footing from which to judge. The practice of defining such groups pejoratively is indicative of Foucault's claims about how power/knowledge assertions 'make us what we are'. We cannot generalize a universal moral assumption from the recognition of the practice, but we can see how these cultural practices are part of what it means to say that we 'know' that being on welfare represents a lesser choice. The act of forming such cultural definitions creates the language domain within which acts of knowledge or power operate.

Poverty 'wars': the denial of social rights

Colloquially, we might ask whether the 'war against poverty' has now inevitably become the 'war against the poor' (Asen, 1996; Loney, 1987). Derrida argued passionately that 'no degree of progress allows one to ignore that never before, in absolute figures, have so many men, women, and children been subjugated, starved, or exterminated on the earth' (1994: 85).[9] Various discourses of risk have been used to set out the nature of that 'war', to alter our perceptions about being dependent, or in need, so that now in our privatized certainty of normality we can rail against the 'social junk'. These sad and bizarre examples of the problems of welfare dependency are meant to be hidden away – to be the responsibility of our residual welfare 'safety nets', but certainly not to encroach on the public space of our neo-liberal individual freedoms. The welfare 'other' is to be defended against, seen as part of the context of risk, and is not to be understood, seen or recognized. This reindividualizing of risk in the face of the massive concerns about risk society reveals a paradox. The private palimpsest of risk overlays and distorts the public one. Vilification of welfare dependency suits the legitimating politics. Specific realities of human need and survival no longer compel a public political response. We are, seemingly, inured in our watching. Derrida comments that:

> this triumphant conjuration is striving in truth to disavow, and therefore to hide from, the fact that never, never in history, has the horizon of the thing whose survival is being celebrated (namely all the old models of the capitalist and liberal world) been as dark, threatening and threatened. (1994: 52)

The language of risk and its various epistemologies reflects defence against risk, not satisfaction of needs. The effect of this in terms of the discourses about welfare dependency is a grand 'emptying out' of the validity of social rights. Rights discourse in this new arena of the dominant risk society is increasingly allied with themes of protection not satisfaction. Previously, the legitimization of rights presupposed the welfare state. The nature of welfare discourse has totally changed. Now the perspectives on governance, in an age of risk, imply that the proper role of the state is not the meeting of needs, and the satisfaction of rights, but protection against risk.

While we might argue that the new attitudes toward dependency imply the 'emptying out' of former rights and an attempt to 'hide away' welfare failure within the compliant self of the claimant, the discourse about welfare dependency is not hidden away. It has become very much part of the justifications for the massive deregulation of the welfare state. The contradiction is important, since the nature of that contradiction reveals the reflexiveness of the arguments about the 'perils' of welfare

dependency. Its emergence is a response to risk, but it also is fundamentally part of the way that neo-liberal politics establishes a Foucauldian
'governance' that limits our understanding of need and survival. That
requires a reworking of welfare discourses away from needs and rights,
towards threat and risk. Foucault's important insights about how the
modern state establishes systems of governance is directly related to the
recasting of welfare discourses. This means that welfare

> knowledges are no longer to be regarded as part of the order of representation
> or signification. The idea is to treat discursive materials less as representing the
> things on which they bear, than as a means of attempting to *organise* them.
> (Minson, 1985: 124)

Public discussion about welfare dependency is designed to inculcate a
sense of the overwhelming threat that welfare transfer payments create –
a fundamental risk to a healthy economy. The discourse is no longer
about the legitimization of individual needs but about the necessity to
publicly organize against the risks involved in maintaining excessive
levels of financial transfer. To deny the legitimacy of 'representation' or
'signification', in the dominant discourses, is the means by which a new
reflexive discourse of welfare dependency is created.

Neo-liberal 'story lines': welfare epistemologies

The idea of a 'story line' which occurs in theories of discourse analysis is
useful in charting the range of assumptions that are part of the debate
about welfare dependency. Neo-liberal welfare 'story lines' constantly
portray welfare negatively by constructing a discourse about the perils of
dependency. Hajer provides a possible model to explicate the new order
of welfare dependency. While his concerns are to discuss issues of
ecological modernization (and outline the production of new social
orders with respect to ecology), his schema can be transferred to this
specific social policy debate. He contends that it is necessary 'to reconstruct the social construction of the reductions, exclusions and choices'
that typify these new social orders before generating any 'interweaving
of correlations' (1996: 257).

   The following three discourses clarify our understanding of welfare
dependency. Dependency can be depicted as an issue of reduction; it can
be depicted as an aspect of social exclusion; and it can reflect the specifics
of choice as well as the epistemology of choosing. These three aspects of
dependency correspond in significant ways to the 'registers of meaning'
first formulated by Fraser and Gordon, when establishing their model of
dependency. They describe four aspects: an economic register, where the
requirements for survival depend on the action of another; a 'socio-legal
status', where personal identity is construed on the basis of status;
dependency resulting from political subjection; and, finally, dependency

defined as a moral/psychological question depicting personal inadequacy and consequent neediness (1994a: 312). The categories of reduction, exclusion and choice clearly correspond to these four 'registers'. The overlay of all these various aspects of risk is significant to the further explication of a genealogy of dependency.

Dependency: risk and reduction

The issues surrounding dependency are often framed as risk reduction – borrowing from the jargon of the business world the need to limit exposure to risk. The stigma of dependency, as we have seen, is a reflexive counterpoint to success. Here legitimate needs and social dependence are defined as 'sectorial interest', not rights or legitimate areas for recognition. The counter-argument to these economistic views is the basic concern of social policy, which is that:

> dependency and social needs are not merely caused by social forces and do not exist as pure facts. They are constructed within the discourse of social policy as categories, classification systems and forms of knowledge by individuals and groups within the political, administrative and economic spheres. (Hewitt, 1983: 67–8)

Dependency: an aspect of social exclusion

The subjectification of welfare dependency becomes an aspect of the self rather than any social or needful situation that might be assumed to have also created it. Dependency therefore is related not only to poverty, youth, ill-health etc. but to the 'problem' of having poverty, youth and ill-health as an expression of the self. We cannot simply talk of 'dependency as a social relation of subordination' (Fraser and Gordon, 1994a). The subordination is now in the self of the person who is a welfare claimant. That this self is quintessentially female has been well attested. As Mink argues, 'exhortations against single pregnancy, and for marriage and child support, all reflect persistent faith that the economic security of women and children depends upon their relation to men' (1994: 121). We need to see the 'truths' of Foucault's urgent perspective to free the surveilled, measured and dominated subjects of our 'welfare wars'. Or more particularly, we need to see how normalizing welfare practices establish the very scourge of so-called dependency that we want to avoid.

Dependency: the need for choices

Within this aspect falls all the understandings of dependency associated with what Fraser and Gordon (1994a; 1994b) describe as the movement from the 'natural and proper' usage of dependency, in the industrial age, to a post-industrial usage where all aspects of dependency are described as 'avoidable and blameworthy'. The correspondence to my thesis about risk and the construction of a genealogy of dependency is clear. We have seen how fundamentally risk has been reconstructed to reflect the generation of a personal focus on autonomy and survival. That such autonomy is quintessentially male is also significant. As Fraser has suggested:

> Participants in the 'masculine' subsystem are positioned as *rights-bearing beneficiaries and purchasing consumers of services*. Participants in the 'feminine' subsystem, on the other hand, are positioned as *dependent clients*. (1987: 113)

Conclusion: the false separation of the one and the many

Can welfare clients ever be 'recognized' (in Honneth's terms) or is Foucault correct in arguing that welfare is fundamentally a disciplinary activity (a different institution of violence), first of liberal and now of neo-liberal social policy? However we seek to answer that question it is clear, from the foregoing, that rejection of welfare recipients into a 'dependency class' is reflexive.[10] It constitutes the neo-liberal individual in the way that Foucault could argue the *Narrenschiff* created an opportunity for the commerce and dialogue of the rejected to reinforce the normal. Sequestration of welfare beneficiaries into the unseen and unknowable is necessary in order to sustain the neo-liberal individual project. Without the rejected obverse, the 'independence' of the successful collapses into only a private and encapsulated hedge against risk. The contextualizing of the rejected other (the welfare dependent – who are really a collectivized other) is necessary to assert claims for individual autonomy. Thus the neo-liberal project needs the risk society, indeed has even created the necessity for it, in order to prove the irreducible truth of its own presumption.

This brings us back into the paradoxical heart of risk analysis in that it stigmatizes welfare dependency on the basis of a generalized analysis of risk, which Foucault argues is not really possible. Like the triumphant individual of public choice theory who seeks to maximize their own advantage, who is seen to be unique, random, capricious (utterly personal) – so too must the welfare client be construed. We cannot logically argue for a category of uniqueness to apply to one subset of individual risk and not the other (cf. Bauman, 1997). Welfare dependency is only a general category because we choose to frame it that way. That it is possible to universalize welfare need, but particularize individual educational or employment success, is essentially an epistemology, a language of market winners and losers: both are socially constructed 'domains of speech'.

Foucault's 'archaeological step' really poses the question that there can be no undifferentiated starting point – no equal stepping off into the dark. We may share 'common practices' in our search for education, employment, survival and meaning but there is no one single point of departure. In that respect the advent of our life journeys *is* singular and particular. There is no 'level playing field' that thrusts us all, similarly equipped, into random competition. Risk and randomness are the twin 'devils' of chance that is the context of the lived life. To be successful or dependent has little to do with some presumed category or quality of personality, or with individual power and courage. Success and dependency arise out of Beck's risk society with a suddenness and brutality that ought to give us pause – one which leads us into aspects of Honneth's paradigm of recognition, as well as Goodin's (1985) reflections on the importance of acknowledging mutual vulnerabilities.

Risk and threat are common and not singular. This commonness arises out of a personal recognition of mutual uniqueness that does not lead into the defensiveness of risk and loss, but rather uses that sense of risk and loss to associate with the other. Individual uniqueness is always necessarily reflexive. We define ourselves as individuals not by rejecting the uniqueness of the other, but by claiming the singularity of the other as reflective of our own idiosyncrasy. We can only be truly enlightened in the Kantian sense by perceiving that individual rationality and uniqueness require recognition, and not undifferentiated defence. Beyond the power to use each other lies the possibility of validating our mutual political and social dependency. Perhaps at the end of all our speculative 'journeys' we come back to the beginning of a pragmatic common-sense and know it for the first time. Rorty can have the last word here:

> the rich democracies of the present day already contain the sorts of institutions necessary to their own reform . . . communication among the citizens of those democracies is not 'distorted' by anything more esoteric than greed, fear, ignorance and resentment . . . the principal institutions of contemporary democratic societies do not require 'unmasking' but rather strenuous utilization, supplemented by luck. (1995: 459)

Notes

1 A palimpsest is an original manuscript that is effaced and overwritten. The imagery seems singularly appropriate in this discussion of risk and dependency, particularly as these concepts of risk are continually being 'overwritten' to serve new political ends. Zygmunt Bauman has coined the phrase 'palimpsest identity' to refer to an aspect of personal self-image 'where the art of forgetting is an asset' within 'postmodern uncertainty' (1997: 25).

2 Habermas has argued that the 'project of the welfare state' has 'grown reflexive' in the necessity to abandon the previous utopian dreams of a universal labouring society (1986: 15).

3 See Le Grand (1997: 158).

4 Honneth, for instance, has argued 'that motives for social resistance and rebellion are formed in the context of moral experiences stemming from the violation of deeply rooted expectations regarding recognition' (1995b: 163).

5 A 'story line' is a concept related to discourse analysis which represents not only the content of the specific ways that welfare dependency (for example) is depicted but also how the stories come to have an independent 'life of their own' (cf. Hajer, 1995; 1996: 63).

6 The evocative phrase comes from this quote of Pratt's:

the subjection of economics to market forces and the cutting back of welfare programmes of assistance have led to the re-creation of risks which welfare had alleviated – poverty, unemployment and the formation of a new indigent class – vagrants, beggars, the homeless, the mentally ill with criminal tendencies who now find themselves left to roam the streets, holding conversations with imaginary colleagues, an assorted collection of 'social junk'. (1996: 258)

7 The question of polemics and critical theory is clearly important, but in the 'passion for change' the polemicist 'relies on a legitimacy that . . . the adversary is by definition denied'. Foucault goes on to suggest that:

Polemics defines alliances, recruits partisans, unites interests or opinions, represents a party; it establishes the other as an enemy, an upholder of opposed interest against which one must fight until the moment this enemy is defeated and either surrenders or disappears. (1984e: 382–3).

8 There are many valuable studies of how 'dependency relationships are enculturated into social habits and identities'. As Wynne suggests, many smaller communities, who are dependent on one major employer, when faced with massive redundancy have developed a 'long-standing sense of self-denigration at "allowing" their own dependency on such an untrustworthy owner and employer' (1996: 51).

9 That is not to lay the blame for this at the 'doorstep' of welfare!

10 Heclo comments that:

in the organized way through which power is exercised . . . poor people do not matter very much . . . Antipoverty policies are less a matter of demands poor people make in the political process and more a function of what other people decide to do to and for them. (1994: 397)

AFTERWORD

FOUCAULT'S COLDEST OF ALL COLD MONSTERS!

> Now we all live, comparatively speaking, in far too great security for us ever to acquire a sound knowledge of man . . . As long as truths do not cut into our flesh with knives, we retain a secret contempt for them: they still appear to us too much like 'winged dreams', as though we were free to have them or not have them.
>
> (Nietzsche, 1997: 192)

For Foucault the 'coldest of all cold monsters' was of course the state! He did not assume that it was possible to 'defeat' the disciplinary society and replace it with a truly human one. Like Nietzsche (from whom he borrowed the phrase)[1] he might well have seen risk (and the need for security) as fashioning a politic that made 'sound knowledge' of each other impossible. He found the antinomy of 'large destructive mechanisms and institutions oriented toward the care of individual life', coexisting in politics, genuinely puzzling and needing investigation (1988c: 147).

We have seen how risk is an intrinsic part of the genesis of 'self-politicization' within neo-liberalism. Diverse practices of governance, developed out of the political protection of that radical 'self-politicization', are reflexive. Different antinomies of control and care do coexist. The welfare 'other', subject to the disciplinary politics of the state, is the obverse, not the separate object of that 'self-politicization'. Understanding that our divisive politics *are* founded on complex reifications of risk – both to defend the project of self-politicization, and to attack recognized social need – allows us to recognize the political legitimacy of that obverse. It would require, as Foucault argued, that the 'discourse of subjectivity . . . be cut loose from its moorings in bourgeois individualism' (Richters, 1988: 632). Allowing for a thorough examination of the politics of security and risk, and especially how this has created our deep social divisions, might yet let us 'acquire a sound knowledge of' each other.

The 'truths', which I have been canvassing in respect of risk, are ultimately normative in that they come from a determination to respect the true nature of the welfare 'other'. The character degradation that typifies so much of the argument for the need to reimpose a moral revaluation of welfare is vapid. The media 'sound bytes' that create such instantaneous assumptions about the perfidy of welfare claimants can be rejected. Suggesting that we listen to the 'truths' of those who must survive as welfare beneficiaries may seem hopelessly romantic – the 'winged dreams' of Nietzsche that are so apparently evanescent. Yet the moral vision that welfare might express the desire for a more civil and nurturing society need not be abandoned. Social policy requires a new language if we are to 'encounter the otherness of need in each other' (Goodin, 1985; 1988; Hewitt, 1994: 54).

Fundamentally, the issue is whether we can find a position for critical theory that can elucidate the whole, one that can set out the reasons why the normativeness of its inclusive stance should be respected. It may well be that espousing a critical position requires an adoption of a stance, an attitude, rather than seeking to complete an analysis that could be normative (cf. Valero-Silva, 1996). Foucault explicitly rejected the possibility of a normative stance, let alone the possibility of explicating policy on the basis of such assumptions! However, I think Fraser is correct in her rejection of this pessimism (1996: 533). It is rather an attitude towards dependency that is an appropriate normative concern. This is not to argue for the possibility of 'undistorted discourse'. Given our constant propensity to establish 'meta-narratives' (our own 'story lines') we can take an ironic, yet passionate, position towards them. Foucault did not reject the valid search for some 'understanding of what a modern ethic would look like' (Nielsen, 1997: 9). In searching for such an ethic, social policy must articulate how the 'sovereign' common-sense of neo-liberalism can be challenged. Ironically it is Foucault who has sketched out the clearest perspective on how this might be achieved.

Risk and social policies: what is to be done?

In previous chapters we have discussed aspects of Foucault's thinking about governmentality, and the notions of sovereignty that it entailed. In one of his most famous papers, 'On governmentality', he made the observation that 'whereas the end of sovereignty is internal to itself and possesses its own . . . laws, the finality of government resides in the things it manages and in the pursuit of . . . tactics' (1979: 13). The depiction of the 'arts' of government as *tactics* rather than *laws* might seem odd, given the legislative and mandating power of the state. Making the point of distinguishing between law and tactics is important. It opens up the possibility of challenge and counter-tactic. For example, if the neo-liberal rhetoric of common-sense can be defined as tactical, rather than a law of governance, then dissent can more easily be lodged against its 'truth-claims'. The polemic of common-sense had reified risks, their definition, their locales and their resolution into the tight logic of specific policy. It is possible, as a counter-tactic, to raise such reifications for scrutiny. Another is to argue that such reifications are in fact immanent discourses, which neglect the social 'realities' of the welfare 'other'.

We could perhaps retreat into the security of Foucault's canard that academic discourse ought not to be a vehicle for practical injunction: 'love this; hate that; do this; refuse that' (Gordon, 1991: 6). However, in the preface to the edited volume which includes Gordon's classic paper, the editors state that:

> Foucault observed that there is a parcel of thought in even the crassest and most obtuse parts of social reality, which is why criticism can be a real power for change, depriving some practices of their self-evidence, extending the bounds of the thinkable to permit the invention of others. (Burchell et al., 1991: x)

In the end, the continuing viability of neo-liberal welfare policy will depend on whether individual autonomy and security can be linked together in the development of policies that are mutually enhancing. To suggest this is not an 'illusory' contradiction. It is rather an invitation to both aspects of that policy continuum to submit their 'practices', their 'arts' of government, to mutual scrutiny. One vehicle for this is a thorough analysis of risk and how the palimpsests of each can be merged and rewritten.

The enormous logic of change unleashed by neo-liberal 'mentalities of rule' is rational and premised on a valorization of common-sense. However, there is another aspect to how such particular 'mentalities of rule', the 'practices' of governance, can be challenged. Neo-liberal 'mentalities of rule' have reified the logic of common-sense into a set of explicit norms. However, hidden in these norms is a longing for transcendence – a paradoxical desire to 'escape' the contingent and risky mundane. Common-sense has become part of the 'sovereignty' of neo-liberal politics. The contingent is accorded universal significance. This reflects Kant's assumption that 'the finite human being cannot avoid the illusion of the infinite (i.e. sovereign) subject precisely because it is infinite'. Foucault agrees that reifying political power 'is indeed possible on the condition that human beings are finite'. However, he also contends that '*it is precisely for this reason* that one should not accept the notion of an "infinite subject" of power' (Cousins and Hussain, 1984: 263; Doxiadis, 1997: 539–40). Neo-liberalism, like any political ideology, cannot lay total claim to common-sense.

Those reifications that depended upon the hidden 'sovereignty of the infinite' are illogical. They are only one more ideological throw of the contingent philosophical dice. This is the simple, but powerful, challenge to the awful rhetorical hegemony of neo-liberalism, which rejects the legitimacy of the welfare 'other'. The 'sovereignty' of that rejection is unsustainable. Neo-liberal social policy demonstrates the 'despotism' intrinsic to the moral practices of governance inherent in 'the paradigmatic liberal subject's relation to himself' (Valverde, 1996: 359). Such despotism creates a crisis view of welfare support that is akin to a mentality of triage. This is the paradox: only those who can be 'saved' by their own efforts will get the help they need.

'Governing through freedom': some preliminary thoughts

This apparent paradox is, as we have seen, at the heart of the governmentality literature. Various environmental, ecological and risk debates, which fashion the nature of modern politics, reflect a much wider problem. These concern, as Wynne argues,

> the larger crises of legitimacy facing modern, economic, scientific-technical and political institutions, and the search for new forms of legitimate order and authority . . . new forms of emergent political order, with new configurations of global vision and local rootedness, will emerge – are perhaps emerging – in which further imaginations of the relationships between knowledge and human values will be vital. In seeking the basis of more legitimate, less alienating forms of public knowledge, and stable authority out of present conditions of incoherence and disorientation, new constitutional norms of valid knowledge may be articulated. (1996: 78)

Making prognostications is often not wise, but I think we can discern something of the shape of our future politics which arises out of the contracting out and privatization of health and social services. There we see renewed demands for a 'managerial commodification' emphasizing the sick as consumers of health 'goods' and no longer patients to be served. Nevertheless, in the management of health services (and in the provision of social welfare services), despite all the language of 'product', the notion of 'service' has never been completely swamped. The valorization of 'service' is arguably part of the 'freedom' of highly qualified professionals to respond to health needs on the basis of their ethical commitments.[2] Quite complex forces of managerialism and organizational theory are wrapped up in these ideas. I do not intend to try 'unwrapping' them here. What I suggest is that these micro-aspects of governance, through contract, have the potential to redraft our future social policies – how they are being 'mapped' and will be implemented. The question is not either *product* or *service* but how these are being expressed within new management structures.

The glimmerings of Wynne's point that 'new forms of emergent political order, with new configurations of global vision and local rootedness, will emerge' can be seen in the health services. My speculative contention (really only a *jeu d'esprit*) is that health and social service professionals have the capacity to become 'unionized' at the level of client need, and not specifically in their own self-interest. The neo-liberal 'management' of politics has the capacity to introduce new and unintended opportunities for political coalitions that do not arise in protest from 'below'. Challenges to the power of the former liberal state were, in part, the consequence of the rise of unionized labour. New challenges to neo-liberal states may well come from coalitions born out of the frustration at not being able to deliver quality services – mandated by the respective codes of ethics of professional groups. Foucault said of these professions, and their disciplinary nature, that 'human science . . . constitutes their domain, and clinical knowledge their jurisprudence' (1980: 107). The 'sacred' language of *service* still jousts, for its defenders, with the 'profane' language of managed *product*, and vice versa.[3] Social service *clients* now are reframed as *users* and *consumers*. Once these professionals equate the provision of their specialist services as a way to manage the world, as an aspect of governance, then the potential is there for both intended and unintended systemic challenges. The complete marketization of the social world that the penetration of the public sector has witnessed as a result of neo-liberal attacks on social provision still has these issues of professional service 'stuck in its throat'!

Professionals have, individually, been used to the 'public fight'. However, what may be different is the suggestion that we are witnessing a move from personal sporadic outbursts in the media towards a clearer realization that 'management' is an intrinsic part of the professional medical role. It is the doctors (in the hospital systems) who commit resources and prioritize spending. Doctors are realizing how necessary it is to place themselves within 'the control room' of the health reforms and not to stand to one side. There are interesting examples of this occurring in New Zealand where health professionals, operating within a 'funder/ provider' contracting system of governance, are taking on the role of chief executive officers and senior management. It is doctors (in these roles) who are managing public opinion to pressure governments for more resources. While that is a more uncertain general strategy (at a macro-level of demand for their hospitals for example) it will be different if the professionals themselves start to manage the publicity for the needs of client/patients.

The challenges that came from the 'socialism of the dispossessed', Foucault's 'subjugated knowledges', are spent. A new discourse for that is yet to be outlined. But the challenges that will come from professional opinion, *collectivized within a new understanding of managerial* power, will be considerable. Opposition to the constricting and eviscerating rhetoric of neo-liberalism is only now being enjoined at these professional levels.

It is a contentious power, lying in wait. The destruction of a service ethos is well proven within public sector bureaucracies. Whether it is yet dead, within the professionals' own requirements to deliver high quality and verifiable health and welfare services, remains to be seen. As Beck concluded:

> are we dependent on the experts for every detail in issues concerning survival, or does the culturally manufactured perceptibility of hazards restore to us the competence to judge for ourselves? Are the only alternatives now an authoritarian or a critical technocracy? Or is there a way of counteracting the disempowerment and expropriation of everyday life in hazard civilization? (1995a: 184)

This challenge to 'disempowerment', if it comes, will be the more powerful for neo-liberal managerialism because it will be a revolt, not from the easily dismissed 'other' but from 'their own'. That may well fracture the tight logic of the managerial consensus. Client representation on boards of social agencies was a failed community experiment. Countervailing 'voices' are still needed at the level of policy analysis. Social policy needs to expose how 'unified epistemologically' are the social experts who pronounce on welfare issues. This new professional disquiet may provide the impetus for a revaluation of welfare social service ethos.

What we may see emerge is a new politics of professional competition – a politics in 'which new imaginations of the relationships between universal knowledge and human values' are expressed in new coalitions. Risk is no longer devolved onto the client but increasingly involves the professional who delivers the service.[4] There is a reflexiveness of mutual responsibility for outcome, which is a simulacrum of contract. That is where the epistemology of neo-liberalism will be caught because it is very hard for it to maintain its hegemony without maintaining (to use *its* sacred language) the fundament of contract relationships. The relationship of this potential new form of public mobilzation is an interesting reversal of Foucault's 'gaze' which we discussed earlier.

What nature of 'canvas': private or public?

Posing the possibility of alternatives in current welfare policy runs the risk of appearing to present aspects that can be dismissed as social policy *redux*. We are so feverishly painting private canvases that anyone setting out to inscribe tentative marks on a public one is dismissed *tout court*. Beck, less uncertain about the 'problems' in doing this (within the looming shadow of his risk society), has set out three future strategies. His aim was to 'beat it into the heads of these pseudo-free democrats, who turn a deaf ear to historical experience, that the market fundamentalism they idolize is a form of democratic illiteracy' (1997a: 53).

Quite how he intended to do that is not clear! Beck does rightly identify that where there were once two 'employers', capitalism and the state, there is now only one. However, his panegyric to a lost capitalist vision, where the state had been in 'social competition' within what he calls 'jobless capitalism', has aspects of a sociological 'Chicken Little'. Perhaps the 'sky will fall': but such rhetorical challenges seem never to have escaped from the seductions of a philosophical *manqué*. We need a more robust language!

Beck offers a choice for what he calls the invigoration of 'public work', as an alternative to passivity.[5] This involves three aspects: active compassion, practical critique and active democracy. Active compassion means 'active resistance to indifference' – all the ways that 'civil society' can be reclaimed through strategies of active involvement. Practical critique represents the aspects of citizen inquiry and lobbying and 'resistance'. Active democracy refers to all the explicit ways that a concept of civil society can be brought back onto the political agenda. Beck's conclusion is that the injustices arising from 'globalization must be made accountable for the general welfare' (1997a: 56).[6] In order to 'paint on the larger canvas', he suggests that reinvigoration of civil society will require alteration to taxation systems. He raises the 'unspoken' issue that has social coherence but no current political feasibility.[7] In summary, he wants an increase in tax abatement for contributions to the general welfare. He also wants a 'tax-financed basic support payment' so that people who are involved in voluntary social organizations can receive a 'public stipend'. His third aspect, a category of general 'citizen's support', is an unambiguous manifesto for a civil society paid for by an increase in taxation! No matter how laudable this is, the dominant rhetoric picks it off so easily with variations of the 'nice but not affordable argument', or more pejoratively with 'Why should my money go to pay for a life-style choice of non-work?'

Social 'knights' and private 'knaves'

In an illuminating article Le Grand (1997) picks up this theme and describes three categories of motivation and behaviour (*knights, knaves* and *pawns*). His thesis is that major changes in welfare systems have resulted from politicians and policy-makers assuming the worst about the motivations of those who need welfare assistance. Describing that opinion, he says 'in most situations of relevance to welfare, the individuals concerned are more likely to be self-interested than public-spirited' (1997: 160). He also sets out an exposition of 'legal welfare' and the possibilities of what he calls new 'robust' welfare strategies.[8] Both aspects of his paper merit some comment in this postscript about risk and social policy and the implications of this for future welfare strategies.

I agree that we do not know whether 'in welfare-relevant situations' it is possible to ascribe such universal assumptions about basic perfidy, or if other motivations obtain that we do not see. Social policy needs more empirical studies of the 'story lines' of welfare recipients – an inter-weaving of quantitative research and social criticism. That our public depictions are so fraught and disrespectful reveals the urgent need for this. The rhetoric is so limiting and deadening. We need to apply these discourses, as I have argued previously, to generate a new Foucauldian 'genealogy' of welfare dependency. Epistemological challenges to neo-liberalism's assumption that welfare recipients are all knaves are easily fended away. Le Grand's use of Etzioni's assumptions, to push for re-education in the civic virtues by some process of conversion from the moral status of knave to knight, is the weakest aspect of his paper. The task is not to mount a direct challenge to these 'normative' belief systems but to explode what they mean through an analysis of their 'practice', not their intent. Attacking 'false' or selfish 'knavish' behaviour directly simply will not work: it is difficult, as Foucault said, to 'get into people's heads' to try and refashion belief.

When Le Grand turns to an analysis of 'legal' welfare and the possibility of new partnership welfare strategies his argument is much more convincing.[9] These new strategies, while having an implicit hope of attitudinal change, are practical and achievable – or at the very least they are debatable at the policy level. So too is his consideration of *obligation alimentaire*.[10] However, the question still remains (in some minds at least): if we learn to recognize and respect the legitimacy of 'being on welfare' through greater public recognition of the welfare 'story lines', would we be willing to pay more for quality social support? Or will we still rather maintain a punitive, minimal welfare state? Were we ever, in Le Grand's terms, knights and can we regain our 'social knighthoods'? One suspects a certain resignation in the 'structure' of the analysis that posits knights, knaves and pawns. The continuum is really a binary one between knaves and knights. Pawns' motivations are always consequent to the prior action of the others. This raises the question as to whether we can generate social policy theorizing that can encompass Foucault's genealogy of the 'practices' of welfare.

The achievement of that will depend upon the successful challenge to the malign connection of incontrovertible common-sense and 'expert knowledges'. How well fresh intellectual campaigns can be mounted against the multitudinous restrictions that expertise entails is vital. Wynne has mounted the most articulate counter-argument to the Gordian knot of expertise and common-sense. He sets out a complex argument, against Beck's and Giddens' notions of reflexive modernization, and defends the importance of lay knowledge against arrogant and norm-ative interpretative expertise. He argues that in the 'hiddenness' of such lay knowledges lie the seeds for transforming 'modernity's ahuman and alienating universals' of common-sense. Opposing the 'solutions of expertise' may allow us to reveal some aspects of how to achieve Honneth's 'recognition', or understand other discourses by listening to Hajer's 'story lines'. Wynne's hope is that we gain 'inspiration to find the collective self-conceptions that can sustain universals that do not bury the traces of their own human commitment and responsibility' (1996: 78).

Notwithstanding the significant integration of present welfare and social policy that Le Grand has achieved, basing the analysis too squarely on the quicksands of human motivations is a strength (in that we require that information for an accurate assessment of welfare 'story lines') and is also strategically flawed. Relying on an analysis of the stereotypes of labelling theory focuses on the subjective nature of welfare disciplinary knowledges and not on their defining function within society. There is a sense in which such analyses implicitly reinforce rather than challenge dominant political 'practices'. We do need to find ways to challenge the hermeneutics of negativity that surrounds the welfare recipient. What Le Grand points to is the necessity to know more about the personal motivations of these recipients. Good and much needed though such surveys of attitudes and beliefs might be, we need a more compelling analysis. Le Grand may indeed be correct in assuming that this is not feasible. But if not, then the impossibility of this must be proven on a wider canvas than the variability of human motivation. Whether Beck's 'larger canvas' will suffice requires further work. This exploration into risk has sought to find one means, at least, to lever that vigorous neo-liberal rhetoric of common-sense.

The shape of future welfare discourses

This study of risk and social policy is obviously only tentative, aimed more at generating debate than foreclosing it. The subtext of my argument, throughout, is that neo-liberalism is not *ultimately* just a political philosophy of the individual subjective self. *It is side, back and middle of the whole canvas!* It stands revealed for what it is, a totalizing and normative political epistemology – a sophisticated Foucauldian set of governmental 'practices' waiting to be deconstructed. The opportunity is there for us to do this work.

It will be important for us to reflect 'on why so many crucial questions have been posed in such profoundly distorted ways' (Maguire, 1996: 171). The pejorativeness of anti-welfare rhetoric depends upon the structure of an argument that the 'fault' of the system lies with those who apparently misuse it. My purpose has been to sketch out the possibility that the 'fault' lies in the system itself and that misuse is predicated by its very structure. As Wynne has commented:

the powerless always tend to rationalise and thus consolidate their own impotence and apathy because to do otherwise is to expose themselves to the greater pain of *explicit* recognition of their own neglect and marginality. (1996: 53)

It is the cultural narrative of both sides of the welfare 'divide' that are required to be set alongside each other. The neo-liberal 'logic' behind the association of security, not with the social but with individual independence, can now be seen as a necessary part of the questions which social policy can address. Focusing only on welfare dependency misses the point. The more important question is whether we can, or will, address the wider issue. Given our current focus on independent individualism, it is not easy to see how we can.

We have destroyed the general community ethic of mutual responsibility that did inform the ethos of those who framed social democratic welfare state policies. Fragmenting 'responsibility' into a personal privatized reality has clearly generated an enormous creative energy in those now free to pursue the opportunities that a deregulated society and economy offer. The productive creativity of that cannot be gainsaid. But risks are still 'delivered', so to speak, in an obviously unequal way. The obvious inequalities of genetic, social and familial inheritance are not easily dismissed. However, our social policies are increasingly framed within discourses of equality – especially the discourses of equality associated with the rhetoric of individual responsibility and opportunity. The concept of welfare 'safety net' is not a sufficient idea to contain the reality of the denied 'voice' of welfare discourses. Constraining the manifold differences of that 'voice' within such narrow ideas of risk, security and individual responsibility serves a much narrower and tighter purpose.

The current debates about welfare dependency and risk will only produce some 'light' if we are willing to consider the whole interactive policy system surrounding welfare. As Lowi (1990) has trenchantly concluded, the 'problem' in the present climate is that there are two apparently incompatible public policy issues: one is systemic, universal and general; the other specific, regulatory and 'piecemeal'. The welfare state was an 'insurance state'. It involved a raft of social polices which attempted, systemically, to

democratize the burden of bad outcomes by removing most of the blame and indemnifying as many of the victims as possible. But this half of the public policy approach to risk works precisely because the welfare state, functioning as it does through the reality and the conceptualization of insurance, works best at the level of the largest possible universe. The welfare state was, in effect, made to order for the emergent systems approach to social policy. (1990: 38)

The oversight, monitoring and implementation of these systemic policies are always individual and particular. The whole complex of regulations surrounding welfare 'cannot grapple with the system at all but only with specific conducts that may, cumulatively, improve the system someday, somewhere down the line'. Fundamentally, Lowi presents the paradox 'regulation can't deal directly with risk at all. Risk is a system concept, and regulation has to concern itself with specific conduct' (1990: 39). This is a significant argument, daily recorded in the problems faced by welfare bureaucracies. Examining the welfare claimant in the 'harsh winds' of a regulatory climate, which cannot individualize the welfare claimant, might well lead to a wider evaluation of the welfare state. Rationales for the institution of the 'old' welfare state involved aspects of a moral viewpoint, even perhaps a collective 'disgust' about the crude facts of social and economic disadvantage. Contemporary welfare systems do not express such altruistic social motivations. However, as Lowi has demonstrated, they face an almost impossible task. We require a thorough evaluation of the limits of such welfare practices.

Conclusion

The impetus of the Enlightenment project was to prove that politics would ultimately be answerable to reason. But government as a 'conduct' of 'conduct' turns the rationality of government into an individual 'affair' involving all the 'irrationality' of private fears about risk. As Gordon (1991) concludes, despite his disavowal of any normative intention or prescriptive injunction, 'politics becomes, in a new sense, answerable to ethics'. The ineluctable may be more malleable than we think. Beck's ubiquitous risk society might make us more aware that we are 'more contingent, recent and modifiable than we think' (1991: 48). The wildness of difference in post-modernity need not blind us to the obvious fact that such differences do exist together, within the same time frame of experience, if little else. To 'engage the post-modern arts,' as Dumm suggests, 'may be to participate in the always sceptical but always affirmative project of making the potential moment of freedom actual' (1988: 224). How we are to make possible a comprehensive recognition of difference (and recognition of similarity) will obviously preoccupy our immediate and long-term social debates. We do not know how to accomplish this but perhaps it must start with *that* acknowledgement at the very least. What we currently do to each other in our welfare discourses is repeat the mistakes of the past. We need at the very least, as Donzelot argues, to '*make use of our conflicts instead of trying to eliminate them*' (1991: 178, my italics). We are in danger of institutionalizing a new/old version of 'disciplinary welfare' that is fundamentally driven by an angry uncertainty we neither acknowledge nor will admit.

We need to go on articulating the values as well as the practicality of welfare. The ideological debates are crucial. But so too is the patient unravelling of the 'genealogies' of welfare policy and discourse. Only by maintaining both an ideological scrutiny and an analysis of government 'practice' can we expect to challenge the present. In Bauman's words, we need to go on 'asking such questions as fear final answers more than they fear the prospect of remaining unanswered' (1997: 84). This is not to argue for a return to the past, but to seek to expose the values that support the politics of common-sense. *All does need to be in question, all of the time.* That is our security against wilful hegemonies that would make of the present a truth that will admit of no change.

Notes

1 See Nietzsche (1958), *Thus Spake Zarathustra*: 41.

2 We need not be naïve about professional power! The humorous note 7 in Le Grand's (1997: 167) article, about preoccupation with more monetary resources, is a useful reminder that public spirited altruism is not easy to find! My point here may not be defensible but there is a new possibility of political coalitions that might alter the structure of entitlement.

3 A great deal of interesting work remains to be done to elaborate how neo-liberalism appropriated the former language of the left. I have, earlier, given an example of how neo-liberalism took over the former linguistic content of *security*. With this 'make-over' security was associated no longer with protection, but with risk! Another is how phrases which had an ethical 'weight' when they were previously used in reference to welfare are now altered: 'alleviation from distress' is recast as 'release from obligation'. Health, education and social welfare professionals have aspects of their self-knowledge which we can call sacred. This reflects aspects of motivation and action that cannot easily be squeezed into a 'rational utility maximizer' box. By the same token, neo-liberal 'management speak' has a similar 'sacred language'. Throughout this book I have been depicting this 'sacred language' as the mantra of common-sense. It assumes that all things, people, activities and services have a price – that they can be commodified. Both protagonists cry foul when their *sacred language* is abrogated.

4 These questions are no longer simply rhetorical. For many social workers:

> the *experience* of risk and danger is now a central element of what it is to do welfare work. It is not simply that notions of risk are built into the operations, systems and activities of welfare workers, but it is *felt* as a central element of what it is to *do* welfare work at the grass roots, and *be* a social worker. (Kemshall et al., 1997: 228)

5 This was covered more extensively in Chapter 6.

6 Globalization now poses the question of whether the 'coldest of all cold monsters' is no longer the state but the reified effects of a global market and international capital transfer which can undercut any real attempt to re-establish social democratic policies. As Huber et al. argue:

> Market-oriented economic policies supported by international pressures and by local constituencies gaining from them tend not only to undercut social

democratic reform policies, but also to threaten the foundation of even formal democracy. (1997: 338–9)

7 See Le Grand (1997: 158).

8 Hirst and Thompson suggest that as we move into a 'more complex and pluralistic social and political system then the rule of law will become more important rather than less' (1995: 435).

9 In relation to the notion of 'legal welfare', which does serve to reinforce the aspects of Foucauldian 'surveillance', Beck has postulated the development of a 'social court'. This is parallel to the legal system and would function in a similar way, with 'cases' and with 'legal' defence of the 'social charges' being held in front of 'lay judges'. While speculative, it is an imaginative idea that may well find substance if the hopes of an active democracy eventuate.

10 This refers to the set of social polices where those who can afford to provide financial support to needy relatives are required by law to do so.

REFERENCES

Arendt, H. (1959) *The Human Condition*. New York: Doubleday Anchor.

Asen, R. (1996) 'Constructing the objects of our discourse: the welfare wars, the orphanage and the silenced welfare mom', *Political Communication*, 13: 293–307.

Bader, V. (1995) 'Citizenship and exclusion: radical democracy, community and justice. Or, what is wrong with communitarianism?', *Political Theory*, 23 (2): 211–46.

Barnes, J. (1985) *Flaubert's Parrott*. London: Picador.

Barry, A., Osborne, T. and Rose, N. (1993) 'Liberalism, neo-liberalism and governmentality: introduction', *Economy and Society*, 22 (3): 265–6.

Barry, A., Osborne, T. and Rose, N. (1996) *Foucault and Political Reason: Liberalism, Neo-Liberalism and Rationalities of Government*. Chicago: University of Chicago Press.

Barry, N. (1997) 'Conservative thought and the welfare state', *Political Studies*, 45 (2): 331–45.

Baudrillard, J. (1993) *Symbolic Exchange and Death*. London: Sage.

Bauman, Z. (1992) *Intimations of Postmodernity*. London: Routledge.

Bauman, Z. (1997) *Postmodernity and its Discontents*. New York: New York University Press.

Beck, U. (1992) *Risk Society: Towards a New Modernity*. London: Sage.

Beck, U. (1995a) *Ecological Politics in an Age of Risk*. Cambridge: Polity.

Beck, U. (1995b) 'Freedom for technology', *Dissent*, Fall: 503–7.

Beck, U. (1996a) 'World risk society as cosmopolitan society? Ecological questions in a framework of manufactured uncertainties', *Theory, Culture and Society*, 13 (4): 1–32.

Beck, U. (1996b) 'Risk society and the provident state', in S. Lash, B. Szerszynski and B. Wynne (eds), *Risk, Environment and Modernity*. London: Sage. pp. 27–43.

Beck, U. (1997a) 'Capitalism without work', *Dissent*, 44 (1): 51–6.

Beck, U. (1997b) *The Reinvention of Politics: Rethinking Modernity in the Global Social Order*. Cambridge: Polity.

Beck, U. (1998) 'Politics of risk society', in J. Franklin (ed.), *The Politics of Risk Society*. Cambridge: Polity. pp. 9–22.

Beck, U., Giddens, A. and Lash, S. (1994) *Reflexive Modernization: Politics, Tradition and Aesthetics in the Modern Social Order*. Cambridge: Polity.

Bernstein, P.L. (1996) 'A new religion of risk management', *Harvard Business Review*, March–April: pp. 47–51.

Braun, J. (1996) 'Review of Beck, U., Giddens, A. and Lash, S., *Reflexive Moderniza-tion: Politics, Tradition and Aesthetics in the Modern Social Order'*, *Theory and Society*, 25 (5): 752–60.

Bronner, S.E. (1995) 'Ecology, politics and risk: the social theory of Ulrich Beck', *Capitalism Nature Socialism: A Journal of Socialist Ecology*, 6 (1): 67–86.

Burchell, G. (1991) 'Civil society and the "system of natural liberty" ', in G. Burchell, C. Gordon and P. Miller (eds), *The Foucault Effect: Studies in Govern-mentality*. Hemel Hempstead: Harvester Wheatsheaf. pp. 119–50.

Burchell, G. (1993) 'Liberalism, neo-liberalism and governmentality: introduc-tion', *Economy and Society*, 22 (3): 267–82.

Burchell, G. (1996) 'Liberal government and the techniques of the self', in A. Barry, T. Osborne and N. Rose (eds), *Foucault and Political Reason: Liberalism, Neo-Liberalism and Rationalities of Government*. Chicago: University of Chicago Press. pp. 19–36.

Burchell, G., Gordon, C. and Miller, P. (eds) (1991) *The Foucault Effect: Studies in Governmentality*. Hemel Hempstead: Harvester Wheatsheaf.

Calhoun, C.J. (ed.) (1992) *Habermas and the Public Sphere*. Cambridge, MA: MIT Press.

Castel, R. (1991) 'From dangerousness to risk', in G. Burchell, C. Gordon and P. Miller (eds), *The Foucault Effect: Studies in Governmentality*. Chicago: University of Chicago Press. pp. 281–98.

Castel, R. (1994) ' "Problematization" as a mode of reading history', in J. Goldstein (ed.), *Foucault and the Writing of History*. Oxford: Basil Blackwell. pp. 237–52.

Cohen, M.J. (1997) 'Risk society and ecological modernisation', *Futures*, 29 (2): 105–19.

Cooke, M. (1997) 'Authenticity and autonomy', *Political Theory*, 25 (2): 258–88.

Coote, A. (1998) 'Risk and public policy: towards a high-trust democracy', in J. Franklin (ed.), *The Politics of Risk Society*. Cambridge: Polity. pp. 124–31.

Cousins, M. and Hussain, A. (1984) *Michel Foucault*. Basingstoke: Macmillan.

Culpitt, I. (1992) *Welfare and Citizenship: Beyond the Crisis of the Welfare State*. London: Sage.

Davis, G., Sullivan, B. and Yeatman, A. (1997) *The New Contractualism?* Mel-bourne: Macmillan.

Dean, M. (1995) 'Governing the unemployed self in an active society', *Economy and Society*, 24 (4): 559–83.

Deleuze, G. (1979) 'Foreword: the rise of the social', in J. Donzelot, *The Policing of Families*. New York: Pantheon Books. pp. ix–xvii.

Deleuze, G. (1988) *Foucault*. Minneapolis: University of Minnesota Press.

Deleuze, G. (1992) 'What is a dispositif?', in T.J. Armstrong (ed.), *Michel Foucault, Philosopher*. New York: Routledge. pp. 159–66.

de Oliveira, N. (1997) 'Review of M. Kelly (ed.), *Critique and Power: Recasting the Foucault/Habermas Debate'*, *Constellations*, 4 (1): 141–3.

Derrida, J. (1982) *Margins of Philosophy*. Chicago: University of Chicago Press.

Derrida, J. (1984) 'My chances/*mes chances*: a rendezvous with some epicurean stereophonies', in J.H. Smith and W. Kerrigan (eds), *Taking Chances: Derrida, Psychoanalysis and Literature*. Baltimore: Johns Hopkins University Press. pp. 1–32.

Derrida, J. (1994) *Specters of Marx: the State of the Debt, the Work of Mourning, and the New International*. New York and London: Routledge.

Descombes, V. (1987) 'Je m'en Foucault' (review article), *London Review of Books*, 5 March: pp. 20–1.

Donzelot, J. (1979) *The Policing of Families*. New York: Pantheon.

Donzelot, J. (1988) 'The promotion of the social' (trans. G. Burchell), *Economy and Society*, 17 (3): 395–427.

Donzelot, J. (1991) 'The mobilization of society', in G. Burchell, C. Gordon and P. Miller (eds), *The Foucault Effect: Studies in Governmentality*. Chicago: University of Chicago Press. pp. 169–79.

Douglas, M. (ed.) (1982) *Essays in the Sociology of Perception*. London: Routledge and Kegan Paul.

Douglas, M. (1986) *Risk Acceptability According to the Social Sciences*. London: Routledge and Kegan Paul.

Douglas, M. (1990) 'Risk as a forensic resource', *Daedalus*, 119 (4): 1–16.

Douglas, M. (1992) *Risk and Blame: Essays in Cultural Theory*. London: Routledge.

Douglas, M. and Wildavsky, A.B. (1982) *Risk and Culture: an Essay on the Selection of Technical and Environmental Dangers*. Berkeley, CA: University of California Press.

Doxiadis, K. (1997) 'Foucault and the three-headed king: state, ideology and theory as targets of critique', *Economy and Society*, 26 (4): 518–45.

Draper, E. (1993) 'Risk, society and social theory', *Contemporary Sociology: A Journal of Reviews*, 22 (5): 641–4.

Dreyfus, H.L. and Rabinow, P. (1982) *Michel Foucault: Beyond Structuralism and Hermeneutics*. Chicago: University of Chicago Press.

Dreyfus, H.L. and Rabinow, P. (1986) 'What is maturity? Habermas and Foucault on "What is Enlightenment?" ', in D.C. Hoy (ed.), *Foucault: a Critical Reader*. Oxford: Blackwell. pp. 109–21.

Drover, G. and Kerans, P. (eds) (1993) *New Approaches to Welfare Theory*. Aldershot: Edward Elgar.

Dryzek, J.S. (1995) 'Toward an ecological modernity – book review essay', *Policy Sciences*, 28 (2): 231–42.

Dumm, T.L. (1988) 'The politics of post-modern aesthetics', *Political Theory*, 16 (2): 209–28.

Eder, K. (1993) *The New Politics of Class: Social Movements and Cultural Dynamics in Advanced Societies*. London: Sage.

Esping-Andersen, G. (1996) *Welfare States in Transition: National Adaptations in Global Economies*. London: Sage.

Ewald, F. (1991) 'Insurance and risk', in G. Burchell, C. Gordon and P. Miller (eds), *The Foucault Effect: Studies in Governmentality*. Chicago: University of Chicago Press. pp. 197–210.

Ewald, F. (1992) 'A power without an exterior', in T.J. Armstrong (ed.), *Michel Foucault, Philosopher*. New York: Routledge. pp. 169–75.

Fleming, M. (1996) 'Working in the philosophical discourse of modernity: Habermas, Foucault, and Derrida', *Philosophy Today*, 40 (1): 169–78.

Forster, E.M. (1965) *Howards End*. London: Edward Arnold.

Foucault, M. (1973) *The Birth of the Clinic*. London: Tavistock.

Foucault, M. (1976) *The Archaeology of Knowledge and The Discourse on Language*. New York: Harper Colophon.

Foucault, M. (1979) 'On governmentality', *Ideology and Consciousness*, 6: 5–21.

Foucault, M. (1980) *Power/Knowledge: Selected Interviews and Other Writings 1972–1977* (ed. C. Gordon). Brighton: Harvester.

Foucault, M. (1981a) *The History of Sexuality. Volume One: An Introduction.* London: Pelican.

Foucault, M. (1981b) 'Omnes et singulatim: towards a criticism of "political reason" ', in *The Tanner Lectures on Human Values*, Part II. Salt Lake City: University of Utah Press. pp. 223–54.

Foucault, M. (1983) 'The subject and power', in H.L. Dreyfus and P. Rabinow (eds), *Michel Foucault: Beyond Structuralism and Hermeneutics*, 2nd edn. Chicago: University of Chicago Press. pp. 208–26.

Foucault, M. (1984a) 'What is Enlightenment?', in P. Rabinow (ed.), *The Foucault Reader*. New York: Pantheon. pp. 32–50.

Foucault, M. (1984b) 'Truth and power', in P. Rabinow (ed.), *The Foucault Reader*. New York: Pantheon. pp. 51–75.

Foucault, M. (1984c) 'Nietzsche, genealogy, history', in P. Rabinow (ed.), *The Foucault Reader*. New York: Pantheon. pp. 76–100.

Foucault, M. (1984d) 'On the genealogy of ethics: an overview of work in progress', in P. Rabinow (ed.), *The Foucault Reader*. New York: Pantheon. pp. 340–72.

Foucault, M. (1984e) 'Polemics, politics, and problemizations', in P. Rabinow (ed.), *The Foucault Reader*. New York: Pantheon. pp. 381–90.

Foucault, M. (1986) 'Kant on enlightenment and revolution' (trans. Colin Gordon), *Economy and Society*, 15 (1): 88–96.

Foucault, M. (1988a) 'Social security', in L. Kritzman (ed.), *Michel Foucault, Politics, Philosophy, Culture: Interviews and Other Writings 1977–1984*. New York: Routledge. pp. 159–77.

Foucault, M. (1988b) 'Technologies of the self', in L.H. Martin, H. Gutman and P.H. Hutton (eds), *Technologies of the Self: A Seminar with Michel Foucault*. Amherst: University of Massachusetts Press. pp. 16–49.

Foucault, M. (1988c) 'The political technology of individuals', in L.H. Martin, H. Gutman and P.H. Hutton (eds), *Technologies of the Self: A Seminar with Michel Foucault*. Amherst: University of Massachusetts Press. pp. 145–62.

Foucault, M. (1988d) *Madness and Civilization: A History of Insanity in the Age of Reason*. New York: Vintage Books.

Foucault, M. (1991a) 'Politics and the study of discourse', in G. Burchell, C. Gordon and P. Miller (eds), *The Foucault Effect: Studies in Governmentality*. Chicago: University of Chicago Press. pp. 53–72.

Foucault, M. (1991b) 'Questions of method', in G. Burchell, C. Gordon and P. Miller (eds), *The Foucault Effect: Studies in Governmentality*. Chicago: University of Chicago Press. pp. 73–86.

Foucault, M. (1991c) 'Governmentality', in G. Burchell, C. Gordon and P. Miller (eds), *The Foucault Effect: Studies in Governmentality*. Chicago: University of Chicago Press. pp. 87–104.

Foucault, M. (1993) 'About the beginning of the hermeneutics of the self', *Political Theory*, 21 (2): 198–227.

Fraser, N. (1987) 'Women, welfare and the politics of need interpretation', *Hypatia: A Journal of Feminist Philosophy*, 2 (1): 103–21.

Fraser, N. (1989a) 'Talking about needs: interpretive contests as political conflicts in welfare-state societies', *Ethics*, 99 (2): 291–313.

Fraser, N. (1989b) *Unruly Practices: Power, Discourse and Gender in Contemporary Social Theory*. Cambridge: Polity.

Fraser, N. (1992) 'Rethinking the public sphere: a contribution to the critique of actually existing democracy', in C.J. Calhoun (ed.), *Habermas and the Public Sphere*. Cambridge, MA: MIT Press. pp. 109–42.

Fraser, N. (1993) 'Clintonism, welfare, and the antisocial wage: the emergence of a neoliberal political imaginary', *Rethinking Marxism*, 6 (1): 9–23.

Fraser, N. (1995a) 'Politics, culture, and the public sphere: toward a postmodern conception', in L. Nicholson and S. Seidman (eds), *Social Postmodernism: Beyond Identity Politics*. Cambridge: Cambridge University Press. pp. 287–312.

Fraser, N. (1995b) 'From redistribution to recognition – dilemmas of justice in a post-socialist age', *New Left Review*, 212: 68–93.

Fraser, N. (1996) 'Reply to Zylan', *Signs*, 21 (2): 531–6.

Fraser, N. and Gordon, L. (1992) 'Contract versus charity: why is there no social citizenship in the United States?', *Socialist Review*, 22: 45–68.

Fraser, N. and Gordon, L. (1994a) 'A genealogy of dependency: tracing a keyword of the U.S. welfare state', *Signs*, 19 (2): 309–36.

Fraser, N. and Gordon, L. (1994b) ' "Dependency" demystified: inscriptions of power in a keyword of the welfare state', *Social Political International Studies in Gender, State and Society*, 1 (1): 4–31.

Garland, D. (1985) *Punishment and Welfare: A History of Penal Strategies*. Aldershot: Gower.

Garland, D. (1997) ' "Governmentality" and the problem of crime: Foucault, criminology, sociology', *Theoretical Criminology*, 1 (2): 173–214.

George, V. and Taylor-Gooby, P. (1996) *European Welfare Policy: Squaring the Welfare Circle*. Basingstoke: Macmillan.

Giddens, A. (1990) *The Consequences of Modernity*. Cambridge: Polity.

Giddens, A. (1991) *Modernity and Self-Identity*. Cambridge: Polity.

Giddens, A. (1994a) 'Brave new world: the new context of politics', in D. Miliband (ed.), *Reinventing the Left*. Cambridge, MA: Polity. pp. 21–38.

Giddens, A. (1994b) *Beyond Left and Right: the Future of Radical Politics*. Stanford, CA: Stanford University Press.

Giddens, A. (1994c) 'Living in a post-traditional society', in U. Beck, A. Giddens and S. Lash (eds), *Reflexive Modernization: Politics, Tradition and Aesthetics in the Modern Social Order*. Cambridge: Polity. pp. 56–109.

Giddens, A. (1995) *Politics, Sociology and Social Theory*. Stanford, CA: Stanford University Press.

Goldblatt, D. (1996) *Social Theory and the Environment*. Cambridge: Polity.

Goldstein, J. (1984) 'Foucault among the sociologists', *History and Theory*, 23: 170–92.

Goldstein, J. (1994) *Foucault and the Writing of History*. Oxford: Basil Blackwell.

Goodin, R.E. (1985) 'Vulnerabilities and responsibilities: an ethical defense of the welfare state', *The American Political Science Review*, 79 (3): 775–87.

Goodin, R.E. (1988) *Reasons for Welfare: the Political Theory of the Welfare State*. Princeton, NJ: Princeton University Press.

Gordon, C. (ed.) (1980) *Power/Knowledge: Selected Interviews and Other Writings 1972–1977*. Brighton: Harvester.

Gordon, C. (1986) 'Question, ethos, event: Foucault on Kant and enlightenment', *Economy and Society*, 15 (1): 71–87.

Gordon, C. (1991) 'Governmental rationality: an introduction', in G. Burchell, C. Gordon and P. Miller (eds), *The Foucault Effect: Studies in Governmentality*. Chicago: University of Chicago Press. pp. 1–51.

Gordon, C. (1996) 'Foucault in Britain', in A. Barry, T. Osborne and N. Rose (eds), *Foucault and Political Reason: Liberalism, Neo-Liberalism and Rationalities of Government*. Chicago: University of Chicago Press. pp. 253–69.

Habermas, J. (1986) 'The new obscurity: the crisis of the welfare state and the exhaustion of utopian energies', *Philosophy & Social Criticism*, 11: 1–18.

Habermas, J. (1987) *The Theory of Communicative Action. Volume Two: Lifeworld and System: a Critique of Functionalist Reason* (trans. T. McCarthy). Boston: Beacon.

Habermas, J. (1994) 'The tasks of a critical theory', in *The Polity Reader in Social Theory*. Cambridge: Polity. pp. 142–9.

Hacking, I. (1982a) 'Biopower and the avalanche of printed numbers', *Humanities in Society*, 5: 279–85.

Hacking, I. (1982b) 'Why are you scared?', *The New York Review of Books*, 29 (14): 30–3 and 41.

Hacking, I. (1986a) 'The archaeology of Foucault', in D.C. Hoy (ed.), *Foucault: a Critical Reader*. Oxford: Blackwell. pp. 27–40.

Hacking, I. (1986b) 'Self-improvement', in D.C. Hoy (ed.), *Foucault: a Critical Reader*. Oxford: Blackwell. pp. 235–40.

Hacking, I. (1986c) 'Making up people', in T.C. Heller, M. Sosna and D.E. Wellbery (eds), *Reconstructing Individualism: Autonomy, Individuality, and the Self in Western Thought*. Stanford, CA: Stanford University Press. pp. 222–36.

Hacking, I. (1990) *The Taming of Chance*. Cambridge: Cambridge University Press.

Hajer, M.A. (1995) *The Politics of Environmental Discourse: Ecological Modernization and the Policy Process*. Oxford: Clarendon Press.

Hajer, M.A. (1996) 'Ecological modernisation as cultural politics', in S. Lash, B. Szerszynski and B. Wynne (eds), *Risk, Environment and Modernity*. London: Sage. pp. 246–68.

Harris, P. (1997) 'Securing health and happiness: a note on possibilities and limits', *Australia and New Zealand Journal of Sociology*, 33 (2): 153–66.

Heclo, H. (1994) 'Poverty politics', in S.H. Danziger, G.D. Sandefur and D.H. Weinberg (eds), *Confronting Poverty: Prescriptions for Change*. Cambridge, MA: Harvard University Press. pp. 396–437.

Hermer, J. and Hunt, A. (1996) 'Official graffiti of the everyday', *Law & Society Review*, 30 (3): 455–80.

Hewitt, M. (1983) 'Bio-politics and social policy: Foucault's account of welfare', *Theory, Culture & Society*, 2 (1): 67–84.

Hewitt, M. (1992) *Welfare, Ideology and Need: Recent Perspectives on the Welfare State*. Hemel Hempstead: Harvester Wheatsheaf.

Hewitt, M. (1994) 'Social policy and the question of postmodernism', *Social Policy Review*, no. 6: 36–57.

Hillyard, P. and Watson, P. (1996) 'Postmodern social policy', *Journal of Social Policy*, 25 (3): 321–46.

Hindess, B. (1996a) 'Liberalism, socialism and democracy', in A. Barry, T. Osborne and N. Rose (eds), *Foucault and Political Reason: Liberalism, Neo-Liberalism and Rationalities of Government*. Chicago: University of Chicago Press. pp. 65–80.

Hindess, B. (1996b) *Discourses of Power: from Hobbes to Foucault*. Oxford: Blackwell.

Hindess, B. (1997a) 'Politics and governmentality', *Economy and Society*, 26 (2): 257–72.

Hindess, B. (1997b) 'A society governed by contract?', in G. Davis, B. Sullivan and A. Yeatman (eds), *The New Contractualism?* Melbourne: Macmillan. pp. 14–26.

Hirst, P. and Thompson, G. (1995) 'Globalization and the future of the nation state', *Economy and Society,* 24 (3): 408–42.

Honneth, A. (1992) 'Integrity and disrespect: principles of a conception of morality based on the theory of recognition', *Political Theory,* 20 (2): 187–201.

Honneth, A. (1995a) *The Fragmented World of the Social: Essays in Social and Political Philosophy.* Albany, NY: State University of New York.

Honneth, A. (1995b) *The Struggle for Recognition: the Moral Grammar of Social Conflicts.* Cambridge: Polity.

Honneth, A. (1997) 'Recognition and moral obligation', *Social Research,* 64 (1): 16–35.

Hoy, D.C. (1991) 'Foucault: modern or postmodern?', in J. Arac (ed.), *After Foucault: Humanistic Knowledge, Postmodern Challenges.* New Brunswick, NJ: Rutgers University Press. pp. 12–41.

Huber, E., Reuschemeyer, D. and Stephens, J. (1997) 'The paradoxes of contemporary democracy: formal, participatory, and social democracy', *Comparative Politics,* 29 (3): 323–42.

Hughes, D.M. (1995) 'Significant differences: the construction of knowledge, objectivity, and dominance', *Women's Studies International Forum,* 18 (4): 395–406.

Jayasuriya, L. (1996) 'Citizenship and welfare: rediscovering Marshall', *Australian Journal of Social Issues,* 31 (1): 19–38.

Johnson, J. (1994) 'Public sphere, postmodernism and polemic', *American Political Science Review,* 88 (2): 427–30.

Johnson, J. (1997) 'Communication, criticism and the postmodern consensus: an unfashionable interpretation of Michel Foucault', *Political Theory,* 25 (4): 559–83.

Katznelson, I. (1986) 'Rethinking the silences of social and economic policy', *Political Science Quarterly,* 101 (2): 307–25.

Kemshall, H., Parton, P., Walsh, M. and Waterson, J. (1997) 'Concepts of risk in relation to organizational structure and functioning within the personal social services and probation', *Social Policy & Administration,* 31 (3): 213–32.

Landes, J.B. (1992) 'Rethinking Habermas's public sphere', *Political Theory Newsletter,* 4 (1): 51–69.

Lash, S. and Urry, J. (1994) *Economies of Signs and Space.* London: Sage.

Le Grand, J. (1997) 'Knights, knaves or pawns? Human behaviour and social policy', *Journal of Social Policy,* 26 (2): 149–69.

Lidskog, R. (1993) 'Review of Beck's *Risk Society: Towards a New Modernity'*, *Acta Sociologica,* 36 (4): 400–3.

Loney, M. (1987) *The Growing Divide: a Social Audit 1979–1987.* London: Child Poverty Action Group.

Lowi, T. (1990) 'Risks and rights in the history of American governments', *Daedalus,* 119 (4): 17–40.

Luhmann, N. (1986) 'The individuality of the individual: historical meanings and contemporary problems', in T.C. Heller, M. Sosna and D.E. Wellbery (eds), *Reconstructing Individualism: Autonomy, Individuality, and the Self in Western Thought.* Stanford, CA: Stanford University Press. pp. 313–54.

Luhmann, N. (1990) *Political Theory in the Welfare State.* New York: Walter de Gruyter.

Luhmann, N. (1993) *Risk: a Sociological Theory.* New York: Aldine de Gruyter.

Lupton, D. (1997) 'Foucault and the medicalisation critique', in A. Petersen and R. Burton (eds), *Foucault, Health and Medicine*. London: Routledge. pp. 94–110.

Maguire, J. (1996) 'The tears inside the stone: reflections on the ecology of fear', in S. Lash, B. Szersynski and B. Wynne (eds), *Risk, Environment and Modernity: towards a New Ecology*. London: Sage. pp. 169–88.

Marske, C.E. (1991) *Communities of Fate: Readings in the Social Organization of Risk*. Lanham, MD: University Press of America.

McNay, L. (1992) *Foucault and Feminism: Power, Gender and the Self*. Oxford: Polity.

Megill, A. (1985) *Prophets of Extremity: Nietzsche, Heidegger, Foucault, Derrida*. Berkeley, CA: University of California Press.

Megill, A. (1997) 'Surveillance-free subjects', in M. Lloyd and A. Thacker (eds), *The Impact of Michel Foucault on the Social Sciences and Humanities*. London: Macmillan. pp. 54–77.

Meredyth, D. (1997) 'Invoking citizenship: education, competence and social rights', *Economy and Society*, 26 (2): 271–95.

Merquior, J.G. (1985) *Foucault*. London: Fontana/Collins.

Miliband, D. (ed.) (1994) *Reinventing the Left*. Cambridge, MA: Polity.

Miller, J. (1993) *The Passion of Michel Foucault*. New York: Simon and Schuster.

Miller, P. (1987) *Domination and Power*. London: Routledge and Kegan Paul.

Miller, P. and Rose, N. (1990) 'Governing economic life', *Economy and Society*, 19 (1): 1–31.

Mills, P.J. (1994) 'Feminist critical theory', *Science & Society*, 58 (2): 211–17.

Mink, G. (1994) 'Welfare reform in historical perspective', *Social Justice*, 21 (1): 114–31.

Minson, J. (1985) *Genealogies of Morals: Nietzsche, Foucault, Donzelot and the Eccentricity of Ethics*. Basingstoke: Macmillan.

Mottier, V. (1995) 'A tool box of deadly spanners' (a review of Foucault's *Dits et Ecrits 1954–1988*), *The Times Higher Education Supplement*, no. 1197, 13 October.

Mouffe, C. (1995) 'Feminism, citizenship, and radical democratic politics', in L. Nicholson and S. Seidman (eds), *Social Postmodernism: beyond Identity Politics*. Cambridge: Cambridge University Press. pp. 315–31.

Nielsen, K. (1997) 'Habermas and Foucault: how to carry out the Enlightenment project', *The Journal of Value Inquiry*, 31 (1): 5–21.

Nietzsche, F. (1958) *Thus Spake Zarathustra*. London: Dent.

Nietzsche, F. (1997) *Daybreak: Thoughts on the Prejudices of Morality* (eds M. Clark and B. Lester). Cambridge: Cambridge University Press.

Offe, C. (1996) *Modernity and the State*. Cambridge, MA: MIT Press.

O'Malley, P. (1996) 'Risk and responsibility', in A. Barry, T. Osborne and N. Rose (eds), *Foucault and Political Reason: Liberalism, Neo-Liberalism and Rationalities of Government*. Chicago: University of Chicago Press. pp. 189–207.

O'Malley, P., Weir, L. and Shearing, C. (1997) 'Governmentality, criticism, politics', *Economy and Society*, 26 (4): 501–17.

Parton, N. (1996) 'Social work, risk and the "blaming system" ', in N. Parton (ed.), *Social Theory, Social Change and Social Work*. London: Routledge. pp. 98–114.

Pavlich, G. (1995) 'Contemplating a postmodern sociology: genealogy, limits and critique', *The Sociological Review*, 43 (3): 548–72.

Petersen, A.R. (1997) 'Risk, governance and the new public health', in

A.R. Petersen and R. Bunton (eds), *Foucault, Health and Medicine*. London: Routledge. pp. 189–206.

Pleasants, N. (1997) 'The epistemological argument against socialism: a Wittgensteinian critique of Hayek and Giddens', *Inquiry: An Interdisciplinary Journal of Philosophy*, 40 (1): 23–46.

Pratt, J. (1996) 'Reflections on recent trends towards the punishment of persistence', *Crime, Law & Social Change*, 25 (3): 243–64.

Procacci, G. (1994) 'Governing poverty: sources of the social question in nineteenth-century France', in J. Goldstein (eds), *Foucault and the Writing of History*. Oxford: Basil Blackwell. pp. 206–19.

Rabinow, P. (1996) *Essays on the Anthropology of Reason*. Princeton: Princeton University Press.

Rajchman, J. (1985) *Michel Foucault: the Freedom of Philosophy*. New York: Columbia University Press.

Rayner, S. (1992) 'Cultural theory and risk analysis', in S. Krimsky and D. Golding (eds), *Social Theories of Risk*. Westport, CT: Praeger. pp. 83–115.

Reddy, S.G. (1996) 'Claims to expert knowledge and the subversion of democracy – the triumph of risk over uncertainty', *Economy and Society*, 25 (2): 222–54.

Richters, A. (1988) 'Modernity–postmodernity controversies: Habermas and Foucault', *Theory, Culture & Society*, 5: 611–43.

Robson, W.A. (1976) *Welfare State and Welfare Society: Illusion and Reality*. London: Allen and Unwin.

Rorty, R. (1982) *Consequences of Pragmatism: Essays 1972–1980*. Brighton: Harvester.

Rorty, R. (1995) 'Habermas, Derrida, and the functions of philosophy', *Revue Internationale De Philosophie*, 49 (194): 437–59.

Rose, N. (1996a) 'The death of the social? Re-figuring the territory of government', *Economy and Society*, 25 (3): 327–56.

Rose, N. (1996b) 'Governing "advanced" liberal democracies', in A. Barry, T. Osborne and N. Rose (eds), *Foucault and Political Reason: Liberalism, Neo-Liberalism and Rationalities of Government*. Chicago: University of Chicago Press. pp. 37–64.

Rustin, M. (1994) 'Incomplete modernity: Ulrich Beck's "Risk Society" ', *Dissent*: 394–400.

Said, E.W. (1991) 'Michel Foucault, 1926–1984', in J. Arac (ed.), *After Foucault: Humanistic Knowledge, Postmodern Challenges*. New Brunswick, NJ: Rutgers University Press. pp. 1–11.

Saunders, P. (1993) 'Citizenship in a liberal society', in B.S. Turner (ed.), *Citizenship and Social Theory*. London: Sage.

Sawicki, J. (1991) 'Feminism and the power of Foucauldian discourse', in J. Arac (ed.), *After Foucault: Humanistic Knowledge, Postmodern Challenges*. New Brunswick, NJ: Rutgers University Press. pp. 161–78.

Shklar, J. (1989) 'The liberalism of fear', in N.L. Rosenblum (ed.), *Liberalism and the Moral Life*. Cambridge, MA: Harvard University Press. pp. 21–38.

Squires, P. (1990) *Anti-Social Policy: Welfare, Ideology and the Disciplinary State*. New York: Harvester Wheatsheaf.

Taylor, C. (1992) 'The politics of recognition', in A. Gutmann (ed.), *Multiculturalism and 'the Politics of Recognition'*. Princeton, NJ: Princeton University Press.

Taylor, C. (1995) *Philosophical Arguments*. Cambridge, MA: Harvard University Press.

Taylor-Gooby, P. (1993) 'Citizenship, dependency, and the welfare mix: problems of inclusion and exclusion', *International Journal of Health Services*, 23 (3): 455–74.

Thompson, J.B. (1993) 'The theory of the public sphere', *Theory, Culture and Society*, 10 (3): 173–89.

Titmuss, R.M. (1970) *The Gift Relationship*. London: Allen and Unwin.

Turner, B.S. (1993) 'Outline of a theory of human rights', *Sociology*, 27 (3): 489–512.

Turner, B.S. (1994) *Orientalism, Postmodernism and Globalism*. London and New York: Routledge.

Turner, B.S. (1995) *Medical Power and Social Knowledge*, 2nd edn. London: Sage.

Turner, B.S. (1997) 'From governmentality to risk: some reflections on Foucault's contribution to medical sociology', foreword to A.R. Petersen and R. Bunton (eds), *Foucault, Health and Medicine*. London: Routledge. pp. ix–xvi.

Valero-Silva, N. (1996) 'Towards a critique of critical systems thinking within a Foucauldian framework: a "demystification process" or an "instrumental use" of critical theory', *Systems Practice*, 9 (5): 539–46.

Valverde, M. (1996) ' "Despotism" and ethical liberal governance', *Economy and Society*, 25 (3): 357–72.

Veyne, P. (1993) 'The final Foucault and his ethics', *Critical Inquiry*, 20 (1): 1–9.

Wain, K. (1996) 'Foucault, education, the self and modernity', *Journal of Philosophy of Education*, 30 (3): 345–60.

Weberman, D. (1995) 'Foucault's reconception of power', *Philosophical Forum*, 26 (3): 189–217.

White, S.K. (1988a) *The Recent Work of Jurgen Habermas: Reason, Justice and Modernity*. Cambridge: Cambridge University Press.

White, S.K. (1988b) 'Poststructuralism and political reflection', *Political Theory*, 16 (2): 186–208.

Wood, E.M. (1997) 'Modernity, postmodernity or capitalism?', *Review of International Political Economy*, 4 (3): 539–60.

Wynne, B. (1996) 'May the sheep safely graze? A reflexive view of the expert–lay knowledge divide', in S. Lash, B. Szersynski and B. Wynne (eds), *Risk, Environment and Modernity: towards a New Ecology*. London: Sage. pp. 44–83.

Young, I.M. (1990) *Justice and the Politics of Difference*. Princeton, NJ: Princeton University Press.

Young, I.M. (1996) 'Political theory: an overview', in R.E. Goodin and H.-D. Klingemann (eds), *A New Handbook of Political Science*. Oxford: Oxford University Press. pp. 479–502.

INDEX

Note: the letter n *following a page number indicates a reference in the notes.*

Learning Resources
Centre